SEX, SLAVERY AND THE TRAFFICKED WOMAN

About the Author

A human rights lawyer and activist, Ramona Vijeyarasa is the Senior Programme Manager for Women's Rights at ActionAid International. Ramona's career spans corporate law, human rights based non-governmental organisations as well as international organisations, including the Center for Reproductive Rights (New York) and the International Center for Transitional Justice (New York) and the International Organisation for Migration (Hanoi and Kiev). Ramona holds a PhD from the School of Social Sciences at the University of New South Wales (UNSW) in Sydney. She has published extensively in the fields of gender, law and human rights, including in edited volumes, leading international journals and online.

Ramona Vijeyarasa challenges us in every page of her book, deconstructing the system of 'myths, lies and stereotypes' around so called 'modern slavery' with strong evidence and sound field research undertaken in three countries. She emerges with an approach that combines feminist activism and research with patience and determination that dismantles preconceived ideas one by one. A fascinating and adventurous journey, and occasionally an uncomfortable one. Vijeyarasa provides us with a solid, truthful and evidence-based view into the lives of real men and women who are the protagonists of their own stories, and whom you will never again call victims.

Elena Ferreras Carreras, Senior Gender Adviser, EBRD

All readers, whatever their views, will find much to stimulate their thinking in this book. Its breadth and scope, the comparative analysis of the multi-regional data, and the challenging nature of the argument will provoke thought on how we better understand migration and trafficking.

Elizabeth Broderick, Australian Human Rights Commission, Australia

Gender in a Global/Local World

Series Editors: Jane Parpart, Pauline Gardiner Barber
and Marianne H. Marchand

Gender in a Global/Local World critically explores the uneven and often contradictory ways in which global processes and local identities come together. Much has been and is being written about globalization and responses to it but rarely from a critical, historical, gendered perspective. Yet, these processes are profoundly gendered albeit in different ways in particular contexts and times. The changes in social, cultural, economic and political institutions and practices alter the conditions under which women and men make and remake their lives. New spaces have been created – economic, political, social – and previously silent voices are being heard. North-South dichotomies are being undermined as increasing numbers of people and communities are exposed to international processes through migration, travel, and communication, even as marginalization and poverty intensify for many in all parts of the world. The series features monographs and collections which explore the tensions in a "global/local world," and includes contributions from all disciplines in recognition that no single approach can capture these complex processes.

Previous titles are listed at the back of the book

Sex, Slavery and the Trafficked Woman

Myths and Misconceptions about Trafficking and its Victims

RAMONA VIJEYARASA
University of New South Wales, Australia

ASHGATE

Published by
Ashgate Publishing Limited
Wey Court East
Union Road
Farnham
Surrey, GU9 7PT
England

Ashgate Publishing Company
110 Cherry Street
Suite 3-1
Burlington, VT 05401-3818
USA

www.ashgate.com

British Library Cataloguing in Publication Data
A catalogue record for this book is available from the British Library

The Library of Congress has cataloged the printed edition as follows:
Vijeyarasa, Ramona.
  Sex, slavery and the trafficked woman : myths and misconceptions about trafficking and its victims / by Ramona Vijeyarasa.
      pages cm. – (Gender in a global/local world)
  Includes bibliographical references and index.
  ISBN 978-1-4724-4609-1 (hardback) – ISBN 978-1-4724-4610-7 (ebook) – ISBN 978-1-4724-4611-4 (epub) 1. Human trafficking. 2. Prostitution. 3. Women–Crimes against.
I. Title.
  HQ281.V55 2015
  306.3'62–dc23

2014046515

ISBN: 9781472446091 (hbk)
ISBN: 9781472446107 (ebk – PDF)
ISBN: 9781472446114 (ebk – ePUB)

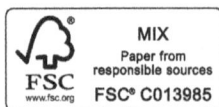

MIX
Paper from
responsible sources
FSC
www.fsc.org   FSC® C013985

Printed in the United Kingdom by Henry Ling Limited,
at the Dorset Press, Dorchester, DT1 1HD

To José-Miguel and Matilda Noa

Contents

List of Figures, Maps and Tables

Figures

Maps

Tables

Acknowledgements

This book has been nothing short of a journey and I owe thanks to several people for their contributions and support.

Thank you to each and every woman and man who so generously offered to participate in my research. I am truly indebted and thankful in particular to the male and female victims who shared with me their experiences on which this book draws. I hope the perspective that I put forward helps to bring about better recognition of and protection for the rights of migrants globally.

Of all the organisations that I have worked with over the years, particular thanks are owed to the International Organisation for Migration, which offered me substantial support in Vietnam and Ukraine. Thank you also to the University of New South Wales, for financial but particularly academic support throughout many years of study at this great institution.

Thanks are owed to several individuals who made valuable contributions to this book: Dr Roberto Barbeito (Universidad Rey Juan Carlos) for his guidance on my methodological design; Dr Anne Gallagher and Dr Ronald Weitzer (George Washington University) for sharing with me their insights that draw on their many years of experience in the field of trafficking; Debbie Budlender for her thorough review and edit of the manuscript; and at Ashgate Publishing, my editors, Kirstin Howgate and Brenda Sharp, for their dedication that helped put my manuscript on the shelf.

A special thanks are owed to my parents, Vije and Rae, and my sisters, Sheila and Vaneeta, for their unconditional support for my human rights pursuits and to Dr Helen Pringle (University of New South Wales) for her invaluable guidance on my scholarship and the countless hours that she was willing to spare me of her already limited time. Thanks are also owed to Dr Geoffrey Brahm Levey (University of New South Wales) who provided thoughtful guidance at numerous points during my research. My thinking on agency and autonomy was challenged and my analysis sharpened due to his work on the topic.

To my daughter, Matilda Noa, who was only in her first few months of life at the time of finalising this book: I hope one day you find this to be an interesting read. May you be driven to make a new and significant contribution to a topic that you love, in whatever field you choose.

Finally, I owe an overwhelming vote of thanks to my partner, José-Miguel. Ideas and projects, even one as big as embarking on a book, have to start somewhere, and in my case, it all began during one of our many debates while preparing a meal. From the moment of conception to getting this book off the printer, he has been my guiding light. There is not a word I have written that he has not read many times over and there was not a moment when he tired of providing me with the emotional and intellectual support needed to get through my field work and to formulate the ideas shared in this book. It is hard to imagine that there is a debate on trafficking that we have not had. No words of thanks are enough. I will be forever indebted.

I remain solely responsible for the interpretations, opinions (and possible mistakes) that appear in this book.

Preface

As an academic and practitioner, it is always confronting when ideas and theories you believe to be correct fall apart the deeper and deeper you investigate. A significant number of the ideas shared in this book are based on many years of study in this field. When I started my research, I intended to examine the factors that shape or limit the choices of women who are trafficked. I had assumed that the mainstream approach to trafficking was an appropriate one and at that stage believed the assumptions that are analysed in this book to be accurate representations of the trafficking phenomenon. The vulnerability of women and girls to being trafficked stirred my interest in the topic. I thought that poverty-driven desperation compelled movement across borders. In fact, my research was originally designed to explore the extent to which socio-demographic 'causes' such as poverty and low levels of education shape trafficking patterns, as opposed to whether they correlate with trafficking at all. In this sense, I was a supporter of the mainstream trafficking framework that I now critique.

As my research progressed, I realised that what I used to believe about trafficking is the very problem with trafficking discourse. I began to see the distinct lack of methodologically sound evidence to demonstrate that the image of the coerced, naive female victim actually reflects the demographics of victims. I became frustrated with the limited effort made to substantiate these stereotypical claims, leaving these assumptions about trafficking and this image of victims unexamined. I felt concern – particularly given the significant investment of donor resources in anti-trafficking programmes – when these inaccurate images were subsequently reiterated by the most dominant voices (loud, influential keynote speakers at more than one or two anti-trafficking conferences). At the end of the day, this mainstream picture has been deemed an accurate description of the trafficking phenomenon, resulting in a clichéd image of victimhood.

I was not the first to ask, 'Where are the stories of men and non-sexual exploitation?' but I certainly felt in the minority when looking for a way to give attention to the active role of the victim in their eventual exploitation. I wanted to find a better way to express the voluntary pursuit of a destiny that sadly ends in exploitative conditions.

I spent time in the field when developing the ideas expressed in this book: in Ukraine from July to September 2009; in Vietnam in 2008 and in October 2009; and finally in Ghana from July to November 2010. I chose these countries, in part, because of my view that among the overwhelming (and arguably excessive) literature on trafficking, there was no truly multi-regional comparative study of the so-called causes. I wanted to ensure that my cross-regional study included both under-researched countries and those countries believed to have some of the highest trafficking prevalence rates in the world. Naturally, I also took into account ethical considerations and what was feasible for me as an individual researcher.

The field research that forms the backdrop to this book involved a steep learning curve. My sex probably meant that female informants were more willing to participate in this research and may also have increased the likelihood that shelters were willing to support my research, particularly when the majority of their victims were females who had suffered sexual exploitation. I was, however, also faced with shelters unwilling to support my research. While I appreciated the ethical reasons behind such decisions, my scepticism about the suitability of many reintegration programmes and the operation of these shelters simultaneously grew. I was also cognisant of the fact that in all three countries I was a foreigner and this would inevitably influence my findings.[1]

My field experience confirmed some of the biggest concerns that I have with the anti-trafficking sector. I sat through many interviews with experts in the field, hearing the continuous repetition of one or two particular views. As this continued, I was doubtful that these were simply individuals expressing original and independent thoughts. To me, it appeared that the anti-trafficking communities in Vietnam, Ghana and Ukraine – all of which are sufficiently small that there is a large amount of information sharing – were all informed by the same widely-read report, the same piece of research, the same speech, workshop or training.

This was particularly evident in Vietnam and Ukraine and could be explained, in part, by the existence of fairly strong – especially in Ukraine – non-governmental reintegration networks that work together in partnership with the government and international organisations in both countries. While understandable, this repetition of ideas also epitomises one of the main problems with current day anti-trafficking discourse – the lack of original, fresh and challenging thoughts. Paul Bernish, Director of Anti-Slavery and Human Trafficking Initiatives at the National Underground Railroad Freedom Centre, a museum in Cincinnati, Ohio, has explained this problem succinctly:

> I feel a growing sense that modern-day abolitionists (... myself included) are existing in an echo chamber where our thoughts, ideas and suggestions are

---

1 A small but illuminating incident occurred during my interview with a Ghanaian informant, Judith Dzokoto, then Assistant Director of Migration at the Ghana Immigration Service. Dzokoto recounted how Ghanaian children living abroad in the US, the UK as well as Australia are a status symbol for their Ghanaian parents. While it is reasonable that she would mention the US or UK, both of which have relatively high prevalence of migration from Ghana, the reference to Australia is surprising. Only 0.06 per cent of Australia's overseas population in 2006 identified as being of Ghanaian origin (Hugo, 2009: Table 7 citing ABS Population Censuses 1986 to 2006). As Australia is not a common destination for Ghanaian migrants, I can only conjecture that the informant was influenced by my own Australian nationality and the fact that I was undertaking my research with an Australian university, as I had explained at the start of the interview. This incident was a significant reminder of the influence researchers may have on the data they collect.

repeated in a continuous loop, with very little that is new or insightful about the issue and what to do about it. (2011)

This notion of an echo chamber was one of the main drivers behind my research. Myths and misconceptions are frequently left unchallenged because of the limited space for researchers and practitioners working on trafficking to debate outside of this 'chamber'. Unquestionably, there have been notable shifts in academic discourse since I first started working on human trafficking. However, this book aims to take that trend to a new level and offer a comprehensive challenge to stereotypical, biased and sensationalised portrayals of human trafficking.

Having said this, despite my growing awareness of the complex relationship between gender and trafficking, the majority of my own data discussed in this book has a focus that is limited to the trafficking of women and girls. This may lead some readers to think that I too have followed this stereotypical line of thought. However, this deliberate decision to focus my attention on gender stereotypes concerning female victims not only challenges the female victim archetype but also has important implications for what we know about the trafficking of men.

In addition, throughout the drafting process, as a lawyer and policy advocate, I have felt the need to outline some pragmatic conclusions from this research. For this reason, I have also set out, in the final section of this book, some recommendations for how the realities of trafficking can be formulated into a more appropriate definition, for legal and non-legal purposes.

I hope that after reading this book readers feel that I have achieved what I set out to do, that is, we know more about what should and should not be considered factors that increase the vulnerability of would-be migrants to exploitation. I hope, too, that I have done justice to the diversity of experiences of women and men who suffer trafficking and trafficking-like conditions, offering an approach that enables us to think outside of the 'mainstream trafficking framework' and providing a methodologically sound alternative way to understand human trafficking.

RAMONA VIJEYARASA

Series Preface

Sex, Slavery and the Trafficked Woman challenges mainstream representations of human trafficking and the equating of victimhood with uneducated, poor, naïve and vulnerable young women and girls who are preyed upon by male traffickers who lure them into sexual exploitation. This well-known image has been reinforced by the media, the entertainment industry, international policy agendas and even academic literature. Ramona Vijeyarasa presents a powerful challenge to these stereotypes and argues that these explanations of human trafficking are based on weak, unsystematic evidence which has produced largely unsubstantiated portrayals of trafficking and its victims. A critical evaluation of the main stakeholders and their agendas – from academic literature and the reports of NGOs to pieces in the popular press – reveals not only the weak foundation underpinning these largely unsupported assumptions, but also the gains to be made by those espousing these characterisations of victims and the supposed 'push' factors that are claimed to drive human trafficking.

Vijeyarasa challenges the mainstream framework of human trafficking, arguing that its focus on coerced victims is misleading. While coercion is a reality in some instances, trafficking more often results from non-coerced migratory movements. Many victims are fully aware that they are taking risks when they agree to their movement or accept conditions of work at the point of destination. How well they understand those risks no doubt varies, but, as Vijeyarasa points out, human trafficking is often a 'choice' rather than a matter of brute force. For example, she discovered that barriers to employment are among the most decisive factors in the decision to risk and accept exploitative conditions. Poverty's relationship with trafficking is far more complex than often perceived and she presents fresh ideas on the important distinctions between absolute and relative poverty.

While recognising additional issues such as legal barriers, ethnic minority status and conflict, Vijeyarasa remains focused on the importance of viewing human trafficking through the lens of 'voluntary victimhood' and unmet expectations. She points out that the exploitation of men and women in trafficking often arises in the course of their voluntary pursuit of economic and social goals. She argues that human trafficking needs to be placed within the field of migration – indeed as a form of failed migration. She also highlights that people who become involved in human trafficking have often made well considered decisions to improve their economic position. Yet these decisions may be based on fraudulent information, leading to uninformed and often dangerous decisions.

The identification of trafficking 'victims' with helplessness and passivity both ignores their agency and more importantly, obscures the misinformation and malpractices that are trapping so many innocent people in very dangerous circumstances. More attention to the traffickers and their behaviour, and the dangers facing willing 'victims' seeking a better life in an unforgiving world, holds out the promise of shifting the argument away from victimhood to a critical engagement with the practices that might help produce very different outcomes. The agency of the 'victims' of human trafficking is the site where rethinking and redesigning responses to human trafficking needs to begin. *Sex, Slavery and the Trafficked Woman* is an important contribution to this debate, and a welcome addition to our series.

JANE L. PARPART
PAULINE GARDINER BARBER
MARIANNE MARCHAND

PART I
Setting the Scene: Trafficking Myths and Misconceptions in Context

Chapter 1
Introduction to Trafficking and the Mainstream Trafficking Framework

Over the last few decades, we have witnessed the rise of a global movement – fragmented though its members may be – working to end human trafficking. Governments worldwide increasingly recognise their responsibility to prevent human trafficking from taking place from across or within their borders, to prosecute traffickers and to protect victims. There is also substantially greater recognition, although notably slow, that human trafficking is a complex and multi-faceted phenomenon that takes many forms, including and beyond sexual exploitation of women and girls.

However, misconceptions remain about the most dominant forms of human trafficking and the most dominant characteristics of its victims, including among governments, policy makers, UN experts and within academic circles. Victims of human trafficking are frequently, and erroneously, viewed as uneducated and poor, naive and susceptible to deception. With the quintessential victims presented as young women and girls, recruited or abducted by male traffickers, the language of vulnerabilities and an emphasis on sexual exploitation remain widespread.

While the manifestation of such imagery in films, on television and in magazines can be dismissed as merely fictional, the persistence of these stereotypes among governments, academics and activists has a significant bearing on anti-trafficking efforts. A fight against 'modern-day slavery' has been declared in policies, programmes and literature. Unsubstantiated portrayals of trafficking form the foundations for significant policy dialogues on the subject, with these stereotypes systemically amplified through repetition. The effect of this reverberation is that these assumptions now sit at the heart of mainstream approaches to trafficking.

This book is a comprehensive effort to dispel some of the most dominant myths and misconceptions about human trafficking, providing evidenced-based examples to challenge those factors that are assumed to be its causes. The terms myths and misconceptions have been chosen not only to highlight the deeply ingrained imagery, particularly slavery imagery, that has helped to fuel these inaccurate portrayals but also to emphasise how even minor errors or non-deliberate misuse of data can reinforce and perpetuate unfounded stereotypes. As will be seen, not only are there numerous areas of contention in this field, but even significant deficiencies in definitions and approaches about which there is relative consensus.

Human Trafficking: Concepts and Realities

Defining Human Trafficking

While the international community long ago came to an agreement that human trafficking involves egregious violations of human rights, it is arguable that a consensus on the definition of trafficking has not yet been reached. Many, however, describe 2000 as a defining moment. Prior to this, various legal instruments (particularly ILO conventions) and resolutions existed to govern the issues of forced and child labour, slavery and practices similar to slavery, including white slavery and commercial sexual exploitation of children and adults. The term 'trafficking', although mentioned, was not yet defined.

In 2000, many in the global community gathered in Palermo, Italy, to discuss and debate growing confusion within this field. Clarity was needed on the overlaps and distinctions between prostitution and trafficking and between trafficking and migrant smuggling, as well as on the relative weight to be accorded to crimes of a sexual and non-sexual nature. This moment was preceded by a resolution introduced by the United States on trafficking in women and children at the April 1998 session of the UN Commission for Crime Prevention and Criminal Justice. The resolution called for the development of a protocol on trafficking in women and children under a proposed UN Convention against Transnational Organised Crime [Transnational Organised Crime Convention]. The draft protocol itself was introduced by the United States and Argentina at the first negotiation session for the Convention in January 1999.

In the lead-up to Palermo, non-governmental organisations (NGOs) lobbied member states on the draft language of the protocol. Abolitionist feminists (who promote the simultaneous criminalisation of both prostitution and trafficking) and pro-sex work feminists (who distinguish voluntary sex work from the involuntariness of trafficking) were unsurprisingly divided.[1] The UN, particularly the UN Office for Drugs and Crime (UNODC), was at the centre of discussions in Palermo, along with the inter-governmental organisation, the International Organisation for Migration (IOM). The outcome of these discussions was the UN Protocol to Prevent, Suppress and Punish Trafficking in Persons. The Protocol supplements the UN Convention against Transnational Organised Crime and was signed by over 80 countries in December 2000 [hereafter, Trafficking Protocol].

The Trafficking Protocol defines trafficking as:

> ... the recruitment, transportation, transfer, harbouring or receipt of persons,
> by means of the threat or use of force or other forms of coercion, of abduction,

---

1   Throughout this book, I use the terms 'prostitute' and 'sex worker' interchangeably to remain true to the original passage and the preferred term of the author(s) being discussed or cited. My preferred terminology is 'sex work' as a reflection that women voluntarily involved in sex work seek recognition of this work as a legitimate livelihood choice.

of fraud, of deception, of the abuse of power or of a position of vulnerability or of the giving or receiving of payments or benefits to achieve the consent of a person having control over another person, for the purpose of exploitation. Exploitation shall include, at a minimum, the exploitation of the prostitution of others or other forms of sexual exploitation, forced labour or services, slavery or practices similar to slavery, servitude or the removal of organs; ... (Article 3(a), Trafficking Protocol)

The Trafficking Protocol sits alongside the Protocol against the Smuggling of Migrants by Land, Sea and Air [Smuggling Protocol] and a third Protocol against the Illicit Manufacturing of and Trafficking in Firearms, their Parts and Components and Ammunition. The Smuggling Protocol defines human smuggling as:

... the procurement, in order to obtain, directly or indirectly, a financial or other material benefit, of the illegal entry of a person into a State Party of which the person is not a national or a permanent resident. (Article 3(a), Smuggling Protocol)

The Trafficking Protocol's definition revolves around three separate elements: first, the action ('recruitment, transportation, transfer, harbouring or receipt of persons'); second, the means; and finally, the purpose of exploitation. For a given situation to be deemed one of trafficking, all three elements (action, means and purpose) must be present, with the exception of cases involving children (those under 18 years of age). In these instances, no means need to be identified (Article 3(a)). That is, the movement of any persons under the age of 18 for the purpose of exploitation is defined as a case of trafficking, regardless of the presence of any consent.

Unsurprisingly given its annexation to a convention focus on organised crime, the Trafficking Protocol adopts a criminal justice perspective oriented towards the prosecution of the alleged trafficker. It therefore focuses on both the actions of the trafficker(s) (*actus rea*) and their mental intent, or the purpose of the crime (*mens rea*). After its enactment, this criminal-law oriented definition found its way, in various forms, into national legislation and policy instruments and is cited in most, if not all, literature as *the* definition of human trafficking.

Where and How Did Trafficking Discourse Go Wrong?

Over the years, the most shocking and stereotypical aspects of human trafficking have attracted widespread interest in the mass media which is dotted with such portrayals. In the film *Human Trafficking* (2005), a single mother in Prague is seduced by a handsome man, a Ukrainian girl is duped by a model agency and an American tourist is kidnapped in the Philippines. In *Lilya 4-Ever* (2002), young, desperate, naive and unsuspecting Lilya from the former Soviet Republic is tricked by her boyfriend into accepting a false job offer in Sweden.

The mass media's focus on 'sexual victimhood' has led to '[s]alacious and controversial statements about trafficking, which often seem intended more to titillate' than inform (Uy, 2011: 209). These statements serve to reinforce the gender stereotype that women need constant male or state (police) protection and that women's independent mobility should be prevented. It therefore tends to have a two-pronged focus: fighting criminals and saving the victims (Pajnik, 2010: 59). Such an approach to trafficking neglects more multifaceted economic and social circumstances and fails to capture the complexity of the decisions of potential migrants that might lead to a situation of exploitation, not to mention their agency. Male vulnerability is also obscured (for more, see Jones, 2010: 1145).

The media's vested interested in trafficking – a topic that can be assumed to increase readership – is at least clear. However, it is particularly surprising that media outlets at times credit themselves as key players in the actual 'fight' against trafficking. The United States of America's Cable News Network, CNN, for example, has run the CNN Freedom Project since 2011, an initiative that uses celebrities to highlight the work of activists – 'CNN heroes' – fighting 'modern day slavery'. At one point, the news source claimed that 'nearly 2,000 people have come out of slavery, either directly or indirectly as a result of the hundreds of stories broadcast on air and published online' (CNN Freedom Project, 2011). The complex relationship between poverty and trafficking and the legal nuances that distinguish trafficking from slavery are ignored in the narratives presented by such outlets as CNN.

Academic Dina Francesca Haynes denounces the 'celebritization' of human trafficking and reproaches not only the media but particularly those law and policy makers who in some instances use anti-trafficking efforts to 'indulge their desire to interact with celebrities' (2014: 38). Haynes highlights the main drawbacks of celebrity engagement with a legal/policy issue of this kind, including celebrities lack of accountability; their unrefined, reductive and at times uninformed narratives; the possibility that celebrity engagement in fact reduces the will of otherwise interested individuals to engage on an issue once it becomes a 'sexy' topic; and the tendency to defer attention away from those solutions that may have been identified by those most affected, the victims themselves. Haynes specifically points out the lack of celebrity interest when human trafficking is framed as a question of the exploitation of migrant labour, uninteresting when compared to more horrifying or more voyeuristic issues like 'sex trafficking', 'sexual abuse' and the 'rescue myth' (2014: 29).

While such clichés and sensationalism may be expected in fictional portrayals and, to some extent, in for-profit media, they are also present in academic literature. Benjamin Skinner, author of *A Crime so Monstrous* (2008), is an influential voice who has bridged journalism, politics as well as academia, including as a Fellow at the Carr Center for Human Rights Policy of the Harvard Kennedy School of Government. Skinner has repeatedly contended that 'there are more slaves today than at any point in human history' (2008a, 2008b, 2010), without offering any data to substantiate his claim about the scope of trafficking or slavery. He applauds the efforts of US President Clinton, among others, in the 'modern American war on slavery' (2008a: xvii). While conceding the limitations of the scope of his research, Skinner describes how he 'visited twelve countries and recorded interviews with over a hundred slaves, slave dealers and survivors' (2008: xvii).

As a result of the work of authors like Skinner, there has been a domino effect in the adoption of the language of enslavement in trafficking discourse. I have elsewhere undertaken an analysis of the problem of conflating slavery and trafficking (see Vijeyarasa and Bello y Villarino, 2012). An extensive analysis is beyond the scope of this book but a number of examples are worth noting. Jeana Fowler and her co-authors who estimate – using an uncited source – that approximately 800,000–900,000 people are currently living as modern day slaves, argue:

> … in nearly every country of the world, this modern-day slavery epidemic is present in some way due to unscrupulous criminals who are benefiting from a lucrative, but illegal, enterprise while stripping away the rights of innocent victims. (Fowler, Che and Fowler, 2010: 1346)

An academic in the field of social work, David Androff, discussing this 'modern-day slavery', contends, '[m]uch of slavery, from ancient to modern times, has involved the forced transportation of people across political boundaries' (2011: 210). He continues by explaining what I see as a misuse of both the terms slavery and trafficking by saying:

> [M]any prefer the term 'slavery' to 'trafficking' as the former serves to both connect the current problem to the historical context of forced labor and to highlight the brutal reality and human suffering. The term 'trafficking' can reflect a sanitized version of the problem. (Androff, 2011: 212)

The interchangeable use of the language of 'slavery' and trafficking heightens public intolerance for such exploitation, a response that might not exist if we refer instead to the case of a smuggled migrant who falsified his or her visa papers and later found themselves in a situation of labour exploitation. Pursuit of economic opportunities or a better life and even partially reasoned decision-making by the victims barely rate a mention in such enslavement discourse. It is difficult to imagine anyone not supporting a more vigorous fight against the crimes described given the type of imagery used by these authors. Indeed, given the prevalence of such powerful imagery, my stance in questioning these portrayals and searching for a more accurate one might seem inappropriate to some readers.

Such sensationalism and stereotypes extend to the policies and reports of a number of governments. Among them, the US Government plays a particularly influential and, at times, highly damaging role in trafficking debates. Its annual Department of State *Trafficking in Persons* (TIP) report is a frequently cited source, relied upon for its ranking of foreign states on the basis of their efforts to prevent and respond to trafficking (ranking them as Tier 1, Tier 2, Tier 2 Watch List or

Tier 3). Described by some as a 'moral crusade' (Agustín, 2009), the report provides no explanation as to how national data have been compiled and compared across multiple languages, by whom or under what circumstances (Agustín, 2009).

Moreover, authors like Skinner, who praise the annual report, fail to question whether the US Government has access to sufficient data or the political independence to make an accurate assessment. Despites evolutions in US Government thinking and the existence of more cautious voices – the 2009-appointed US Ambassador to Combat Trafficking in Persons, Luis CdeBaca, for example – the whole reporting exercise continues to be a centrepiece of the US Government's approach to trafficking. Its analysis therefore remaining fused with the US' foreign policy agenda[2] and flawed by 'messy slippages with the use of numbers and statistics' (Mahdavi, 2011).

Overall, in terms of how victims are perceived, we can divide these mainstream approaches into two categories. On the one hand, we have those academics and other stakeholders who argue that there is no identifiable voluntariness in the initial movement of trafficked individuals. Instead, trafficking is perceived as involving the kidnapping, abduction or selling of women and girls, that is, coerced movement. The possibility of a woman simultaneously being a victim of trafficking and an agent seeking economic or social betterment is ignored.

On the other hand, we have those academics and stakeholders who see some level of voluntariness in the movement of victims. Such an approach recognises that many victims are aware of the risks of exploitation and in some cases, of their illegal status at the destination. Victimhood is recognised along with the active involvement of women and men in their own movement.

Yet even many of these authors still assume that there are 'push' or 'causal' factors that shape the decisions of victims beyond their own volition. Discussions examine *how free* victims are in making migratory decisions as opposed to whether or not these 'causes' played a role in the decision-making of those victims in the first place. The autonomy of these individuals is questioned because these 'push factors' – such as low levels of education, apparent desperation arising from poverty; gender inequality; discrimination and social and cultural attitudes towards girls; conflict; lack of democracy or social integration; lack of employment opportunities or ethnic minority status – are labelled as the 'causes' of human trafficking.[3] With such an all-encompassing list of 'causes', it is difficult to imagine what areas of poverty, development and inequality have not been named a cause of trafficking. Both of the above approaches – first, the coerced victim for whom no voluntariness is recognised and second, the recognition of

---

2   For example, in 2012, Kosovo, Moldova and Mexico were ranked 'Tier 2', China was ranked 'Tier 2 Watch List' whereas Cuba was ranked 'Tier 3' (US Department of State, 2012).

3   Representative works include European Commission, 2012: §1; UNESCO, 2006; Bernat and Zhilina, 2010: 3; see also Askola, 2007; Hughes, 2001; Zimmerman et al., 2011; Chuang, 2006; Lyttleton 2002; Raymond et al., 2002: 60, 138; and SIREN, 2008b: 1.

voluntary movement but the simultaneous naming of trafficking's so-called causes – dominate mainstream literature.

The Myths and Misconceptions Challenged in this Book

From the statements of government officials to articles in the popular press, from academic writing to films, we see (too often) a wide array of assumptions about human trafficking and its victims. There are several reasons why these portrayals can be described as 'mainstream'. First, these depictions of victims and patterns of trafficking are not one-off examples but rather reflect recurrent imagery found throughout NGO, inter-governmental and UN reports, in popular media (including press, films and novels) and in academic literature. Arguably this is unsurprising, given these portrayals appear victim-friendly and allow for easy endorsement, typically through the creation of a gender dichotomy. Women are framed as victims and men as the trafficking aggressors.

While these (and other) common, assumptions also require analysis and validation or rejection, they fall outside of the scope of this book. Here we focus exclusively on the four assumptions that dominate the mainstream trafficking framework. These relate first to the nature of victims' movement and second, to their demographics:

1. Victims are assumed to be passive individuals, whose 'involuntary arrivals' in destination countries result from their coerced movement *by the trafficker* (for example, through force, abduction or fraud or through payment to another individual in order to control the trafficked person).
2. Victims are assumed to have a lower level of education than their peers, leading to both fewer opportunities and uninformed decision-making.
3. Poverty and the assumed exclusion of victims from access to work in the domestic labour market are driving forces for seeking work abroad.
4. Victims are assumed to be predominantly women and girls.

The Coerced Victim of Trafficking

The first assumption analysed in this book is that of the coerced victim. 'Coercion' is defined as a process in which an outcome is driven by physical, mental, legal and/or psychological restraint. In trafficking discourse, this translates into the ever-present imagery of kidnapping, abduction and the selling of young girls. At its most extreme, the literature describes women who 'are mutilated and murdered as warnings to competing traffickers and pimps and as punishment for refusing to engage in prostitution' (Hughes and Denisova, 2002: 16–17). However, the coerced victim appears across various types of literature. Both US-based clinical professor of law Beverly Balos (2004) and Radhika Coomaraswamy, the former UN Special

Rapporteur on Violence against Women, its Causes and Consequences, draw on the sold victim imagery as the springboard for their arguments:

> A Nepalese girl, Chamoli ran away from home with her boyfriend to India at the age of 16. It was only when she arrived in the city of Poona that Chamoli discovered her boyfriend's intention to sell her to a brothel. (Balos, 2004: 137; Coomaraswamy, 2001: ¶ 12)

Chamoli's experience also closely resembles that described by Siddharth Kara of fellow Nepalese girl Maya who, Kara tells readers, was sold by her parents to a local agent for USD 55, ostensibly to work in a carpet factory. Maya, who Kara explains was forced to work in a brothel in Mumbai's 'red light district', is described by Kara as 'emblematic of the hundreds and thousands of women and children trafficked and forced into prostitution each year' (2009: 3). Despite criticisms that his literature is a 'set of speculations' (Cheng, 2010: 364) that 'rel[y] on salacious material and hero fantasies', Kara's work is praised, for example, by *The Financial Times* as 'an eloquent, campaigning book that addresses an evil that belittles our humanity' (Birchall, 2009).

These representations draw clear links between the *involuntary* victim and trafficking. Voluntariness and the socio-economic drivers that may be relevant to the decisions of these victims do not feature in these narratives nor do the failed hopes and expectations of these potential migrants. In Part II of this book (Chapter 3), I analyse the coerced victim at length and ask important questions about the role of victims' desires and rational choices. It is also at this point that I introduce the concept of the 'voluntary victim'.

The Uneducated Victim

The second assumption analysed in this book concerns the link between access to education, school completion and human trafficking, that is, the view that low levels of education are a typical demographic trait of victims. Numerous authors on trafficking mention the 'rampant' disparities in education that act as a 'risk' or 'vulnerability' factor.[4] In addition, links are made between individual choices and education. Education creates opportunities for potential migrants to access work in the domestic market and, if they choose, to migrate for work abroad. Higher levels of education are assumed to create opportunities for potential migrants to leave under safe conditions. Low levels of education are therefore seen as an

---

4   Representative works include McCabe, 2008: 12; Truong, 2006: 32 on Mozambique; Marshall, 2005: 151 on South-East Asia; Susan Tiefenbrun, 2001: 208 (quoted in Trépanier, 2003: 48); Duong and Khuat, 2008: 205–6 on Vietnam; Poudel and Carryer, 2000: 74–5 on Nepal; Crawford and Kaufman, 2008: 905–6 also on Nepal; Cole, 2006: 222 on Nigerian women; and Lăzăroiu and Alexandru, 2003 on Romania to name just a few examples.

impediment for potential migrants to find work at home and/or migrate safely, creating the risk of trafficking.

Education is also often assumed to give victims a heightened capacity to identify the risks involved when they enter into a transaction. 'Uneducated' victims of trafficking are therefore assumed to be less capable of recognising and overcoming the risk of fraud potentially involved in contracts for work abroad. As Surtees notes in regard to Albanian women: 'Poorly educated victims may be more easily manipulated in the recruitment process as well as less equipped to negotiate trafficking and abuse' (2005: 61). Such an assumption gives rise to the frequent portrayals of victim naivety and the relatively high investment of funds in anti-trafficking programmes focused on education as the counter-trafficking solution (Crawford, 2010). Both of these above depictions are addressed in Chapter 4.

The Poor Victim of Trafficking

The third assumption analysed relates to both poverty and women's experience of the domestic labour market. It is widely assumed that 'lack of employment opportunities increase the vulnerability to being trafficked' (UNGIFT, 2008: 8). Gendered practices prohibit women's entry into some occupations and concentrate them in others. In some instances, weak economies, economic decline or war are said to cause market shifts and marginalise certain groups, and particularly women, from employment (Kligman and Limoncelli, 2005: 128).

Women are particularly affected during times of high unemployment, suffering discrimination in hiring and disproportionate lay-offs, including illegal dismissals during maternity leave (Luda di Cortemiglia, n.d. 16; see also Clark, 2003: 252). This contributes to high poverty rates and unemployment, leaving women vulnerable to the enticements of traffickers who take advantage of their desire for better working and living conditions abroad (Kligman and Limoncelli, 2005: 129). Some authors deem economic necessity *the* 'underlying factor that informs most women and girls who engage in the sex industry whether voluntarily or by coercion' (Elabor-Idemudia, 2003: 120). This approach opens the door for direct links to be made between trafficking and sex work.

If we view trafficking as resulting from a voluntary pursuit of economic betterment, a relationship between barriers to decent work in the domestic market and trafficking is logical. Within this framework, however, the relationship drawn between poverty and trafficking is a simplistic one and ignores underlying complexities, including distinctions between absolute and relative poverty and the role of false expectations of work, pay and life abroad that may play a role in the decisions of these women in the first place. I unpack the myths and misconceptions underlying this assumption, as well as the truths behind it, in Chapter 5.

The Female Victim

The final assumption analysed in this book, which can be seen as an overarching theme across the mainstream discourse, is the gendered nature of trafficking. First, women are deemed 'easy targets' for traffickers (US Department of State, 2009: 36) due to gender inequality. Second, and interrelated with this assumption, socio-cultural values frequently imposed on women are considered one of trafficking's causes. These cultural values, expectations and traditions are assumed to shape women's freedom in deciding whether or not to migrate and what conditions of work to accept abroad, particularly in light of social pressures to support families' economic needs. Finally, the dynamics of trafficking themselves are assumed to be gendered, with women framed as victims suffering at the hands of male perpetrators.

Links between gender inequality and trafficking have been made ad nauseam, frequently by feminist theorists, women's rights advocates, UN agencies and government authorities, with research insisting that women are 'more vulnerable than men to being trafficked' (Mediterranean Institute of Gender Studies, 2007: 6). Discussing Nepal, Pratima Poudel and Jenny Carryer argue that trafficking 'has its roots in gender politics and sexual inequalities, linked to widespread economic poverty' (2000: 74). Similarly, the US Government's annual *Trafficking in Persons Report* draws attention to the 'gender imbalance in human trafficking' and states in generalising terms that women 'often have no individual protection or recognition under the law, inadequate access to healthcare and education, poor employment prospects, little opportunity to own property' as well as 'high levels of social isolation. All this makes some women easy targets for harassment, violence, and human trafficking' (US Department of State, 2009: 36).

Such statements often lack a causal chain in their reasoning. Indeed, some authors concede that there is a lack of reliable data to enable us to draw conclusions as to the sex of the majority of victims. They nonetheless argue that women and child victims dominate and therefore contend that the focus on women and girls is warranted: 'But inasmuch as the admittedly questionable data available suggest that more women and children are trafficked than men, and that trafficked women are more likely to be subjected to gross physical abuse than men are, the focus here can be justified' (Holmes, 2010: 15; see Vijeyarasa, 2011c for a review of the Holmes compilation).

Despite what may be warranted attention to the inequality experienced by women as a factor that exacerbates vulnerability to trafficking, what has emerged is the female victim archetype. The perception of trafficking as synonymous with the movement of women is exacerbated by the dearth of literature on the trafficking of men and the stark absence of empirical research on this subject (examples include Surtees, 2009 on trafficking of men from Ukraine and Belarus and Horwood, 2009 on irregular migration of men from East Africa and the Horn of Africa to South Africa). I challenge the myths and misconceptions that sustain the female victim archetype in Chapter 6.

As a whole, the coerced victim, uneducated victim and poor, economic migrant – all female – present a composite picture of the mainstream trafficking framework that is called into question in this book. Before moving on, it is important to clarify that, although I emphasise the voluntariness often exercised by victims in their departure, at no stage in this book or in the course of my research did I set out to determine, quantifiably, the number of women who fit within this category of what I consider simultaneously agents and victims. As I note below, estimates of the absolute numbers of trafficked victims are extremely controversial and looking to quantifiably disaggregate the experiences of victims is even more difficult. While exact quantification is impossible, the existence of a very high number of victims of trafficking, maybe a vast majority who fall outside of the mainstream trafficking framework, must be recognised and efforts made to gain a reliable insight into their experiences.

Finally, before continuing, it is also important to note that within academic scholarship, there has been an important evolution in the conceptualisation of trafficking. A decade ago, few academics adopted the line of thought that I promote in this book. Since that time, a growing body of authors has begun to question the assumed involuntariness of victims' movement and the so-called 'causes' of human trafficking. For example, Perdis Mahdavi (2011) discusses the exploitation suffered by workers in Dubai in an analysis that links labour, migration and trafficking; Robert Uy (2011) offers a legal perspective on why trafficking discourse needs to shift away from a focus on sexual exploitation and the 'perfect victim'; and Janie Chuang (2010) critiques the common 'slippage' between trafficking and prostitution so striking in the popular press.

However, it is important, too, to observe that mainstream representations and those academics who question these sensationalist portrayals at times offer opposite, but equally biased or erroneous interpretations. For example, Laura Agustín directs many legitimate challenges towards the US government and the implications mainstream approaches have on the freedoms of migrant sex workers. She nonetheless offers a simplistic analysis of trafficking by portraying the central issue as a question of sex workers who are marginalised in their migration pursuits. While the coerced/kidnapped victim should be considered atypical of human trafficking, this more extreme experience is completely ignored in Agustín's framework.

Analysing Trafficking Through the Lens of Autonomy, Agency and Causality

This book adopts two theoretical approaches: the first concerns the autonomy exercised by victims in the decision-making process. The second involves a focus on causality, as typically understood in the social sciences.

Autonomy, Agency and Victim Decision-Making

The concept of autonomy has been the subject of a long history of philosophical debate among liberal and feminist theorists.[5] For obvious reasons, I will not embark here on a full-scale theoretical exploration. However, it is important to explain how the term 'autonomy' is used in this book. Throughout Part II, I approach the question of victims' decision-making and choices by examining the levels of autonomy they exercise when making those decisions.

I use the 'autonomy' approach primarily in two contexts in this book, although with slightly different implications. First, the book examines evidence of what is described as 'voluntary' decision-making on the part of victims, concretely in the initial period prior to departure. I present the 'voluntary victim' who sits in opposition to the coerced victim archetype which, as I argue, almost always incorrectly presents victims as exercising no (or very limited) free or self-determined movement.

By their very definition, the two concepts of voluntariness and victimhood may seem directly at odds. The very idea of victim voluntariness may cause offence even to those academics in the field of trafficking who strongly support a migration-centred approach to the topic. However, my purpose is to highlight, and give weight and value to, the reality that trafficking often begins with a non-coerced decision on the part of a voluntary migrant. This recognition allows us to more accurately examine and discuss the drivers of that migration, including factors that may have led to the eventual exploitation of the victim contrary to their initial expectations prior to leaving home.

Second, I use the concept of autonomy in my analysis of the three remaining assumptions explored in Part II of this book concerning victims' demographics. As discussed above, education levels, experiences of poverty and labour market access, and gender inequality are assumed to be causes or drivers of human trafficking. In Part II, I examine the extent to which this is true. Were victim's decisions shaped or influenced by these 'causes' and should they therefore be considered non-autonomous or partially autonomous decisions? Are these so-called push factors therefore the real drivers of trafficking or are these 'causes' a misconception?

The concept of autonomy is therefore helpful in this analysis of whether and to what extent the myths and misconceptions examined prove accurate. The first understanding of autonomy is more 'absolute' – there is autonomy (voluntary victims) or there is an absence of autonomy (coerced victims) in victims' initial departures from home. The second proves to be a more 'relative' analysis, with the so-called causes discussed affecting, to various degrees, the levels of autonomy exercised in the decision-making of victims.

---

5   For more recent work in this area, see Madhok, Phillips and Wilson (2012); Mackenzie (2010); Superson (2010); and Phillips (2007). Other foundational authors include Meyers (1987); Schulhofer (1998) and Arneson (1994).

Before moving on, it is important to reiterate that at no point do I contend that the male and female victims who contributed to this research are not victims of exploitation. Recognition of any form of voluntary decision-making ought not to be seen as pushing 'victims' outside of the realm of victimhood. To the contrary, I intentionally use the word victim. While the term is often associated with naivety, lack of voluntariness or agency, it is important to recognise the violation of victims' rights involved in human trafficking and as a result, their right to legal redress. The term 'victimhood' is not used to define trafficked women as inactive and without agency. Rather, it is one dimension of a multi-dimensional experience of migration and exploitation.

Causation and Causality: The Push and Pull Factors of Trafficking

Turning to my second lens of analysis, it is important to provide clarification on the use of the language of 'causation' in this book. One of the main challenges in the social sciences in general and with human trafficking in particular, is the idea of 'causality'. Factors such as levels of education, poverty, labour market barriers and gender inequality are carelessly labelled as 'causing', 'influencing' 'impinging', 'pushing' or 'driving' human trafficking. There is a frequent disregard for the significance of these terms which are used interchangeably and without justification.

I categorise the various approaches authors take when using causal language in the literature on trafficking in three main ways. First, there is a body of thought that frames education levels, labour market barriers and gender inequality as *direct* causes of human trafficking. For example, we read of the 'root causes' that make women and girls 'more susceptible to fall into trafficking' (UNESCO, 2006a: 31; see also La Strada, 2008). In a foreword to the United Nations Office on Drugs and Crime's (UNODC) compilation of the UN Convention against Transnational Organised Crime, the former UN Secretary-General Kofi Annan described trafficking as:

> rooted in social and economic conditions in the countries from which the victims come, facilitated by practices that discriminate against women and driven by cruel indifference to human suffering on the part of those who exploit the services that the victims are forced to provide. (UNODC, 2004: iv)

Janie Chuang (2006) writes of the socio-economic 'causal' factors that 'impel' migration. This is sometimes packaged in the language of 'push and pull': 'These push and pull factors lay the causal foundation for trafficking' (Jordan, 2002: 28). Sometimes a third category is added: 'push, pull *and* facilitating factors' (Jordan, 2002: 28, emphasis added). Similarly, Alexis Aronowitz argues that all forms of 'migration and trafficking are driven by "push" and "pull" factors' and that 'the causes that propel people to leave their country either through legitimate or illicit channels are the same' (2001: 170). Other authors merge several ideas that refer to causality, suggesting that such 'factors', 'constraints and considerations' 'promote alternative migration practices that lead towards exploitation and trafficking' (Jones, Engstrom, Hilliard and Diaz, 2007: 112).

Authors who adopt the language of structural factors or structural inequalities are placed in the second category. For example, Phyllis Coontz and Catherine Griebel refer to the 'structural economic inequalities that create the endless supply of women vulnerable to the trafficking market in Africa, Eastern Europe, Asia and Latin America' (2004: 56). Kristof van Impe argues that trafficking is 'a structural problem caused by a diverse set of economic and social realities, commonly called "the gap between the rich and the poor"' (2000: 123). Even more nuanced feminist writing uses this language. Grace Chang and Kathleen Kim, in a critique of the attention given to the 'unproven link' between prostitution and trafficking by the Bush administration, argue that focusing on abolishing prostitution as a central part of the anti-trafficking agenda 'has diverted attention away from an assessment of structural factors that facilitate trafficking such as poverty, discrimination, and civil and political unrest of certain developing regions' (2007: 321). In earlier writings, I myself have referred to the 'structural inequality' involved in the trafficking of women in Vietnam (2010b: 5), language which I now believe should be adopted with caution.

In the third category are those authors who choose not to adopt the language of 'causation' but nonetheless see a link, particularly in relation to increased vulnerability. Phil Marshall, for example, counsels against inappropriate use of the language of 'causes' in his work on Southeast Asia. He argues that 'trafficking involves gross abuses of human rights, including physical and mental abuse, rape, forced drug use, deprivation of liberties and sometimes even murder' (Marshall, 2005: 150). He claims that to suggest that these abuses are 'caused' by factors such as 'poverty' or lack of employment opportunities is simply inaccurate (Marshall, 2005: 150). Marshall, however, maintains that these factors, 'along with others such as lack of education, lack of legal status and problematic individual situations, certainly *contribute* to the vulnerability of individuals and groups to being trafficked' (Marshal, 2005: 150–51, emphasis added). Heightened vulnerability is the key issue for the authors in this category.

When analysing the mainstream trafficking framework, I use a variety of terms in order to stay true to the chosen language of the author (causal, push and pull, structural factors and exacerbated vulnerability). However, in an attempt to address the confusion in existing trafficking debates and to assess the validity of these various lines of thought, I primarily use the term 'correlation' in this book. This term, to a certain extent, is an umbrella concept for the abovementioned terms. At the same time, the term 'correlation' reflects my view that while a particular demographic trait(s) may be commonly identified with trafficking, it does not necessarily mean that this trait *results* in trafficking. Rather, it may be that an unrelated factor is 'causing' trafficking. As such, 'correlation' provides us with a more verifiable hypothesis: is there a *direct* correlation between low levels of education, poverty, labour market barriers and gender inequality and the traffic of women and girls? I assess whether such a correlation exists or whether these are merely myths and misconceptions.

Structure of this Book

Part I of this book is dedicated to setting the scene and provides readers with background context on trafficking, the main actors and major debates. Chapter 2 in particular is dedicated to a detailed analysis of the mainstream trafficking framework. I begin by examining the origins of mainstream approaches to trafficking: What are the reasons for the overwhelming dominance of the naive victim archetype and who are the main drivers of this stereotype? My assessment reveals how the assumptions tested in this book are promoted by a cross-section of stakeholders engaged in this field, aligning otherwise naturally opposed stakeholders, such as abolitionist feminists calling for the criminalisation of 'prostitution' and pro-sex work feminists calling for the legalisation or at least decriminalisation of sex work. Other stakeholders who are analysed for their role in promoting this victim archetype include governments, intergovernmental organisations including the UN, the religious right, the 'rescue industry' and the media. A detailed legal analysis is provided in Chapter 3.

Part II of this book is focused on dispelling the myths and misconceptions set out in Part I. Chapter 4 focuses on coercive movement and challenges the involuntariness often assumed to be at the heart of the movement of victims. Chapter 5 focuses on education levels and the assumed naivety of victims. Chapter 6 explores the link between poverty and trafficking, introducing often ignored distinctions like absolute and relative poverty. Chapter 7 focuses on the female victim archetype and calls for greater attention to the male victim, the female trafficker and victim stigma.

Having laid out the inconsistencies within the mainstream trafficking framework, in Part III I offer an alternative approach to trafficking. In Chapter 8, I analyse the criminal law approach to trafficking, identifying what is missing in this framework and how these gaps may be addressed by concepts such as unmet expectations and the voluntary victim. In Chapter 9, I outline a new lens of analysis in the form of a migration framework. This is not only an alternative theoretical approach but has potential judicial application as well.

As noted above, the ideas presented in this text draw largely from field research conducted in Ukraine, Vietnam and Ghana. For the purposes of this research, I designed a questionnaire that explored several topics and was disseminated among returned victims of trafficking housed in reintegration shelters or otherwise accessing reintegration support (a copy in English is set out in Annex 1). Reintegration is defined as a process that begins after the initial stages of identification of trafficked persons. In the context of support to refugees, it has been defined as a long-term and multi-faceted process that is not complete until the person becomes an active member of the economic, cultural, civil and political life of a country and perceives that she has reoriented and is accepted by her community (Zimmerman 2007, 153) or in many cases, a new community. Reintegration has become a fundamental component of the response by many governments to the traffic of its citizens.

Complementary to the quantitative data collected from returned victims, I also sought to collect qualitative data. I conducted interviews in all three countries with key informants who were policy, programming or academic experts in the areas of counter-trafficking, reintegration and migration; education; labour rights and labour market access; and gender equality. For various reasons, the quantitative data collection yielded important findings in Ukraine, but less so in Vietnam, and was impossible to complete in Ghana. Annex 2 sets out a summary of the quantitative and qualitative data collected in each of the three countries, as well as the cumulative data collected across all three.

The Way Forward

As we have seen in this introductory chapter, this book joins a small but growing body of academics who are challenging the stereotypical and inaccurate depictions of human trafficking that have proliferated in volume since the enactment of the Trafficking Protocol. I provide empirical evidence to challenge not only the coerced victim archetype but also the unfounded assumptions about the so-called 'causes' of trafficking that sit at the centre of mainstream portrayals of the phenomenon.

To take the positions that I present in this book is to contest a normalised perspective of trafficking. The guiltless, agency-less victim is an image that neither challenges public preconceptions, nor demands a shift in our thinking on an emotional or intellectual level. However, the misrepresentation of the decisions taken by these men and women engaged in irregular migration and the stereotypical portrayals of the demographics of these victims call for an analysis of this nature, grounded in evidence-based research. By drawing on my field experience to argue for and defend the value of a migration spectrum approach, I demonstrate the need for a critical shift in thinking by questioning the very applicability of the term 'trafficking'.

I hope that this book provides solid empirical and theoretical grounding to support a more precise understanding of trafficking. In this respect, I argue for a move away from the evocation of the forced or abducted victim archetype towards a more accurate assessment of the socio-demographic factors assumed to make victims susceptible to exploitation. As such, the primary proposition put forward is that the typicality of human trafficking is best represented as 'failed migration', with cases falling outside of this framework being atypical. Countering the inadequate and singular criminal justice approach – which in practice, often fails to be victim-centred and rights based – this book calls for an approach to exploitation that recognises victim's unmet expectations. These 'unmet expectations' of the 'voluntary victim' are central to how we define human trafficking and provide key conceptual tools for determining victimhood and redress.

Chapter 2
The Main Agendas and Those Behind Them

Over the last two decades, human trafficking has attracted the attention of numerous actors – from NGOs to international organisations, from government bodies to donor organisations, from academics to celebrity activists. It is important to appreciate as a starting point that their engagement in the topic is conditioned by their vested interest in how trafficking is framed both conceptually and practically. This includes how such issues as sex work, migration, trafficking, slavery, gender and feminism, victimhood, legal and monetary redress and policing are addressed.

Vanessa Munro has described trafficking for sexual exploitation as a 'contemporary battle-ground for competing agendas on issues as diverse as globalization, migration, labour relations and the regulation of sexuality' (2005: 93).[1] This chapter attempts to navigate and examine that battleground and identify the sources and vested interests of relevant groups, or what I refer to in this chapter as stakeholders. As we will see, these agendas are closely linked to the stereotypical assumptions most reiterated in the mainstreaming trafficking discourse. Moreover, these stakeholders not only analyse the phenomenon of human trafficking and debate among themselves about the causes and consequences but in fact establish the lens through which society understands human trafficking; they shape the very concept under discussion.

For the purpose of this analysis, I have categorised the primary agendas present in human trafficking discourse as follows: (a) abolitionist feminists promoting the criminalisation of both prostitution and trafficking; (b) pro-sex work feminists who distinguish voluntary sex work from the involuntariness of trafficking; (c) the religious right and 'rescue industry' who advocate for interventions to remove sex workers from prostitution; (d) the media (including films and popular press) and their role in promoting sensationalist portrayals of trafficking, with the focus

---

1   In this study, Vanessa Munro focuses on domestic responses to trafficking of women for sexual exploitation in the UK and Australia. Munro's discussion is situated in what she terms 'contemporary obstacles' to combat human trafficking, including the feminisation of poverty and the 'deconstruction of sex work as legitimate labour' (2005: 92). Relevant to this chapter, she also situates her discussion within the 'problematic juxtaposition of policing, immigration and human rights imperatives that is manifest in the phenomenon of trafficking' (Munro, 2005: 93). Her primary focus is the divide between the Global Alliance Against the Trafficking in Women (GAATW) which supports a non-sexual-service-specific definition of trafficking and conceives sex work to be legitimate labour and the Coalition Against the Trafficking in Women (CATW), which opposes both trafficking and prostitution. Partly theoretical and partly practical, Munro's discussion is most valuable for its emphasis on competing ideologies within trafficking debates.

in this chapter largely on profit-driven media; (e) Governments, particularly those in destination countries, seeking to stop 'illegal' immigration through more regulated or 'closed' borders and to control the practice of sex work; and, finally, (f) international organisations and related bodies, among which we have seen an evolution in approaches to trafficking but also the persistence of inaccurate portrayals and a bias in their emphasis. We can add to these six categories a seventh, which is not discussed in detail in the existing literature, that of victim self-imagery. Few researchers have looked into the factors that may drive victims to exaggerate or even falsify their own stories of being trafficked. These factors have direct implications for how we should view victims' testimonies.

These seven categories do not capture the entire trafficking discourse. Moreover, the divergence of views, quality of data collected and accuracy of depictions of human trafficking within any one category must be noted. However, these agendas are identified as having the most weight and as those most commonly amplified through repetition. The potential gains for stakeholders in the way trafficking debates, research, discourse and imagery unfold should not be underestimated. While many stakeholders have a genuine interest in countering trafficking, we have simultaneously seen human trafficking presented in a sensationalised or biased light to obtain particular gains.

To conceptualise the different interests in how trafficking is presented, the term agenda is applied. The analysis in the following pages demonstrates that these agendas are not only accompanied by inaccurate assumptions made about trafficking and its victims, but that those who endorse them carry great weight and play a central role in establishing the archetypal victim. Further, these agendas directly affect the very meaning of the term 'trafficking'. Such assumptions easily become self-fulfilling: where Siddharth Kara searches for 'slaves', he finds slaves; if we searched for trafficked women who fit the victim archetype, we would indeed find them.[2]

The agendas underlying these positions are not mutually exclusive. Robert Uy, for example, notes that '[f]or the Religious Right, human trafficking is a "clear cut, uncontroversial, terrible thing going on in the world"' while for many feminists in the 'progressive left', 'trafficking is simply an extension of women's inequality, which is a "product of domination of women by men – inequality is presented as political and sexual in nature"' (2011: 205). Like others before him (for example, O'Connell Davidson, 2003), Uy points out this 'unusual alliance' of the religious right and abolitionist feminists (2011: 205). What results is a popular discourse on human trafficking focused on the 'need to "rescue and restore" sex slaves to their normal lives' (2011: 205).

---

2   In a similar vein, writing about abolitionists' framing of sex work as a form of oppression, Ronald Weitzer notes how authors rigidly adhere to their position, even when confronted by clearly contradictory evidence, which is conveniently ignored (2012: 1339).

Few other comprehensive analyses of the various agendas involved in human trafficking debates exist.[3] Yet, in the context of this book this chapter serves two main purposes. First, this discussion demonstrates the diversity, but also interrelatedness, of the positions presented in the literature on trafficking. Second, it explores who is promoting the assumptions analysed in this book and what do they have to gain. We will see that what is at stake is not merely a question, for example, of allocation of funding for anti-trafficking efforts but our very knowledge of the phenomenon under scrutiny.

Academic Discourse: Feminist Debates on Sex Work and Trafficking

Academic discourse with respect to human trafficking is multi-disciplinary. The phenomenon of trafficking spans such fields as sociology, human and labour rights, criminal law and criminology, international relations along with feminist theory. Numerous academics engaged on the issue therefore fall outside of the field of feminist critical engagement which is the focus of this section.

For example, there are a number of academics whose work on migration and trafficking cannot be classified as feminist in orientation, nor would these academics be classified as feminist theorists. This includes those writers whose work has made a positive contribution in deconstructing methodological approaches to trafficking research (see Tyldum and Brunovskis, 2005; Andrees and van der Linden, 2005). In other instances, academics engaged in the topic may be critically aware of the question of gender but do not take an explicit stance on prostitution and sex work (Gallagher, 2010: 54–64, 153, 191–7).[4] In the analysis that follows, I focus specifically on those actors whose contributions to the academic literature on migration and trafficking have become a central point of feminist critical engagement with the topic.

A significant role in promoting the image of the coerced victim can be attributed to feminist theorists on both sides of the divide when it comes to the acceptability

---

3   Marjan Wijers and Lin Lap-Chew (1997: 156–78), writing specifically in the context of trafficking for sexual exploitation, outline different approaches to trafficking and the strategies these imply. These range from moral perspectives regarding trafficking and prostitution as 'evil', which overlap with criminal approaches which risk labelling women as the guilty parties, to migration approaches that demand stricter border controls. They also note human rights perspectives, public order/health approaches – whose purpose is control by medical examination – and labour rights arguments that demand rights for women in prostitution (Wijers and Lap-Chew, 1997: 174). This analysis by Wijers and Lap-Chew provides a sense of the multi-disciplinary and multi-issue nature of trafficking, but not necessarily of how much is at stake for those groups promoting these various lenses of analysis.

4   Even in these cases, however, we see a heavy focus on criminal justice perspectives (Gallagher, 2011; Gallagher, 2008) that tend to ignore other dimensions of human trafficking and fail to provide a more holistic, victim-oriented approach.

of sex work and prostitution. Put simply, a dichotomy situates those feminists who seek the decriminalisation of sex work as a voluntary and legitimate form of labour – 'pro-sex work' or 'decriminalisation feminists' (for example, Doezema, 1998; Doezema, 2005; Agustín, 2007; Kempadoo and Doezema, 1998) on the one side, and those who characterise prostitution as a form of violence against women and see little difference, if any, in the lack of freedoms for women involved in prostitution and those involved in trafficking (for example Farley, 2004; Raymond, 2004; Jeffreys, 1997 and 2000; Balos, 2004) – 'abolitionist feminists' – on the other. While the abolitionist conflation of trafficking and prostitution shows little recognition of the voluntariness or agency exercised by sex workers, the promotion by pro-sex work feminists of a distinction between voluntary sex work and the involuntariness involved in trafficking has also reinforced the voluntary/involuntary dichotomy which I outline further below.

The Abolitionist Agenda: The Conflation of Prostitution and Trafficking

The abolitionist agenda largely contends that to distinguish human trafficking from prostitution is to draw a false divide. In short, prostitutes are framed by abolitionists as mostly agency-less; the harms of prostitution and trafficking are said to be overlapping. For abolitionists, women in prostitution are not free agents operating on a level playing field in which they rationally 'choose' prostitution over other occupations for the advantages it offers (Barry, 1995). Economic coercion renders hollow any idea of this so-called agency or free choice (Jeffreys, 2000: 368–9). Rather, socio-economic inequality drives the decision-making that leads women into the sex industry in the first place and also shapes their conditions within the institution of prostitution.

Even where abolitionists recognise women's agency, it is not within the context of their choice to become a sex worker, but rather, their potential to escape prostitution. In an interview with Angela Miles, abolitionist Janice Raymond argues that, '[t]o acknowledge systematic victimization of women in the sex industry doesn't mean that you deny the victims' agency' (Raymond cited in Miles, 2003: 28). Rather, women act against this 'oppression' and many who had been in the sex industry 'managed to resist, survive, and rebuild their lives' (Raymond cited in Miles, 2003: 28).

With regard to harm, abolitionists such as Melissa Farley and Beverly Balos argue that the physical, social and psychological harms of prostitution cannot be controlled in a way that enhances the autonomy or safety of women (Farley, 2004: 1087; Balos, 2004: 138–9). In light of such harms involved in prostitution, they argue that it is contradictory to oppose trafficking while promoting prostitution as a justifiable form of labour (Farley, 2004: 1094–109). Arguments that frame prostitution as a form of work are deemed 'attempts to remove all obstacles to conducting the business of prostitution' (Farley, 2004: 1091) and a last-resort attempt to normalise women's exploitation adopted 'out of despair' (Barry, 1995: 296).

These authors argue that exploitation should be actionable whether it is against women or children and strong critiques are directed towards distinctions drawn between adult and child trafficking on the basis of capacity to consent (Balos, 2004; Raymond quoted in Miles, 2003: 26; see also Jeffreys, 2000). Moreover, prostitution is not only harmful to the prostituted women themselves, but makes all women vulnerable to subordination (Barry, 1995: 317).

Through this approach to both agency and harm, abolitionists blur experiences of women in 'prostitution' with those who have been trafficked. Both prostitution and trafficking are framed as involving an involuntary choice. Such an approach negates the possibility of women sitting within a migration spectrum. For their portrayal of trafficked women as vulnerable, exploited and non-autonomous agents, abolitionists are frequently described as part of a 'western feminist crusade' and the 'rescue industry' (Sutherland, 2004: 164; Trépanier, 2003: 50; Busza, 2004, 243; Chuang, 2010: 16).

Through both deliberate and careless use of statistics, the abolitionist is ever-present within the literature and wider public debates on trafficking. Wendy Chapkis, for example, notes the manipulation and mis-application of statistics to portray particular images about trafficking in the US in the lead-up to the drafting of the *Trafficking Victims' Protection Act 2000*. The US-based National Organization for Women (NOW), for example, claimed in 2000 that sex trafficking victimises 50,000 women and girls every year in the US alone. Chapkis responds that this figure was 'inaccurately based on data from a 1999 CIA briefing on global trafficking in which the CIA estimated that between 45,000 and 50,000 women and children are trafficked into the United States for *sweatshop labor, domestic servitude, agricultural work and prostitution* every year' (2003: 926, emphasis added). The misleading claim that all of these exploited documented workers are 'sex slaves' and that global trafficking is 'all about women and children' (Chapkis, 2003: 926; see also Godziak and Collett, 2005: 108), persists within and beyond the US, with research frequently giving inadequate attention to male victims.

Jo Doezema (2001) adds a further dimension, highlighting the racialised nature of the distinction between the 'free' and the 'involuntary' with the construction of the 'Third World prostitute' i.e. abolitionists' framing of prostitution and trafficking frequently describes the victimised woman in the Global South. Importantly, Doezema notes that abolitionists are not alone in constructing the image of the 'suffering prostitute body' (2001: 17–18). Even feminists who support the idea of sex work as a legitimate profession promote a dichotomy between the 'voluntary' western sex worker and 'victimized' third world sex worker (Doezema, 2001: 18). This 'suffering prostitute body', she also argues, appears in non-western, national discourse, used in the fight against the 'global march of capitalism, and its negative effects on women' (2001: 18, 22). To the contrary, Doezema writes that sex worker organisations from the Global South reject these racist portrayals of themselves as 'deluded and despairing' and the view that they 'are victims of their (backward, barbaric) cultures' (Doezema, 2001: 30).[5]

In brief, the abolitionist approach to prostitution and trafficking suggests that they are intimately linked, including in relation to their physical, social and psychological harms; victims, regardless of age, demonstrate no agency; and *both* prostitution and trafficking should be eradicated. Decisions of victims are said, at best, to be driven by the exploitation of vulnerabilities, particularly limited education, the need to escape from domestic violence and other socio-economic inequalities. What emerges is the picture of the coerced female, with at times racialised undertones.

Pro-Sex Work Feminists: The Voluntary Sex Worker and Involuntary Victim of Trafficking

Pro-sex work feminists argue that sex work is not inherently bad for women; if legalised, or at least, decriminalised, the rights of sex workers can be better protected and those engaging in the profession de-stigmatised (O'Connell Davidson, 2003; Kempadoo and Doezema, 1998). In an effort to promote this agenda, pro-sex work feminists draw a divide between 'voluntary' migration for sex work and trafficking for forced sexual exploitation.

Unlike sex work, they argue, trafficking is premised on exploitation and coercion or deceit about the nature of the work or working conditions (Segrave and Milivojevic, 2005: 11). If we fail to distinguish the two, Ratna Kapur – whose writing focuses on sexuality and the regulation of migration, particularly in relation to Indian women – contends that instead 'the woman and the movement of women are viewed through the lens of criminality and stigma, and the woman herself is rendered both a victim as well as an immoral subject' (2005: 147).

Other academics in this field maintain that it is primarily criminalisation, rather than the nature of the sex industry, that connects sex work and trafficking and puts voluntary sex workers at risk. For example, Kamala Kempadoo and Jo Doezema argue that as a result of criminalisation of sex work, the violence suffered by migrant women at the hands of recruiters, smugglers, employers, clients and immigration officials is exacerbated (Kempadoo and Doezema, 1998). In this respect, the Brazilian organisation Associação Brasileira de Defesa da Mulher, da Infância e da Juventude (ASBRAD) refers to the triple stigma – 'criminosa, puta e imigrante' (criminal, whore and immigrant) – that promotes inhumane treatment of sex workers (ASBRAD, 2008: 261).

However, such a distinction drawn by pro-sex work feminists between trafficking and its coercive practices and voluntary sex work downplays the agency and decision-making involved in migration linked to trafficking. The economic

---

5   On the topic of race, see also Patience Elabor-Idemudia's discussion of the traffic of Nigerian women in which she notes the role of 'class, gender, and ethnic concerns that marginalize women in particular from employment and education' (2003: 116).

rationality of women who later become victims of trafficking is paradoxically diminished. Ironically, this distinction made by pro-sex work feminists, which inevitably requires trafficking to be framed as *always* involving an act of coercion, has fostered the very stereotype of trafficked women chained to beds that these feminists deride.

Laura Agustín, who has engaged extensively in trafficking debates (2003a; 2003b; 2004; 2005; 2006; 2007; 2009), situates herself slightly more narrowly within this body of literature. Rather than focusing on the divide between trafficking and sex work, she is sceptical about the relevance of the term 'trafficking' altogether; rather she argues that migrant sex workers experience varying degrees of exploitation and are often able to resist economic, social and physical forms of compulsion. Criticising the closed borders that migrants often face, Agustín contends that it is the 'illegal' status attributed to the *migrant* sex worker that should be seen as the 'single overarching problem': their 'irregular status, not sex, is the heart of the issue' (2005: 98). This approach challenges stereotypical assumptions held about sex workers' agency. Yet Agustín's analysis is rather simplistic, leaving little space for non-voluntary cases and failing to recognise the shifts that may occur between voluntary and non-voluntary within an individual's experience.

In this sense, it is important not to ignore the empirical reality of the coerced victim of trafficking. However, it is problematic when this picture is generalised and presented as capturing all or most victims' experiences. As will be explained below, other actors in pursuit of their agendas play a substantial role in creating and reinforcing the coerced female victim archetype. However, I would argue that these two dichotomous groups of feminist theorists and the intensity of their debates have, intentionally or otherwise, played the most central role in shifting attention away from all forms of exploitative experiences towards trafficking for sexual exploitation, in turn promoting the idea of the quintessential female victim.

Government Agendas: Controlling Sex Work and Migration Using Anti-Trafficking Policies

This section focuses on government agendas and the misuse of anti-trafficking legislation to target both 'illegal migration' and sex work. Government efforts to combat trafficking – often framed as prevention, prosecution and protection – include the passage of legislation to criminalise the practice; fostering discussions on human trafficking as a normative issue; the creation of domestic campaigns to raise awareness; and the development of domestic programs for victims.

The analysis in this section focuses on the particular role of the executive and legislative arms of government. This is not to ignore the role of judiciaries and the impact case law can have in challenging or reinforcing the stereotypes analysed in this book. However, an analysis of individual cases from the lens of the mainstream framework is beyond the scope of the discussion presented here (see

Vijeyarasa and Bello y Villarino, 2012). Rather, my analysis focuses on the use, by some governments, of trafficking policies and debates to promote agendas related to criminalisation of sex work and tighter controls on migration. This section concerns these moral-political controversies over border control and prostitution that governments are frequently required or choose to straddle (Molland, 2012: 9). Specific laws and policies are discussed in the following chapter.

Human trafficking is a form of irregular – often termed illegal – migration. A significant driver of human trafficking, put simply, is border control and the way in which opportunities are created for the exploitation of individuals as a result of difficult, and for many potential migrants, unreachable requirements for regular, or legal, migration. Yet, the Trafficking Protocol shifts responsibility for trafficking away from nation states' restrictive immigration policies towards those who facilitate the movement of victims. This in turn fosters a criminal justice focus in anti-trafficking programs (as opposed to a migration and labour-centred focus), one that has been widely criticised in the literature (Burn, Blay and Simmons, 2005: 548; Coontz and Griebel, 2004: 52).

Based on an examination of anti-trafficking information and awareness-raising campaigns designed to prevent 'unwanted migration' from Central and Eastern Europe, Céline Nieuwenhuys and Antoine Pécoud discuss how the global recognition of trafficking as a human rights violation has been abused to legitimise the control of undocumented migration at large (2007: 1689). Scrutinising the campaigns organised by the inter-governmental organisation, IOM, they identify a clash between the goal of promoting the rights of individual migrants and the dominant goal of ensuring public security[6] and social cohesion. Nieuwenhuys and Pécoud highlight the limited value of information campaigns as these initiatives, in their view, incorrectly presume that migrants make rational decisions on the basis of available knowledge (2007: 1685).

Rather it is the migrants' interpretation of the situation as opposed to objective factors that really counts. Nieuwenhuys and Pécoud claim that this process of interpretation is grounded in a 'social context characterized by socioeconomic dead ends and exposure to signs of a better life' (Nieuwenhuys and Pécoud 2007: 1686). To the contrary, 'information' campaigns reinforce stereotypical victim imagery, buttress the fear among potential migrants of the risk of coercion and exploitation and use this fear as a deterrent for their decisions to migrate.

Rutvica Andrijasevic and Bridget Anderson similarly critique anti-trafficking campaigns, focusing on the manner in which they 'eroticize and fetishize women's bodies' (2009: 151). They note the failure of these campaigns to accurately reflect the reality of many victims' experiences and in turn how legal and policy

---

6   Other authors have similarly analysed how government officials have embraced the framing of human trafficking as a question of national security. Amy Farrell and Stephanie Fahy, for example, refer to how US officials have 'co-opt[ed] anti-trafficking under the guise of homeland security', with news articles in the US, between 2002 and 2006, discussing trafficking as an explicit national security threat (2009: 622).

frameworks set standards that many victims of exploitation do not meet: 'Not all those horrendously abused or caught in what some people describe as "modern day slavery" will count administratively as victims of trafficking even when they are migrants who are grossly exploited' (Andrijasevic and Anderson, 2009: 154). Andrijasevic and others note how anti-trafficking campaigns promote a stereotypical and rigid view of 'Eastern' European societies as patriarchal and crime-ridden, with women presented as naive victims (Sharma, 2003: 55; Nieuwenhuys and Pécoud, 2007: 1684; Andrijasevic and Anderson, 2009: 151). In masking women's economic rationality, the State is said to pursue its own agenda under the pretext of protecting women and children as well as its citizens and their homeland (see also Berman, 2010: 87 on this point).

As a result, these information campaigns (government and otherwise) promote a narrow view of trafficking that leaves out many victims of exploitation and simultaneously fosters a gender stereotypical perspective. The victim of trafficking, through this lens, is not a voluntary, decision-making migrant but rather is a duped, naive and innocent woman whose vulnerability is exploited.

We have also witnessed how a 'moral panic' against sex work fuels the push for anti-trafficking legislation (Amar, 2010; see also Berman, 2010). Efforts to curb sex work are driven by the goal of preserving 'social morals', maintaining public order, containing the spread of sexually transmitted infections (STIs) and protecting women from exploitation (Outshoorn, 2005: 141).

In the case, for example, of Vietnam, the government's agenda is driven by its designation of sex work as a 'social evil'. This perspective, in part, represents but also shapes and reinforces societal attitudes towards sex workers generally and in turn directly affects victims of trafficking (Vijeyarasa, 2010b). In an effort to criminalise and eradicate sex work, both trafficking and sex work are united as a government target. Like sex work, trafficking is viewed as an 'urgent and pressing problem, badly affecting the society, customs, tradition, social morals and Government laws, destroying family happiness, increasing the risks of HIV/AIDS transmission and resulting in potential impacts on national and social security' (National Plan of Action 2004 -2010: Part I, § 1).

Somewhat similarly, US federal government approaches to trafficking unquestionably emphasise trafficking for sexual exploitation over other forms of labour (Chang and Kim, 2007: 318), neglecting trafficking into agriculture, domestic work, restaurants, hotels, manufacturing and construction. While the US government is one of many major global players in this area, its weight in shaping global trafficking discourse should not be underestimated. It is the only government that produces an annual ranking of every government's interventions in the field of trafficking.

The role that US government donor aid plays in distorting global priorities has also been highlighted elsewhere. One study of Latin American local governments' anti-trafficking programmes has been described as 'adopted under a certain degree of external force or coercion', raising concerns about resource allocation in the face of aid dependency and the aggressive pursuit of inaccurate data to meet the demands of the donor (Guinn, 2008: 121). Both the domestic examples of Vietnam and the US are dealt with in greater detail in Chapter 3.

Evidently, not all governments follow the same approach to either migration or sex work. The purpose of this analysis, however, has been to demonstrate how the existence of both anti-immigration and anti-sex work goals within some government agendas has led to an exaggeration of the scope of coercion evident in trafficking cases. Within anti-immigration campaigns, the economic and social goals of potential migrants are overlooked. Criminalising both trafficking and sex work alike and in cases like Vietnam, linking the two as 'social evils', furthers the stereotype that trafficking is largely about sexual exploitation and the victimisation of women and girls. In the desire to achieve legal convictions, evidence of a victim's voluntariness may be ignored. Consequently, the image of a coerced female victim of sexual exploitation is reinforced as the quintessential victim of trafficking.

The Influence of the UN, Inter-Governmental and Non-Governmental Organisations and Donors

The UN, which encompasses a variety of agencies (from the United Nations High Commission for Refugees through to UN Women, UNICEF and ILO), has a substantial influence on global trafficking debates, discourse and practice. It is doubtful that a 'common approach' can be identified, particularly given each UN agency has a different mandate and focus. UNICEF, for example, is more focused on child trafficking, while the UN Office on Drugs and Crime (UNODC) is mandated to assist member states 'in their struggle against illicit drugs, crime and terrorism'. Nevertheless, many of the agencies (UNODC, UNHCR, UNICEF, UNICRI, UNIFEM, ILO, IOM and OHCHR) came together in 2009 as co-authors of the International Framework for Action to Implement the Trafficking in Persons Protocol, designed to tackle key challenges in the implementation of the Trafficking Protocol.

Beyond their technical role, UN agencies are also key players in shaping popular understanding of issues that fall within their mandates. It is precisely through these efforts that more nuanced contributions can be undermined. UNODC, for example, through its endorsement of the Blue Heart Campaign against Human Trafficking, offered supporters a simplistic view that reinforced the conflation of trafficking and slavery and failed to concede the lack of scientific evidence of the scope of the phenomenon: 'Millions of victims are entrapped and exploited every year in this modern form of slavery' (UNODC, 2013a). UNODC in fact introduced a new element of 'acquiring' in its definition of trafficking: 'Human trafficking is the acquisition of people by improper means such as force, fraud or deception, with the aim of exploiting them' (UNODC, 2013b). Given the challenges that already exist with the Trafficking Protocol's definition, the introduction of additional elements by UNODC is highly problematic and opens the door for further confusion among lay persons and practitioners alike.

We also cannot ignore the influence of other international organisations, especially IOM. An inter-governmental agency formed in 1951 whose membership increased to 157 States in 2015, IOM has established itself as a key entity in combating human trafficking. Its influence in the trafficking landscape is so great that in certain countries, such as Ukraine and Ghana, it would be reasonable to argue that where IOM places its focus is where the focus of the entire country's approach to trafficking lies. Frequently quoted for its trafficking statistics, the mere fact of being an IOM (as is the case with ILO) source adds weight to the data circulated and gives them an air of credibility that is not always a reflection of sound methodological approaches. This problem has been recognised before and a good example of an attempt to address this concern was the creation of the UNESCO Trafficking Statistics Project, designed to analyse and evaluate the methodologies behind these oft-cited statistics and address the inconsistencies in estimates on trafficking, particularly those offered by UN agencies (UNESCO, n.d.).

In general, it seems logical that there is a link between the agendas of the most preeminent organisations who deal with trafficking in a particular country or region and the meaning given to trafficking in that locality. In Latin America, ILO and IOM are not the leading players in the trafficking landscape. Instead, in this region a significant part of the international efforts to combat trafficking is led by other intergovernmental organisations such as the Inter-American Commission of Women and the Inter-American Children's Institute of the Organization of American States; NGOs such as Save the Children; as well as UNICEF (Guinn, 2008: 129). With these groups focused on children and women victims, it is inevitable that the Latin-American approach to trafficking, and the perception of trafficking itself, will be different: 'i]nsofar as they are among the primary sources of data on the problem, analysis of that data will necessarily highlight their concerns' (Guinn, 2008: 130). As a result, women and children are frequently presented as the quintessential victims in the region.

NGOs, both local and international, are the primary conduit for donor funding in many source countries (although there has been a shift in recent years on the funding front in light of aid effectiveness principles). Donors therefore also play a role in shaping the work of NGOs, including international NGOs and therefore need to be examined as part of our assessment of how trafficking concepts are created and reinforced. The pursuit of donor resources may skew NGO priorities towards addressing issues of particular concern to funders, such as 'favoring efforts to help children or address sex trafficking – issues with strong emotional appeal to donor organizations and their supporters and funders – rather than issues of labor abuse' (Guinn, 2008: 140).

David Guinn notes how 'topic fragmentation by funders also impairs the effort to develop a coordinated, coherent national and regional plan for the overall anti-trafficking effort' (2008: 140). The skewing of priorities due to donor funding is clearly evident in Ghana, with informants on the ground identifying child trafficking with funding opportunities: 'People think that if they work on child trafficking and children's issues, then they will get sponsorship. They will get money. So they ignore adult trafficking' (Anon., Ghana Police Anti-Human Trafficking Unit, 27 August 2010). Sverre Molland adds to this his honest reflections on NGO anti-trafficking programme staff in Laos, himself having come from that sector. These workers, Molland notes, 'depend on the imagery of the trafficked victim to give legitimacy to the very existence of anti-trafficking programmes' (2012: 19). He therefore argues 'it is perfectly reasonable to ask who needs whom' (2012: 19).

The work of the numerous UN Rapporteurs whose mandates directly or indirectly engage the topic of human trafficking, must also be noted here. Within the portfolios of the Special Rapporteur on Trafficking in Persons, especially Women and Children; the Special Rapporteur on Contemporary Forms of Slavery, its Causes and Consequences; and the Special Rapporteur on the Sale of Children, Child Prostitution and Child Pornography, we have seen some careful considerations of the links between trafficking, migration and human rights (see for example Ngozi Ezeilo, 2012b: ¶ 10). Appointed by the UN Secretary General, these mandate holders are meant to act independently of their governments through fact-finding missions and their advisory roles. However, the cumulative work of these rapporteurs reveals substantial divergence in the extent to which they reinforce or challenge stereotypical portrayals of trafficking and its victims.

The Special Rapporteur on Violence against Women, for example, has issued a number of reports to address the issue of trafficking in women. The initial reports produced by the violence against women mandate-holder in the late 1990s reflected a lack of alignment with either group of feminists described above in relation to debates on whether sex work can be freely chosen and consensual. However, reports from 2000 onwards recognise sex work as a labour rights issue. The work of Coomaraswamy, Special Rapporteur on Violence against Women from 1994 to 2003, gives credence to the notion of a migration spectrum. Yet at the same time, and arguably because the mandate is focused on violence against women, the reports tend to reinforce gender stereotypes by identifying various examples of gender inequality as the 'causes' of human trafficking.

The natural focus on women and children of the Special Rapporteur on Trafficking in Women and Children is self-explanatory. To the contrary, the Special Rapporteur on the Human Rights of Migrants, who does not carry such a narrow mandate, is well-placed to broaden the analysis and challenge narrow portrayals. Unfortunately, however, the 2011 Report of Special Rapporteur Jorge Bustamante continued to emphasise the role of the third party – traffickers, smugglers, clandestine trafficking networks – largely ignoring the important role of the victim themselves and the significance of this for our understanding of drivers of migratory movement (Bustamante, 2011). It does, nonetheless, call for a rights-based approach, challenging government policies that in reality fail to deter smuggling and trafficking and in fact exacerbate violence and abuse of victims (Bustamante, 2011). The report of the 2014 mandate-holder, François Crépeau on labour exploitation, importantly emphasised the close interrelationship between trafficking and deception regarding salaries, working hours, days off and the nature of the work, as well as vulnerability of migrants to non-payment of salaries (Crépeau, 2014: ¶ 46).

The Special Rapporteur on Trafficking, Joy Ngozi Ezeilo, who held the mandate from 2008 to 2014, should be commended for challenging the narrow focus on a criminal justice solution to trafficking by advocating for a more victim-centred approach and by condemning the criminalisation and detention of victims. However, the tendency to label certain unfounded 'causes' as responsible for trafficking persisted in her work, including references to gender inequality and poverty (Ngozi Ezeilo, 2009: 25; see also Ngozi Ezeilo, 2011: ¶ 21–2).).

In this category, I have placed a broad mix of UN agencies, UN experts, international and national NGOs and the donor community. Despite the divergences in mandates, roles and purposes, we still see a focus on women and children, whether due to the parameters of their mandate, the drive for donor funding or the search for a justification for the very existence of the actors' efforts to combat trafficking. It is essential that organisations like IOM and ILO are held to account for a higher standard of accuracy when reporting numbers and patterns of movement, particularly given the weight they hold as major players in the field. Lack of a strong evidence base for statistics, inaccuracies in definitions and biases towards certain types of trafficking raise stark concerns about how certain agendas rather than the realities of the phenomenon itself may be a driving force behind what we understand to be trafficking.

The Rescue Industry

The fifth agenda that is the subject of this discussion is that of the 'rescue industry', which has received only minimal attention at the academic level. The term 'rescue industry' is used to group NGOs and other civil society organisations and those of influence[7] in favour of 'rescuing' women from the sex industry (male and transgender sex workers are less often targeted for rescue). The narrative of the rescue industry often involves the Western feminist rescuer (Sutherland, 2004: 164; Trépanier, 2003: 50; Busza, 2004: 243; Chuang, 2010: 16) or (white) male rescuer (Overs, 2009: 13), the latter frequently tied to faith-based (often Christian) organisations (Ahmed and Seshu, 2012: 159–61). Among other things, they advocate for, and even participate in, raids on brothels in order to extract women from their 'captors'. These kinds of activities may also be done with the assistance of the police.

A deconstruction of the approaches of the rescue industry reveals a constant shift between the rescue of the women themselves and the 'rescue' of their purity. The goals are therefore both practical – saving victims and punishing wrongdoers –

---

7 The term has also been applied by Laura Agustín to journalist Nicholas Kristof (Agustín, 2012).

and symbolic – defining normative boundaries and moral standards (Weitzer and Ditmore, 2010: 325; see also Weitzer, 2007). It is the symbolic ones that are particularly pertinent to this analysis of underlying agendas, contributing to the victim archetype, especially with regard to the sex of victims, an overemphasis on coerced movement and a focus on sexual rather than other forms of exploitation.

The influence of the 'rescue' industry on trafficking discourse should not be underestimated: '[A]ctivists have met with remarkable success in getting their views and demands incorporated in government policy, legislation, and law enforcement practices' (Weitzer, 2007: 447). The 'rescue industry' is a stakeholder that does not operate on its own. Julia O'Connell Davidson, for example, notes the alliances often formed between 'moral conservatives', feminist abolitionists, police and anti-immigration politicians as 'strange' 'bed fellows' (2003, 61).

Some academics and practitioners are less critical of the rescue approach. In a study that focuses on minors within the sex industry, Holly Burkhalter responds to criticisms directed towards the role that police play in rescues and raids by naming this as only one of several potential sources of violence against adults and children in the sex industry (2012: 132). Burkhalter insists on the necessity of the presence of police, despite the concerns raised by sex worker groups and academics towards such interventions (see for example Chuang, 2010: 1716). She sees the solution as lying with reform of local police.

Nonetheless, academics like Melissa Ditmore and Juhu Thukral (2012) discuss research which reveals how raids conducted by local law enforcement agencies are an ineffective means of locating and identifying trafficked persons. Such evidence of harmful raids and rescues leads us to question Burkhalter's position that 'professionalization of the police … is attainable' and that, in the meantime, 'children and trafficked adults being raped for profit should not have to wait until police everywhere in the world have been pronounced good enough to protect them' (2012: 133). Burkhalter seems to suggest that the possible risk of harm to or abuse of consensual sex workers from a brothel raid is justified by the potential rescue of victims.

Illustrative of the rescue industry at its worse is the work of Jeffrey Cole (2006) in regard to Nigeria. An academic in the field of anthropology, Cole states that his aim is to 'assess a project that offers medical care, free condoms, advice on safe practices and other forms of assistance to Nigerian prostitutes' (2006: 217). However, his piece is sensationalist and trades in stereotypes. Making no distinction between sex work and trafficking, he contends that the women in the project 'encounter unanticipated and brutal exploitation at the hands of their co-national female exploiter, the "madam" and her male associates' (Cole, 2006: 217). Cole's piece is an insensitive article that is not justified on the basis of accuracy or a scientific approach. Writing of the reluctance of the 'Nigerian prostitutes' to get involved in the NGO project, he comments:

> Mediators describe the women as very aggressive, at least initially. They shout, taunt and even strike at their would-be helpers. When it suits them, they speak

insistently in Pidgin English, pretending they cannot understand a word the team utters in Italian, English or French. Nor do they hide their suspicions. More than once they have rifled through the project vehicle, searching for surveillance equipment (there was none) ... The female mediator described women who touch and rub up against her, saying they have AIDS. (Cole, 2006: 220)

Cole makes no effort to understand the lack of trust the women workers have in the NGO. Nor does he reflect on how such moral judgment, when weighed against the little offered in return, may make the NGO programme undesirable for these women who may wish to remain sex workers.

Economic considerations are also frequently ignored by the rescue industry model. The rescue and repatriation approach fails to provide women with compensation for their labour, protection from retaliation or immigration relief and may further the economic difficulties these women may face (Zheng, 2010: 2, 10; see also Busza, 2004: 243–4). Pardis Mahdavi, in her analysis of trafficking in Dubai, particularly critiques efforts to legitimise brothel raids by organisations like Free the Slaves and authors like Siddharth Kara through the framing of women as 'ignorant or duped into terrible situations' (2011: 68; see also Phoenix, 2009 for an analysis of the UK rescue industry). Busza and colleagues also contend that many 'rescued' women 'usually returned to their brothel as quickly as possible' after a raid (Busza, Castle and Diarra, 2004: 1370), highlighting the limited value that this approach has in achieving the underlying goal.

Several key observations emerge from this analysis. First, the rescue industry's approach reinforces the focus on sexual exploitation and the female victim. Second, we see a merging of the discourse around sex work, migration and trafficking, with little, if any, recognition of the distinctions between these experiences or the possibility of voluntary decision-making. Collectively, all women involved must be rescued from abuse as agency-less, passive recipients of help. Where distinctions between non-coerced sex workers and trafficked victims are made, rescues and raids are treated as the lesser of two evils, with the potential harm to some voluntary sex workers justified by the rescue of trafficked victims.

Third, such discourse frequently reproduces the white slavery imagery of earlier decades, thereby frequently conflating slavery and trafficking; the rescue industry seeks to end those practices that 'endanger the welfare of the individual, the family and the community' (Trafficking Convention, 1949: Preamble). Finally, the synergies between the coverage of trafficking by the media and the agendas of the rescue industry must be noted. The media amplifies the views of the 'rescue industry' through the disproportionately large amount of coverage given to it relative to its size as an actor in the trafficking phenomenon. This final point is discussed in more detail in the following section.

The Media

When it comes to profit-driven media, its stake is clear: sensationalist portrayals of human trafficking draw readership better than moderate accounts of the phenomenon. Media reporting globally shows disproportionate attention to trafficking for sexual exploitation when compared to the non-sex sector (Chuang, 2010: 1696–7; Gulati, 2011), 'manufacturing the belief that most if not all trafficking is sex trafficking by always keeping sex in the limelight' (Uy, 2011: 209). In popular press descriptions of trafficking, the attention is either on the 'bad migrant sex worker' (see Agustín, 2003b: 377) or the 'innocent victim' and on the scandalous sex industry that has exploited them. The latter is evident in the writings of journalist and academic Benjamin Skinner, in his expositions on the 'modern American war on slavery' (2008a: xvii).

With reference to Nicholas Kristof's series in *The New York Times* on 'sex slavery' in Cambodia and Peter Landesman's *New York Times Magazine* piece on 'sex slavery' in the United States, Janie Chuang notes how abolitionists have 'shaped and fed public scepticism over whether meaningful consent to prostitution is possible' (2010: 1769; see also Hallgrímsdóttir, Phillips, Benoit and Walby, 2008 discussion of media narratives about prostitution and their relationship to prostitution stigmas). Chuang identifies the common 'slippage' between prostitution and trafficking in the media that 'sweeps any exercise of agency by the putative victim under a totalizing narrative of victimization that refuses to engage in any marking of relative control or freedom' (2010: 1700). As a result, patterns of trafficking are described by the media as 'men dominat[ing] and all prostitute women […] subordinate, oppressed and unfree' (Chuang, 2010: 1700).

As noted above, the media often amplifies the goals of the rescue industry. Tom O'Neill's analysis of media reporting on the 'traffic' of Nepali women and girls to Kuwait offers an excellent example of the sweeping generalisations and tendency of the press to ignore salient details. O'Neill discusses the media's treatment of the 'rescue' of 15 teenage girls from Helambu in Nepal by the then Government of Nepal and NGO Maiti Nepal from a 'scheme to traffic them to work in Kuwait as domestic workers' in the late 1990s. O'Neill argues that while the media accurately noted that the decision to leave Nepal was made largely by the girls' parents, this did not necessarily mean that the girls were forced 'against their own will' (2001: 162). The whole scheme was conflated with forced prostitution, with the young girls 'presented as child like innocents who were victimized by more powerful and more knowledgeable agents who prey upon that innocence' (O'Neill, 2001: 162). In addition, the experiences of all 15 girls were conflated with that of a Nepalese female migrant, Kani Sherpa who, in an earlier incident, had been raped and abused by the men in the family where she was working in Kuwait and later committed suicide in November 1998.

Mojca Pajnik's analysis (2010) of the representation of trafficking in the Slovenian press is also illustrative here. Trafficking, according to Pajnik, is presented within four dominant frames: criminalisation, nationalisation, victimisation and regularisation (2010: 51) and primarily involving a problem of illegal migration. As a consequence, Pajnik notes that 'more complex social and economic circumstances are neglected ... the anti-trafficking paradigm is promoted as a "natural" response, one that is necessary for the survival of the nation-state and of the world social order, and that is also in the interest of the victims' (2010: 49). Such a construction of trafficking fails to reflect the multiple dimensions of migration-related decisions and clearly supports a governmental agenda around fighting crime, heightened security and closed borders.

Finally, it is important to note that the media's role in some countries is more extreme where the press is not free and is required to reproduce the views of the government, thereby acting as a tool to promote government agendas. In Vietnam, for example, public statistics become suspect while the language of 'social evils' and corrupted families is replicated, with the press, for example, reporting on 'women falling prey to city evils' (Viet Nam Net Bride, 7 January 2009).

In this category, I also include the extensive number of films (English language and foreign) about trafficking. While the films differ in quality and emphasis, and certainly not all films promote the stereotypes questioned in this book, a large majority focus on trafficking into industries related to sexual exploitation with very little concern for labour trafficking (see also Chuang, 2010: 1697 for a critique of trafficking films). These films present a formulaic picture with common traits: trafficking equals sexual exploitation; its victims are women and frequently from Southeast Asia and Eastern Europe; and its perpetrators are mainly men. Rarely deviating from this mould, at least in their focus on the female victim, they generate and strengthen the stereotypes promoted about trafficking.

Perhaps the most famous human trafficking film is *Lilja 4-Ever* about an Estonian girl trafficked for sexual exploitation to Sweden. In the case of *Lilja 4-Ever*, the concern stems beyond the question of popular appeal. The film has been treated as 'factual evidence' of contemporary human slavery for education purposes by governments, members of parliament (MPs) and groups like IOM (Small, 2012).

Other examples include *Taken* (2008), about an ex-CIA agent whose daughter is kidnapped while on vacation in Paris – a city not known to be a major trafficking hub – by a group of Albanian traffickers, which evokes white slavery imagery; *Not for Sale* (2007) which emphasises the language of enslavement and has led to a world-wide campaign that conflates ending slavery with combating trafficking, particularly from Eastern Europe; and finally *Human Trafficking* (2005), which similarly draws heavily on stereotypes of trafficking of Eastern European women.

Through a valuable analysis of *Lilja 4-Ever*, *Human Trafficking* and *Born into Brothels*, Jamie Small notes how the treatment of these narratives of abuse are 'monolithic'. They 'leav[e] little or no room ... for nuances and complexities of individual lives' or 'institutional and structural conditions that reproduce inequality' (Small, 2012: 439). Instead, the construction of at-risk victims as child-like, the conflation of youth and femininity with victimisation and the manner in which sexuality 'haunts the characters' are treated as authentic truths by the films' producers (Small, 2013: 417).

More valuable contributions, which nonetheless retain a focus on sexual exploitation and reinforce this stereotype, include *The Whistleblower* (2010) about an American police officer who takes a job working as a peacekeeper in post-war Bosnia and *The Jammed* (2008). The latter was promoted as 'a thriller about trafficking, governmental deportation and the sex slave trade in Melbourne', furthering the salacious depiction of human trafficking.

The media is a key shaper of public opinions and the failure of media representations of trafficking to reflect a divergence of experiences is a grave concern. The biased involvement of the media in promoting these narrow views exists at both national and global levels. At times, the media's approach is intimately connected to the agendas of the rescue industry; in other instances, we see close links to government goals related to border security, migration and sex work. Among the assumptions that inform mainstream trafficking discourse are the notions that the entry of all women into the sex industry is predominantly forced and that trafficked women are only too happy to be rescued, reintegrated or rehabilitated. Racialised undertones tend towards a focus on Eastern Europe and to a degree Southeast Asia. The multi-dimensional nature of the phenomenon and its links to labour and migration are all diluted in this mainstream portrayal.

Victim Self-Imagery: The Good Woman, Innocent Victim and Inviolable Man

This final section focuses on a frequently neglected issue in trafficking debates: the priorities of the victims themselves and the role this plays in shaping victim imagery. Few authors critique the unquestioned acceptance of the stories of victims. Arguably this is because it is often deemed unfriendly to victims and therefore inappropriate to challenge their stories. However, particularly for returned victims of trafficking, there may be a need to exaggerate experiences abroad in order to be considered a 'true' victim. That is, victims may feel the need to ensure that their story corresponds with that of the archetypal victim in order to receive compensation or victim support or to avoid being deported as an unlawful immigrant.

There is limited literature discussing the types of biases that emerge in the testimonies of victims. One of the very few examples is Ted Leggett, a US academic who has previously written about sex workers in South Africa. Discussing the need to draft a new anti-trafficking law in South Africa, he writes:

> Another major deficiency of the existing research is the uncritical way the narratives of the women are accepted. When asked to explain their activity, sex workers can be expected to portray themselves as victims, and for foreign sex workers, this portrayal is likely to fit the broad definitions of trafficking. Particularly when encountering law enforcement, foreign sex workers will most

likely chose to be repatriated as trafficked innocents, rather than opportunistic prostitutes. (Leggett, 2004)

While Leggett's analysis is simplistic in its dichotomy of innocents and opportunists and has a critical undertone directed towards sex workers, it is important to note how a country's laws and policies on trafficking and sex work and the treatment of victims may encourage voluntary sex workers and victims of trafficking to create or alter stories of their experiences in order to protect themselves from other rights violations. On the one hand, there may be a need to exaggerate or falsify one's story in order to be accepted as a victim in a trafficking reintegration programme. On the other hand, out of shame or embarrassment, there may be an incentive to downplay their own voluntary contribution to the situation that led to their exploitation as proof of 'added innocence'. Victims may also be more likely to perceive their situation prior to leaving their country of origin as worse, justifying their decision to leave and accept a fraudulent contract for work abroad.

In comparison to the limited attention paid to possible biases in trafficking victims' stories, a larger body of academic work exists on research biases in investigations on sex work. Laura Agustín, for example, has noted that '[i]t has long been recognised that people who are considered "victims" or "deviants" are likely to tell members of mainstream society what they believe they want to hear' (2004: 6). Agustín argues that in light of the contemporary focus of research on the personal motivations of sex workers and why they entered the sex industry, 'many make their present circumstances appear to be the fatal or desperate result of a past event' (2004: 6). Agustín refers to the comments of one Dominican research participant, who said, '[a]fter all, if we were forced to be what we are now, we cannot be blamed for it' (2004: 6).

Wendy Brown's analysis elaborates this idea further. The porn star who feels exploited 'invariably monopolizes the feminist truth about sex work', while sexual abuse and violation are the prevailing themes when it comes to feminist discourse on women and sexuality (2005: 92). That is, despite feminist attempts to ensure diverse representations of women and women's experiences, what results is 'a unified discourse in which the story of greatest suffering becomes the true story of woman' (Brown, 2005: 92). Reinforcing the view of the Dominican research participant cited above, Brown further suggests that shame and suffering are in some sense 'required', otherwise one would be excluded as a bona fide member of the category. She gives examples of the adult woman who does not continue to suffer from her childhood sexual abuse or the lesbian who feels no shame for her sexuality (Brown, 2005: 92).

The questions that emerge from Agustín's and Brown's analyses equally apply to research on trafficking. The exploited victim of trafficking, whether they have suffered sexual, labour or both forms of exploitation, may feel compelled to 'feel' and express shame and suffering, even if these emotions were a limited or non-existent part of their experience. Consequently, the tradition of 'breaking silence' acts only to 'silence and exclude the very persons these traditions mean to empower' (Brown, 2005: 92). Brown argues for 'story telling' 'that is neither confessional nor normative in a moralizing sense' (2005: 96); we must therefore seek trafficking testimonies in a mode that neither demands that victims admit guilt nor requires them to conform to a particular victim mould.

While the status of the female victim 'requires' shame and suffering, the contrary can be said of male victims. Stereotypes regarding men's demeanour as 'macho' often undermine their ability to self-identify as victims, thereby reaffirming the stereotype that it is predominantly women who are victims of trafficking. This is summarised succinctly in the comment of an informant from Ukraine: 'Men are less willing to recognise themselves as victims. Men are less visible and they tend to keep to themselves whereas women come out easier and bond with others' (T. Ivanyuk, IOM, Ukraine, 3 September 2009).

Insights by one of my informants brought many of these issues to light, suggesting that there may indeed be multiple truths to what an individual has experienced or suffered:

> I was working in a shelter in Spain. You know how many times a victim told her story? Thousands. They say it to the police, to the social worker. A lot of the women were more or less – not inventing – but after so many conversations, they had a story. They were building a story, a story that was acceptable for society. It is very difficult after this to go away from the story that they have told. It does not mean that they are lying. You have your personal story but after you have contact with other women, you say something that is more consistent … (E. Ferreras, Programme Director, Multilateral Cooperation and Gender, AECID, 9 October 2009)

Victim testimony is also affected by fear of criminalisation and justifiable desires for redress, both legal and economic. In this respect, one informant in Vietnam made a rather controversial statement, suggesting that the incentives associated with 'victimhood' must not be ignored:

> … Some people, they pretend that they are trafficked and three days later they return to the country and they claim the package. I have heard stories of that here in Vietnam where there were four sex workers. One of them sold three others to a brothel in China but they had worked in the brothels before. They are regular migrants. They cross the borders regularly and the tricks of migrants do not deceive them but they got back and claimed the government support. (Anon., National Trafficking Project Coordinator, United Nations Agency, 16 October 2009)

While this was the only such example offered during my field research, it identifies the possible role economic incentives play in skewing victim testimony and consequently victim imagery.

Sexual stereotypes concerning the 'good woman', the 'innocent victim', and the 'inviolable man' have a significant influence on trafficking narratives and those of its victims, as well as the ability of certain individuals to identify as victims. This latter problem has created a major barrier to the identification of male victims and possibly also a broader demographic of female victims as well. While this 'agenda' sits apart from the others articulated in this chapter, it nonetheless has also shaped trafficking debates, research, discourse and imagery and is important to keep in mind as we continue to explore the myths and misconceptions behind the trafficking phenomenon.

Conclusion

The various categories analysed in this chapter (feminist academics, governments, NGOs and related groups involved in raids and rescues, the UN, inter-governmental organisations, donors and the media), identify, promote and amplify the attention given to various 'causes' assumed to link with human trafficking. The moral panic of governments towards sex work and the demands from abolitionists for the criminalisation of prostitution endorse the idea that prostitution and the underlying problem of gender inequality are to blame for trafficking. The coerced victim of trafficking is central to the arguments made by pro-sex work feminists who put forward a neat distinction between voluntary sex work and coerced trafficking-like practices. Meanwhile, abolitionists draw direct links between sex work and its harm to the traffic of women; rescue and rehabilitation of sex workers is justified by a world view that both prostitution and trafficking exploit the secondary and unequal status of women. Anti-immigration campaigning intensifies coerced victim imagery, with naive and uneducated women framed as the most vulnerable to deception. It simultaneously gives governments 'political purchase' for their roles in protecting the homeland and 'saving' a population of innocent, women victims.

While these agendas are in a number of respects distinct, they also frequently come together, amplifying each other and presenting one dominant image of trafficking and its victims that reinforce the assumptions that are discussed in Part II of this book. These stakeholders, given the weight of their views, shape the lens through which trafficking is viewed and debated. In the following chapter, we turn to what may be seen as an eighth 'shaper' of trafficking discourse: the national and international legal landscape and its definitions of trafficking. The focus of the analysis that follows is on how the law contributes to and shapes the mainstream trafficking framework, including who constitutes a victim of trafficking.

Chapter 3

Legislative Approaches to Trafficking: The Role of the Law in Challenging or Reinforcing Myths and Misconceptions

The law plays an important role in consolidating society's understanding of trafficking. However, as will be demonstrated in this chapter, the law plays a more crucial role; it frames the meaning we attribute to the phenomenon itself, even outside of a legal context. In this chapter, I focus on the law's role in influencing trafficking debates and analyse how legislation reinforces mainstream approaches to trafficking. This includes the way in which the law defines *who* is recognised by society as a victim of trafficking and *why* certain factors are labelled as 'causes'.

Trafficking provisions at the national, regional and international levels frequently fail to define human trafficking in a manner that reflects the stories of individual victims, the existing data or case law. At times, trafficking laws cast the net wide, capturing not only victims of trafficking but also exploited migrants within their ambit. At other times, legal provisions attempt to create neat categories, confining victims and their experiences into distinct groups by determining who does or does not meet the legal standards for trafficking. However, we cannot easily divide victims between the involuntary and the voluntary, between those who experience one type of exploitation (for example, sexual) and those who experience other forms. As Rutvica Andrijasevic and Bridget Anderson note in their feminist critique of anti-trafficking campaigns:

> Hierarchies of suffering may reflect more the preconceptions and feelings of those who devise them than those who experience them. But workers, migrant or not, cannot be divided into two entirely separate and distinct groups – those who are trafficked involuntarily into the misery of slavery in an illegal economic sector, and those who voluntarily and legally work in the happy and protected world of the formal economy. Violence, confinement, coercion, deception and exploitation can and do occur within both legally regulated and irregular systems of work. How to draw a line in the sand between 'trafficked' and 'not trafficked but just-the-regular-kind-of-exploitation' migrants? (2009: 154)

This chapter tries to delve further into that very question: 'How does the law attempt to draw a line in the sand?' In order to do this and assess the impact the law has in shaping assumptions about coercion and the factors said to correlate with increased vulnerability to trafficking, this chapter is divided into three sections.

The first section deals with the primary international legal instrument related to human trafficking, the Trafficking Protocol, including the establishment of a 'global' definition. The second part of this chapter involves an analysis of other legal instruments at the international and regional levels that are relevant to the question of how trafficking is conceptualised. Finally, a select number of national laws, in both sending and receiving countries, are examined. This third section involves an analysis of not only how trafficking is defined nationally but also how victims are identified in practice.

There is an extensive body of laws and conventions that have an impact on human trafficking. This includes the ILO Convention Concerning Forced Labour (No. 29) (1930) and the ILO Convention Concerning the Prohibition and Immediate Action for the Elimination of the Worst Forms of Child Labour (No. 182) (1999). While relevant to broader discussions on trafficking as a whole, an overarching study of all trafficking laws is not considered necessary here. Instead, only those laws that have a *significant* and *identifiable* impact on the mainstream trafficking framework are discussed.

The Trafficking Protocol and its Problematic Definition of Trafficking

As noted in the Introduction, the most relied upon global definition of trafficking is provided in the Trafficking Protocol. Trafficking is defined as:

> ... the recruitment, transportation, transfer, harbouring or receipt of persons, by means of the threat or use of force or other forms of coercion, of abduction, of fraud, of deception, of the abuse of power or of a position of vulnerability or of the giving or receiving of payments or benefits to achieve the consent of a person having control over another person, for the purpose of exploitation. Exploitation shall include, at a minimum, the exploitation of the prostitution of others or other forms of sexual exploitation, forced labour or services, slavery or practices similar to slavery, servitude or the removal of organs; ... (Article 3(a), Trafficking Protocol).

In the following sections, I look at the origins of the Protocol, its particular lens of analysis and the impact this has on our understanding of human trafficking.

Prostitution, Sex Work and a Position of Vulnerability

It is important to consider the historical significance of debates concerning the definition of trafficking. Although not to the same extent as the 1949 Convention for the Suppression of the Traffic in Persons and of the Exploitation of the

Prostitution of Others,[1] the definition of trafficking in the Trafficking Protocol, with its explicit reference to 'the exploitation of the prostitution of others', places the spotlight on sexual exploitation within trafficking debates. This is exacerbated by the fact that the definition sits within a protocol with a particular focus on protecting 'especially women and children'.

As noted in the previous chapter, human trafficking has stirred (and continues to stir) considerable debate among the two major schools of feminist thought that address the question of consent in sex work. Feminists on both sides of the abolition/legalisation divide considered the negotiations over the Trafficking Protocol a critical moment in establishing a general principle on whether or not all forms of prostitution/sex work should be considered violence and therefore inextricably linked to trafficking (see for example Doezema (2005) for a discussion of the involvement of the pro-sex work movement in the Trafficking Protocol's negotiations).

In an effort to avoid a definitive answer, numerous terms that are central to how trafficking is framed are left vague or undefined in the Trafficking Protocol. The phrases 'exploitation of the prostitution of others' and 'other forms of sexual exploitation' were intentionally left undefined so as to reflect a 'compromise definition'. This was intended to accommodate the divergence of responses to sex work that exist in national legislation, that is, criminalisation, decriminalisation and/or regulation while simultaneously still achieving a consensus on the definition of trafficking (UNODC, 2006: 347; Gallagher, 2010: 28). Nonetheless, described by some as a 'win' for abolitionists (Jeffreys, 2002: 45; Piscitelli, 2008: 32), the Trafficking Protocol's definition was seen by many pro-sex work groups as conflating sex work with trafficking and as deeming sex work exploitative in whatever context (Ditmore, 2002: 35).

Failure to provide explicit clarity on the relationship between prostitution/sex work and trafficking has fostered the debates that have preoccupied feminist critical thinking prior to and since the Trafficking Protocol's enactment. This has facilitated the bias towards trafficking for sexual exploitation that is critiqued in this book. Such debates have deflected valuable attention away from the larger question of the best means of protecting a broader category of migrants from exploitation (Vijeyarasa, 2010a: 11–12).

In addition to the vague treatment of prostitution within the Trafficking Protocol, the drafters also failed to define adequately one of the elements of the definition, that is, 'abuse of power or of a position of vulnerability'. In addition to the lack of definition, the phrase itself presents problems. With a Protocol focused on protecting 'especially women and children', this phrase emphasises the image of the vulnerable woman targeted by perpetrating males. Further, the Trafficking Protocol deflects attention from the agency and decision-making capacity of

---

1   The 1949 Convention links 'prostitution' with 'the accompanying evil of the traffic in persons for the purposes of prostitution'.

women involved in migration and poses challenges for implementation as discussed in detail in Chapter 8.

The Treatment of Consent

The Trafficking Protocol defines the issue of consent of the victim in these terms:

> The consent of a victim of trafficking in persons to the intended exploitation set forth in subparagraph (a) of this article shall be *irrelevant* where any of the means set forth in subparagraph (a) have been used. (Article 3(b), Trafficking Protocol, emphasis added)

This provision renders the individual's consent *legally* irrelevant to the trafficker's defence if any of the means named in the Trafficking Protocol are used, that is, for example, if there is evidence of coercion, force, deception or fraud.

In determining whether a crime has been perpetrated, it is indeed not only legally practical but also victim-centred to nullify such consent. However, while the intention behind this provision is to deem consent by the victim *legally* irrelevant in a trafficker's defence, this definition of trafficking is used and applied outside of the framework of law. Outside of legal circles, it shifts attention away from any process of autonomous decision-making engaged in by the victim and is inadequate in encapsulating the socio-economic factors that may be relevant to trafficking. It also fails to portray realistically the roles of all parties involved in migration and labour exploitation.

An emerging body of literature demonstrates that trafficking rarely corresponds to the image of the kidnapped and naive young woman, but more frequently involves economic migrants (for example Banerjee, 2006: 192–3; Chapkis, 2003: 931–2; Chuang, 2010: 1659), some of whom may even know that the tourist visa on which they are travelling has been obtained without disclosure of the intention to work in the destination country (see Tang (2007) at 19; also Dorevitch and Foster, 2008: 9). A significant number of victims of trafficking therefore consent to their initial entry into a situation where they risk exploitative conditions of work.

Moreover, the approach encapsulated in the Protocol presents challenges for the victim, despite the legal nullification of consent. As has been noted by various authors (Obokata, 2005: 395; Musto, 2009: 28; Spener, 2011: 175), the greater the apparent voluntariness of the individual migrant, the easier it is – particularly for law enforcement agents – to determine the situation to be a case of smuggling rather than trafficking. It is often deemed 'impossible' in the eyes of the law for a voluntary person to be a victim, particularly when it comes to trafficking. Therefore, when consent is considered legally relevant in a particular case i.e. none of the means listed have been used, the victim is not a minor or lacking legal capacity to consent, victims are frequently left to choose between downplaying or ignoring their voluntary acts or having their status as a victim denied (see in more detail Vijeyarasa, 2010e). In this regard, Jo Doezema argues that the sex worker is left to a 'precarious' existence, with nothing in the Trafficking Protocol to protect them from abuse where they 'fall outside of the narrowly constructed category of "trafficking victim"' (Doezema, 2005: 80). Doezema argues that the Trafficking Protocol thereby 'reproduces the whore/Madonna division' such that only involuntariness is rewarded by protection (1998: 47). This has fostered the coerced victim archetype critiqued in the following chapter.

These weaknesses in the Trafficking Protocol raise the question of how we should define and treat the victim's consent, both within and outside of the law. If an individual is recruited and transported for the purpose of exploitation but none of the means can be proven, what remedies outside of trafficking legislation exist? How do we treat cases where the individual is initially coerced but later knowingly and voluntarily consents to the proposed conditions of work? Does the initially nullified consent become relevant to the trafficker's defence? There has been too great an emphasis on the development and implementation of trafficking laws, with less attention paid to the broader regime of labour laws that might otherwise capture both the coerced and non-coerced scenarios. Failing to recognise the spectrum of trafficking experiences from voluntary to entirely coerced, the Trafficking Protocol's approach either encourages victims to deny this voluntariness in order to be identified as a 'victim of trafficking' and find some protection within the law's framework, or promotes a definition that excludes these particular victims of exploitation and leaves them without redress.

A Criminal Law Approach to Trafficking and Related Challenges

The annexing of the Trafficking Protocol to a convention focused on organised crime prevention and criminal justice was a deliberate step that continues to shape the mainstream trafficking framework and the idea that trafficking 'is a form of organised crime'. There is a growing body of literature that critiques this criminal justice approach to trafficking and 'the identification of criminality and victimisation as critical elements of this issue' (Segrave and Milivojevic, 2005: 12). Many authors highlight the pitfalls of current visa regimes and the focus on illegal entry (Rijken, 2010) and point to the reality that the small-scale involvement of a few 'facilitators' (smugglers, traffickers, migration agents) means that it is better described as 'disorganized' crime (Weitzer, 2014: 12).

Elizabeth Bruch criticises the Trafficking Protocol's law enforcement – rather than human rights or labour rights – approach (2004: 14), but nonetheless concedes that the criminal justice approach is unsurprising given that coercion, kidnapping or ill-treatment of victims often violate domestic criminal law (2004: 17). There is also advantage in the availability of financial, personnel and enforcement resources for prevention. In Bruch's view, some justification is also found in the fact that most states criminalise or otherwise regulate prostitution and trafficking is seemingly connected (Bruch, 2004: 17).

Jo Goodey similarly argues that the key reason for focusing on the criminal aspects of human trafficking is the 'seeming practicality' of prosecutions, since, unlike efforts to prevent trafficking and to support victims, prosecutorial outcomes produce 'tangible results' (2003: 423). However, as a consequence, the Trafficking Protocol revolves largely around the acts of the trafficker as the perpetrator of the crime, with the victim framed largely as passive and acting involuntarily.

The above analysis has highlighted some of the shortcomings of the Trafficking Protocol's treatment of sex work, consent, vulnerability and voluntariness as well as its criminal law orientation. Put simply, the shortcomings include an unjustified focus on the female victim and on trafficking for sexual exploitation, which in turn deflects attention from the agency exercised by victims by suggesting a passive/ active dynamic between victims and traffickers. This approach also tends to shift trafficking debates away from a migration framework into a criminal justice one. This gives fuel to the feminist divide discussed at length in the previous chapter. Further challenges arise from the reality that the Trafficking Protocol's definition of trafficking was designed to guide national-level criminal legislation on trafficking, not to be used more broadly in debates and policy analysis that go beyond the narrower lens of the law. What results is a definition that skews how trafficking is framed in non-legal circles.

Other International and Regional Legal Instruments

In the following section, other legal instruments that play a role in shaping the mainstream framework are briefly examined, including how victims are defined and the causes of trafficking understood. Some of these instruments operate at the global level while others are regional in scope.

The UN Protocol against the Smuggling of Migrants by Land, Air and Sea, supplementing the United Nations Convention against Transnational Organised Crime

The UN Protocol against the Smuggling of Migrants by Land, Air and Sea [hereinafter Smuggling Protocol] defines the 'smuggling of migrants' as 'the procurement, in order to obtain, directly or indirectly, a financial or other material benefit, of the illegal entry of a person into a State Party of which the person is not a national or a permanent resident' (Article 3(a)). The migrants themselves are not liable for criminal prosecution according to the Smuggling Protocol (Article 5), although the entry itself is deemed illegal (Article 3(a) and (b)).

The treatment of smuggling in a separate legal instrument deflects attention away from what is often a blurred and false distinction between trafficking and other forms of irregular migration. This separation clouds situations where a potential migrant might voluntarily use the services of a smuggler and later find themselves in a situation of exploitation. It thereby promotes the inaccurate perception of a dichotomy between the voluntary victim of smuggling and the coerced victim of trafficking.

To the contrary, smuggling and trafficking should be viewed on a continuum, 'shading into and out of one another across a number of dimensions' (Kelly, 2005: 238). Elizabeth Kelly argues that this is particularly so where a journey is relatively long, which increases the opportunities for exploitation and the size of debt and where smuggled persons rely on third parties for employment in destination countries, increasing the potential layers of control (2005: 238). We can easily imagine a migrant assuming a significant level of debt to pay for the services of the smuggler and that debt becoming the tool through which the victim is made to accept exploitative conditions in the destination country. The view that the distinction between smuggling and trafficking is false is supported by many of the findings discussed later in this book, despite the fact that it has been reinforced through the enactment of two separate protocols.

It is important to recall that both the UN Trafficking and Smuggling Protocols are required to be 'interpreted together with the Convention' (Trafficking Protocol, Article 1; Smuggling Protocol, Article 1). While an analysis of the UN Convention against Transnational Organised Crime as a whole is beyond the scope of this more focused discussion, as noted above, situating trafficking within the context of an Organised Crime Convention shifts attention towards the criminal prosecution of the trafficker and away from the victim, including the victim's rational decisions, expectations and desires as a migrant and the rights of migrant workers more generally. By giving both Protocols this context, the Convention and its protocols provide a basis for governments to pursue their agendas of 'cracking down' on illegal migration in the pursuit of closed borders as discussed in the previous chapter.

United Nations Conventions on Slavery

The conflation of slavery and trafficking has increased over the 15 years following the Trafficking Protocol's enactment. 'Slavery' is defined in the 1926 UN Convention to Suppress the Slave Trade and Slavery [hereinafter Slavery Convention] as 'the status or condition of a person over whom any or all of the powers attaching to the right of ownership are exercised' (Art. 1.1). This definition in the Slavery Convention fostered a dependency on legally demonstrable evidence of an exercise of 'powers attached' to an actual 'right of ownership', leaving other extremely exploitative conditions, where there was no evidence of an owner-property relationship, without protection. This shortcoming led to the enactment of the Supplementary Convention on the Abolition of Slavery, the Slave Trade and Institutions and Practices Similar to Slavery [hereinafter Supplementary Slavery Convention] in 1956.

Servitude as a concept is not defined in the Supplementary Slavery Convention. Instead, a 'person of servile status' is defined in Article 7(b) as 'a person in the condition or status resulting from any of the institutions or practices mentioned in article 1 of this Convention', that is, either (a) debt bondage; (b) serfdom; (c) servile marriage; or (d) child servitude. Article 1 of the Supplementary Slavery

Convention provides for states to take all practicable and necessary legislative and other measures to bring about progressively and as soon as possible an end to these four situations. These practices are defined in Article 1 of the Supplementary Slavery Convention:

a. Debt bondage, that is to say, the status or condition arising from a pledge by a debtor of his personal services or of those of a person under his control as security for a debt, if the value of those services as reasonably assessed is not applied towards the liquidation of the debt or the length and nature of those services are not respectively limited and defined;
b. Serfdom, that is to say, the condition or status of a tenant who is by law, custom or agreement bound to live and labour on land belonging to another person and to render some determinate service to such other person, whether for reward or not, and is not free to change his status;
c. Any institution or practice whereby:
    i A woman, without the right to refuse, is promised or given in marriage on payment of a consideration in money or in kind to her parents, guardian, family or any other person or group; or
    ii. The husband of a woman, his family, or his clan, has the right to transfer her to another person for value received or otherwise; or
    iii. A woman on the death of her husband is liable to be inherited by another person;
d. Any institution or practice whereby a child or young person under the age of 18 years, is delivered by either or both of his natural parents or by his guardian to another person, whether for reward or not, with a view to the exploitation of the child or young person or of his labour.

According to the Slavery Convention, in order for a relationship to constitute slavery, there needs, on the one hand, to be evidence of the exercise of 'powers attached to the right of ownership', that is, the existence of a relationship of 'owner and owned' and powers exercised on the basis of that relationship. Although a list of powers is not given, it would certainly include, for example, the power to sell a person. On the other hand, a relationship is defined as holding a person within a situation of 'servile status' (within the framework of the 1956 Supplementary Convention) if it can be placed within one of four pre-established situations listed in subparagraphs (a) to (d) of Article 1 of the Supplementary Slavery Convention above (see Allain, 2009 for a detailed analysis of the Supplementary Slavery Convention and Allain, 2012).[2]

Based on the meaning given to these four circumstances, a situation of servitude could also be a case of slavery (Vijeyarasa and Bello y Villarino, 2012).

---

2   While Allain's analysis is useful, contributions in the Allain, 2012 text continue to reinforce the notion of trafficking as 'modern-day slavery' and lack the nuanced analysis required. See more on this below.

However, this will not necessarily be the case. Deeper analysis allows us also to identify clear examples of situations when trafficking and slavery (or practices 'similar to slavery' defined as holding a person under 'servile status') overlap, and conversely, when trafficking should not be deemed a case of slavery. Beginning with the overlap, we can start with the situation where an individual's movement is arranged with the help of a second person (in this case and for the sake of the law, a 'smuggler' who later becomes the 'trafficker') and the migrant's labour is exploited by that trafficker. If the trafficker also attaches a debt as repayment for the services rendered in moving the individual and the debt is not reduced based on work carried out by that migrant, or the length and nature of the contract is not defined, it is a case of both trafficking and a practice 'similar to slavery' (as per the Supplementary Slavery Convention).

If an individual is enslaved, but has not been moved from point A to B for the purpose of that enslavement (that is, there is no evidence of recruitment, transportation, transfer, harbouring along the way or receipt at the end of that journey), slavery is distinct from trafficking, that is, this will be a case 'similar to slavery' *that is not* a case of trafficking. Finally, if an individual has been moved from point A to B and the individual's labour is exploited, for example, through excessive hours of work or insufficient remuneration, but there is no undefined and unlimited debt that has been attached or there is a debt but it is reduced in accordance with the hours of work, this may be a case of trafficking that falls outside of the realm of slavery as it does not meet the requirements set out in the Supplementary Slavery Convention. In fact, if we wanted to be legally exhaustive, we would need to add another layer of analysis in order to determine whether this is even a case of *trafficking* or 'simply' the *exploitation of a labour migrant*. This would depend on the meaning given to 'for the purpose of exploitation' in the Trafficking Protocol.

These three examples illustrate the complexities involved in the terms trafficking, slavery and servitude and the problems that arise in using them interchangeably. Despite these distinctions, however, trafficking is frequently named 'modern-day slavery' with little knowledge of, or concern for, the exact wording of the Slavery Convention, Supplementary Slavery Convention or the distinctions noted above. (e.g. Androff, 2011: 212; Fowler, Che and Fowler, 2010: 1346; Burn, Blay and Simmons, 2005). This has reached a point where even academic audiences have stopped challenging this equation.[3] The language of 'modern day slavery' has popular appeal but often lacks an evidentiary basis. This has a substantial impact on how we frame trafficking because of the emotional weight that the term slavery carries. Equating trafficking and slavery *a priori* disallows consideration of the idea of autonomous decision-making or the pursuit of economic betterment often involved in trafficking, as will be discussed later in this book.

3 For example, the Gilder Lehrman Centre for the Study of Slavery, Resistance, and Abolition (GLC), part of the MacMillan Centre for International and Area Studies at Yale University, created a Fellowship entitled 'Human Trafficking and Modern Day Slavery'.

Convention on the Elimination of All Forms of Discrimination against Women (CEDAW)

One of the only core international human rights treaties[4] to address trafficking expressly is also the only global gender-specific human rights treaty, the Convention on the Elimination of All Forms of Discrimination against Women [hereinafter CEDAW]. Article 6 of CEDAW (1979) provides that, 'States Parties shall take all appropriate measures, including legislation, to suppress all forms of traffic in women and exploitation of prostitution of women'. Through the inclusion of provisions on prostitution and trafficking in its General Recommendation on Violence against Women No. 19 (1992), the CEDAW Committee links violence to prostitution and trafficking, but by doing so, risks reinforcing the notion that there is little distinction between the two. In the same General Recommendation, the CEDAW Committee labelled 'poverty and unemployment' as responsible for forcing many women, including young girls, *into both prostitution and trafficking* (1992: ¶¶ 14–15, emphasis added), not only conflating the two issues but also establishing poverty as a cause for both.

The narrow focus is a product of its time. At the time of CEDAW's drafting, trafficking into types of exploitation outside of the sex sector was being studied by the Commission on the Status of Women, the Commission on Human Rights and organisations like ILO (Chuang, 2012: 176). Nonetheless, the Convention acts to perpetuate a sexualised view of women that emphasises their victimisation as women as opposed to their agency as human beings. Elizabeth Bruch contends that by confining the discussion of trafficking to a subset of 'violence against women', which is itself a subset of 'women's human rights', it becomes easier to marginalise or ignore the broader issues of women's status, such as agency and resistance (2004: 34).

Janie Chuang is less critical than Bruch, noting that Article 6 of CEDAW, contrary to the attempts of some government delegations, explicitly aimed to restrict its scope to the 'exploitation of prostitution' and not suppress prostitution outright (2012: 176–7). However, the CEDAW Committee has not been consistent in its response to state parties' reports on prostitution and sex work. It has highlighted the stigmatisation of sex workers resulting from efforts aimed at rehabilitation and the risks to due process rights that result from administrative offenses related to sex work (Chuang, 2012: 179). Elsewhere, the CEDAW Committee has positioned itself as opposed to sex work, calling upon states to discourage demand, implement programmes aimed at prevention and to monitor and address the link between sex tourism and sex work (Chuang, 2012: 179). It further frames the 'root causes' of sex work as founded on the sexual objectification of women (Chuang, 2012: 180).

---

4   CEDAW is one of nine international human rights treaties which are currently in force, in addition to the 1948 Universal Declaration of Human Rights (UDHR). The UDHR is not a treaty but is foundational in defining 'fundamental freedoms' and 'human rights'.

In an attempt to broaden the archetypal understanding of trafficking beyond sexual exploitation, in its General Recommendation on Violence against Women, the CEDAW Committee referred also to recruitment for domestic labour and 'organized marriage between women from developing countries and foreign nationals' (CEDAW Committee, 1992: ¶ 14). These are nonetheless similarly gender-stereotypical portrayals, although arguably justifiable given CEDAW is a convention focused on women and girls. It should also be mentioned that this recommendation is now two decades old, pre-dating some of the recent evolutions in thinking on trafficking.

However, problems exist in other later recommendations. In its General Recommendation on Women and Health No. 24 (1999), the CEDAW Committee noted a link between increased vulnerability to HIV/AIDS and other STIs from prostitution and trafficking and stipulated that 'states parties should ensure, without prejudice and discrimination, the right to sexual health information, education and services for all women and girls, including those who have been trafficked, even if they are not legally resident in the country' (CEDAW Committee, 1999: ¶ 18). There are, in fact, limited data that actually establish a link between HIV and trafficking (see Vijeyarasa and Stein, 2010). By naming these inter-related vulnerabilities, this approach risks exacerbating the stigma attached to this entire subset of experiences and promotes the unquestioned acceptance of a correlation between such issues as HIV, sex work and trafficking.

General Recommendation No. 26 on Women Migrant Workers (2008) is a welcomed addition to the existing body of CEDAW recommendations. It helpfully identifies many of the gendered inequalities involved in migration, decisions to depart home countries, experiences abroad and challenges upon return, including compulsory HIV and AIDS testing and moral 'rehabilitation' for women returnees. It also notes the higher personal and social costs facing women migrants when compared to men, without adequate gender-responsive services for these women (CEDAW, 2008: ¶ 11).

International Convention on the Protection of the Rights of All Migrants Workers and Members of their Families

This Convention, adopted in 1990 and entered into force in 2003, is the most comprehensive treaty on migrants' rights within the international human rights framework. It addresses both regular and irregular migration and touches upon a range of issues, not only in the labour market but also in relation to health, education and access to judicial remedies.

Notably, the Convention places the issue of trafficking squarely within the framework of migration. Its preamble explicitly notes:

> ... Bearing in mind that the human problems involved in migration are even more serious in the case of irregular migration and convinced therefore that appropriate action should be encouraged in order to prevent and eliminate

clandestine movements and trafficking in migrant workers, while at the same
time assuring the protection of their fundamental human rights

It provides for the protection of both migrant workers and their families from
violence, physical injury, threats and intimidation (Article 16(2)). The Convention
also clearly calls for the protection of migrants from slavery (Article 11(1)) and
compulsory or forced labour (Article 11(2)). Yet the term debt does not appear
in the Convention and exploitation is mentioned only in the context of taking
advantage of migrants renting housing. Nonetheless, the Convention deals fairly
extensively with the protection of labour rights, opening the door to clear safeguards
for trafficked victims who are exploited by employers in destination countries with
regards to work conditions, hours and pay. This includes equal enjoyment when
compared to citizens of national labour laws (Article 25), freedom of association
with regard to trade unions (Article 26) and social security (Article 27).

However, the Convention is one of the most poorly ratified of the international
human rights treaties; only 47 states parties had ratified the Convention as of
the end of 2014. Numerous authors highlight that financial and administrative
burdens are among the strongest constraints to ratification. The Convention
obliges sending countries to run pre-departure campaigns and training sessions, to
monitor and impose sanctions on brokers and recruiters operating illegally and to
provide embassy services to citizens working abroad. Sending countries also fear
an increase in competition, with their citizens losing out on jobs abroad to other
sending countries who take up their workers' share (Iredale and Piper, 2003: 6).

European Instruments on Trafficking

The most comprehensive European instrument to address trafficking is the Council
of Europe[5] Convention on Action against Trafficking in Human Beings [European
Convention on Trafficking]. It provides guidance on assistance and protection of
victims and the effective investigation of the activities of traffickers. The definition
of trafficking given in the European Convention on Trafficking (which only
entered into force on 1 February 2008) and its Explanatory Report in almost every
respect mirrors that of the Trafficking Protocol, with the one exception being that
the Convention applies to all forms of trafficking at both national and international
levels, thereby exceeding the scope of the Trafficking Protocol.

When we further analyse the European Convention on Trafficking, additional
differences between the instruments become evident. For example, the European
Convention on Trafficking provides a more expansive definition of 'abuse of a
position of vulnerability' than the Trafficking Protocol's *travaux préparatoires*:

---

5   Distinct from the European Union, the Council of Europe has 47 member states
and promotes cooperation in the areas of legal standards on human rights, democratic
development, the rule of law and cultural cooperation. By comparison, the European Union
consisted of only 28 member states as of 2015.

By abuse of a position of vulnerability is meant abuse of any situation in which the person involved has no real and acceptable alternative to submitting to the abuse. The vulnerability may be of any kind, whether physical, psychological, emotional, family-related, social or economic. The situation might, for example, involve insecurity or illegality of the victim's administrative status, economic dependence or fragile health. In short, the situation can be any state of hardship in which a human being is impelled to accept being exploited. Persons abusing such a situation flagrantly infringe human rights and violate human dignity and integrity, which no one can validly renounce. (2005: ¶ 83)

The phrase 'any state of hardship in which a human being is impelled to accept being exploited' is broad and lends itself to an expansive understanding of the meaning of vulnerability. If applied in a legal context, it also places the onus on the trafficker to have understood the mental ('emotional') state of the victim at the time of accepting the contract. While the provision may assume a level of reasonableness will be applied to assess what level of hardship is sufficient to amount to a 'position of vulnerability', no definitional directions are given on this point.

What is perhaps most intriguing is a proviso given under the definition of trafficking: 'It is not necessary that someone have [sic] been exploited for there to be trafficking in human beings. It is enough that they have been subjected to one of the actions referred to in the definition and by one of the means specified "for the purpose of" exploitation"' (European Convention on Trafficking, ¶ 87). By extrapolation, if a future employer arranges the movement (recruitment, transportation, transfer, harbouring or receipt) of a potential employee from place A to B, and the employer, who will benefit from the migrant's labour, knows that the migrant's family is in dire need of additional income, this case could fall within the Convention's definition of human trafficking, even before any exploitation has been suffered. This is despite the fact that the situation described reflects many that underlie regular migration.

Further, based on a strict reading of paragraphs 83 and 87 of the European Convention on Trafficking, it appears that there does not need to be any evidence of an employer's intention to exploit the individual, only that the individual's circumstances are so dire that they might accept exploitation should the opportunity of exploitative work arise. Such a broad approach could result in clamps on migration at large as opposed to targeting only migration that has actually given rise to exploitation.

The European Convention on Trafficking has been noted for enhancing the protections guaranteed to victims (Mattar, 2006: 361, 385). Simultaneously, however, it appears to open the door to national legislation that adopts excessively broad definitions that could deem a wide range of migrants to be victims of trafficking. While several of the provisions can be considered positive developments from a migrant's rights perspective – such as the notion of prosecuting attempted trafficking, even before evidence of actual exploitation emerges or placing the onus on a potential employer to interrogate why a potential employee may accept such conditions of hardship – it is doubtful that the provisions can be practically implemented. We are also left questioning the intentions of the drafters, who were representatives of all European countries except Belarus, including the influence of other migration policy goals.[6]

Another European body, the European Parliament, the directly elected deliberative body[7] of the European Union, has long been involved in putting forward proposals against human trafficking. On 10 February 2010, the European Parliament passed a resolution on 'preventing trafficking in human beings' [hereinafter European Parliament Resolution], naming trafficking 'a modern form of slavery, a serious crime and a severe violation of fundamental human rights' (European Parliament Resolution, ¶ A). While holding less legal weight than the European Convention on Trafficking, the European Parliament Resolution contains several paragraphs of particular note. Namely, slavery and trafficking are explicitly equated. The European Parliament Resolution also refers to the findings of UNODC in its Global Report on Trafficking in Persons, which state that sexual exploitation is 'the most commonly identified form of human trafficking, followed by forced labour' and that '79% of the identified victims of trafficking are women and girls' (European Parliament Resolution, ¶ E). The vulnerabilities to trafficking faced by mail-order brides and children are subsequently elaborated (European Parliament Resolution, ¶¶ F and G).

While the resolution should be commended for calling for an annual report (to be produced by Europol, Eurojust and Frontex) that will include 'root causes' and trends on trafficking (¶ 3), it fails to identify the lack of global certainty on what are these so-called 'root causes'. The reproduction of UNODC data that associates trafficking largely with women and children and sexual exploitation is concerning. The European Parliament Resolution calls for campaigns 'targeting both potential victims of trafficking and potential buyers of services from trafficked persons' without identifying the gap in knowledge about who these 'potential' victims may be. Moreover, the reference to 'potential buyers' hints at targeting the male clientele of sex workers, without discriminating between the different legal approaches of member states of the EU to sex work, with the practice legal or decriminalised in some jurisdictions and illegal or an administrative offence in others.

Finally, at a more general level, the European Convention on Human Rights contains several provisions that are relevant to the issue of human trafficking; notably Article 3 (prohibition on torture or inhuman or degrading treatment), Article 4 (prohibition of slavery, servitude, forced and compulsory labour), Article 5 (right to liberty and security), and Article 8 (right to respect for private and

---

6   To its credit, the European Convention on Trafficking has created a body called the European Group of Experts on Action against Trafficking in Human Beings (GRETA, Article 36) whose intention of enhancing the human rights protections for potential victims of trafficking is clear.

7   The European Parliament is also the budgetary authority and co-legislator in certain areas.

family life). However, inspired by the Universal Declaration of Human Rights, the European Convention in fact does not make *explicit* reference to trafficking. It was in the problematic judgment of the case of *Rantsev v Cyprus and Russia* that the court opined that trafficking itself may run counter to the spirit and purpose of Article 4, despite failing to provide a detailed analysis of the terms slavery, servitude and forced and compulsory labour under the European Convention (more extensive discussions of this case, including a comparative analysis with the Australian High Court judgment in *R v Tang* can be found in Vijeyarasa and Bello y Villarino, 2012; see also Chaudary, 2012, for a less critical discussion of the practical implications of the case of *Rantsev* in the UK context).

The South Asian Association for Regional Cooperation (SAARC) Convention and Coordinated Mekong Ministerial Initiative against Trafficking (COMMIT) Processes

The South Asian Association for Regional Cooperation (SAARC) Convention on Preventing and Combating Trafficking in Women and Children for Prostitution [hereinafter SAARC Convention] reinforces many pre-existing stereotypes regarding the gendered nature of trafficking. This convention, which was adopted by the SAARC states (Afghanistan, Bangladesh, Bhutan, India, the Maldives, Nepal, Pakistan and Sri Lanka) in Nepal in January 2002 and entered into force in late 2005, defines trafficking as 'women and children victimised or forced into prostitution by the traffickers by deception, threat, coercion, kidnapping, sale, fraudulent marriage, child marriage or any other unlawful means' (Article 1(5)). This definition excludes men as well as other forms of trafficking for labour exploitation. The limited definition also creates challenges in addressing trafficking of women and children when sexual exploitation is combined with other forms of exploitation. Some academics also criticise the identical treatment of women and children, ignoring women's greater agency (Gallagher, 2010: 130).

Much of the focus of countries within the Asia-Pacific has been on repatriation. This has translated into numerous memoranda of understanding (MoUs) between destination and source countries to establish agreed protocols for the return of victims (including agreements on intelligence-sharing between law enforcement agencies) and for the protection of victims from prosecution for any offences they may have committed immediately before or during their exploitation (Milivojevic and Segrave, 2011: 47). Among the six countries in the Greater Mekong Sub-Region (Cambodia, China, Lao PDR, Myanmar, Thailand and Vietnam), the best-known agreements are those emerging from the Coordinated Mekong Ministerial Initiative against Trafficking (COMMIT) process. Starting as a series of informal discussions in Bangkok in July 2004, the COMMIT process translated into a MoU established in Myanmar in October 2004.

As a series of multi-lateral agreements, the outcomes of the COMMIT processes do not carry the weight of a legal convention. Rather these agreements bind signatory countries to multi-lateral action. To operationalise the MOUs, the six governments jointly developed a Sub-Regional Plan of Action (COMMIT SPA,

2005–2007), intended to complement, build on and support national responses as well as to coordinate government and non-government counter-trafficking efforts and victim protection activities. Subsequent plans have been established and endorsed. While little detailed analysis of the COMMIT processes exists, one key informant during my field research in Vietnam shared their view that 'COMMIT is not moving. This was the driving force but it has no direction now' (Anon., International NGO, Vietnam, 16 October, 2009).

African Regional Processes

Among African member states, a few agreements exist although it is unclear to what extent national legislation has been harmonised in response. One such agreement is the ECOWAS Declaration on the Fight against Trafficking in Persons which annexed the ECOWAS Initial Plan of Action against Trafficking in Persons (2002–2003) [hereinafter ECOWAS Plan of Action], adopted in December 2001 in Dakar, Senegal. The Declaration calls for a special focus on trafficking of women and children (ECOWAS Plan of Action, Article 19), deferring attention from male victims.

In the west of Africa, high rates of child trafficking and exploitative labour have been noted (particularly in Ghana, Côte d'Ivoire and Burkina Faso in the cocoa and fishing sectors). However, the Multilateral Cooperation Agreement to Combat Child Trafficking in West Africa (2005), which entered into force in July 2006, does little other than to call for greater cooperation among nine countries in the sub-region: Benin, Burkina Faso, Côte d'Ivoire, Ghana, Liberia, Mali, Niger, Nigeria and Togo. Its legal weight and focus mirror the Asia COMMIT processes.

Another instrument, the Ouagadougou Action Plan to Combat Trafficking in Human Beings, Especially Women and Children (2006) [hereinafter Ouagadougou Action Plan], identifies in its general principles a broad range of 'causes' of human trafficking:

> Poverty and vulnerability, an unbalanced distribution of wealth, unemployment, armed conflicts, poor law enforcement system [sic], degraded environment, poor governance, societies under stress as well as non-inclusive societies, corruption, lack of education and human rights violations including discrimination, increased demand for sex trade and sex tourism are among the root causes of trafficking in human beings and must be addressed. (Ouagadougou Action Plan, 2006: General principles)

Adopted in 2006 by the EU and African Union (AU), the shopping list of so-called causes provided in the Ouagadougou Action Plan, as well as the manner in which it links sex work and trafficking, reinforces many of the myths and misconceptions that are questioned in this book. It makes no effort to call for an evidence-based analysis. A meeting to operationalise the Ouagadougou Action Plan took place only in March 2010. The practical implications of this instrument cannot be assessed yet, with these regional processes in Africa coming at a later stage when compared to Europe or Asia.

Although gaining substantially less attention, there is clearly an array of legislation that exists at the international and regional levels alongside the Trafficking Protocol. These laws differ substantially in the extent to which they are binding and the degree to which they protect victims' rights. Moreover, when it comes to certain areas of law, we have witnessed how particular terminology – slave, slavery, servitude and debt bondage – is used in trafficking discourse with little regard to its precise meaning in the law. Some legal instruments offer strong protections for the rights of victims and enable us to understand victims' movement and exploitation within a broader migration framework. Yet, an overwhelming number of these instruments foster a highly stereotypical and gender-biased lens of analysis, the most stark being the SAARC Convention and some of the early general recommendations related to CEDAW.

Regulating Trafficking, Sex Work and Migration at the National Level

In this final section, I examine how the international and regional laws and regulations on human trafficking have impacted definitions of trafficking at the national level. This analysis explores laws currently in force, and particularly those that have been recently enacted, that relate directly to trafficking, as well as migration, labour exploitation and sex work in several different national contexts. Both sending and receiving countries are included in this overview. Since the trafficking phenomenon is shaped not only by current laws but also by former ones, where possible, this analysis covers the evolution of the legislation over the last decade.

The United States of America

Federal legislation passed in the United States in 2000 (*Victims of Trafficking and Violence Protection Act*, often referred to as TVPA) defines human trafficking as the illicit enslavement of individuals into labour or commercial sex through means of force, fraud or coercion. The TVPA introduces the flawed language of 'sex trafficking', moving away from the language of 'trafficking for sexual exploitation'. This in turn dilutes the focus on the movement aspect of trafficking (i.e. movement '*for the purpose of exploitation*') and fosters a conflation of sex work and trafficking for sexual exploitation. Trafficking for sexual exploitation in the United States does not solely consist of, or end with, international trafficking of women and children into the country for sex exploitation. Domestic sex workers – especially children and including foreigners – become classified as victims of trafficking when there is evidence of deceit, fraud, coercion, or transportation of victims interstate or out of the United States to foreign markets (Schaeur and Wheaton, 2006: 154).

As of 2009, just over 1,300 human trafficking victims qualified for victim services in the US and approximately 600 federal convictions for trafficking related crimes had been secured (Farrell and Fahey, 2009: 617). The US Department of State reported 151 convictions for forced labour and/or trafficking for sexual exploitation of adults and minors in 2011, with 141 convictions in 2010 (US Department of State, 2012: 261) These relatively low figures seem to contradict suggestions that trafficking to the US was, at that time, increasing and several academics have argued that the crusade against trafficking for sexual exploitation, particularly under the Bush Administration (2001–2008), transformed into a crusade against all types of commercial sex (Weitzer, 2010: 64, 66). This could explain the exaggerated and at times erroneous use of statistics.

Although remedies for trafficking are still very rare, the United States has expressly granted victims of trafficking the right to private action against their traffickers (*Trafficking Victims Protection Reauthorization Act*, 2003, § 4[1][4]) and has included mandatory restitution to trafficked persons as part of the criminal sentencing of traffickers (VTVPA, 2000, § 1593) (Gallagher and Holmes, 2008: 331). Nonetheless, based on a study of police responses in 12 US counties working on local level enforcement, Farrell and Pfeffer report the misclassification of trafficking victims as 'street-walkers or prostitutes' in the US as a common problem and note the detrimental impact of the limited foreign language capabilities of police when it comes to victims trafficked from outside of the US (Farrell and Pfeffer, 2014, 59).

The US also places trafficking in its foreign policy agenda. Failure of any country to live up to the standards set out in US legislation can lead to the imposition of sanctions and US interference in that country's relationship with major international banks and financial institutions (VTVPA, 2000, § 110) (Gallagher and Holmes, 2008: 319). This global oversight, including the US State Department's annual *Trafficking in Persons Report*, has been endlessly criticised for its unjustified statistics, its colonialist approaches to trafficking in the global south and lack of adequate self-reflection on trafficking within the borders of the United States. At the same time, however, it continues to have considerable weight in global policy debates.

Australia

On 11 December 2002, Australia became a signatory to the Trafficking Protocol and ratified the Protocol on 14 September 2005. In July 2005, the *Criminal Code Amendment (Trafficking in Persons and Debt Bondage) Act 2005* (Cth) was introduced (Division 271 at s 271.2(1)) and inserted into Chapter 8 ('Crimes against humanity and related offences') of the Criminal Code. Prior to this, the *Criminal Code Amendment (Slavery and Sexual Servitude) Act 1999* (Cth) criminalised only slavery, sexual servitude and deceptive recruitment for sexual services (Division 270).

The definition of trafficking in Division 271 of the Criminal Code differs in a number of respects from the UN Protocol's definition. Considered neither clear nor comprehensive, the Australian Human Rights Commission has highlighted that Australia's domestic laws 'may not reflect the full suite of Australia's international legal obligations in this area' (Byrnes, 2009).

Division 271 provides for general and aggravated offences for trafficking; the offence of international and domestic trafficking in children; general and aggravated offences of domestic trafficking in persons; and the offence of debt bondage. These provisions define trafficking as where a person organises or facilitates the actual or proposed entry or exit or the receipt of another person into Australia and uses force or threats to obtain the other person's compliance. The provisions broaden the *mens rea* of trafficking by providing that a person commits the offence where they facilitate the entry or exit of another person and 'the person is *reckless* as to whether the other person will be exploited, either by the first person or another, after that entry or receipt' (emphasis added; Criminal Code Amendment, s 271.2(1B)(b)). The general offence of trafficking also includes deceit regarding the true purposes of the recruitment of the victim.

Like the domestic slavery provisions, the provisions dealing with trafficking for sexual exploitation do not actually prohibit recruitment for the provision of sexual services in general but only under such situations that can be considered coercive recruitment. This distinction allows conformity with the legal status of sex work in several Australian states. The law in fact suggests legislative recognition of the migrant sex worker who enters into a contract to provide sexual services in Australia.[8] Pursuant to Section 271.2 (2B), however, the making of such arrangements will be deemed an offence of trafficking in persons if there are any indications of deceit. This includes deceit as to (i) the nature of the sexual services to be provided; (ii) freedom to leave the place or area of work; (iii) freedom to cease providing sexual services; (iv) freedom to leave his or her place of residence; and (v) if there is a debt owed or claimed to be owed, the quantum of that debt (Criminal Code Amendment, s271.2(2B)). As will be seen in the discussion in Chapter 4, the focus of the Australian trafficking legislation on deception accurately targets what is most central to the phenomenon.

Successful prosecutions for slavery and trafficking are relatively recent developments in Australia. The case against Victorian brothel owner Wei Tang

---

8 This point is specifically made in the Explanatory memorandum to the 2004 amendment regarding section 270.7 on sexual servitude: 'The amended offence criminalises activity that is essentially preparatory to sexual servitude *and is not designed to capture employment disputes in the context of legalised prostitution.* That is, the deceptive recruiting offence will not capture employment disputes in the sex industry where the sex worker disputing the particular contract or arrangement has not been trafficked into Australia' (emphasis added). Explanatory memorandum to the criminal code amendment (trafficking in persons offences) bill 2004, Australasian Legal Information Institute http://www.austlii.edu.au/au/legis/cth/bill_em/ccaipob2004483/memo1.html.

involving five Thai women working in her Melbourne brothel was the first jury conviction under the Criminal Code's slavery offences. This conviction was subsequently appealed (Court of Appeal of the Supreme Court of Victoria) and finally upheld by Australia's High Court in 2008 (*The Queen v Tang*). *R v Dobie* was the first conviction for human trafficking in Australia. The case involved the traffic of two Thai women by Keith Dobie into Australia to provide sexual services in Queensland. His final appeal for an extension of time to appeal was refused in 2011 (for more on the court's analysis of the victims' negotiations with Dobie prior to arriving in Australia, see Vijeyarasa and Bello y Villarino, 2012; see also Cameron and Schloenhardt, 2013 for the sentencing aspects of these cases).

Overall, there is uncertainty about the number of victims of trafficking in Australia. Using approximately a dozen sources, including a number of Refugee Review Tribunal cases, information from Project Respect, an Australian non-profit community based organisation, commentary from the Parliamentary Joint Committee on the Australian Crime Commission and a few academic pieces, Anna Dorevitch and Michelle Foster describe a picture of deception, brutality and violence perpetrated by traffickers and clients and subsequent deportation from Australia. They argue that little protection is offered to victims, despite Australia's international obligations (Dorevitch and Foster, 2008: 8). In addition, several practitioners have questioned why the criminal code in Australia has been used only in relation to trafficking for sexual exploitation and not also to address labour exploitation. Labour-related trafficking has also been given substantially less political consideration in Australia (Cullen and McSherry, 2009: 4, 7).

As noted above, trafficking is treated in Australian law in conformity with the law's approach to sex work. Laws governing sex work differ by state. In Queensland and New South Wales, for example, there is substantial space for legal sex work. This includes licensed legal brothels in Queensland and decriminalisation of most commercial sex businesses and street sex work (Sullivan, 2010). In the State of Victoria, the Victorian *Prostitution Control Act* 1994 regulates the licencing of brothels and escort agents, prohibiting advertisements that induce a person to seek employment as a sex worker or to work for any business that provides sexual services. Street sex work in Victoria is illegal (*Prostitution Control Act*, 1994, Articles 13(1) and (2)).

Ukraine

Prior to March 1998, there was no specific criminal legislation relating to human or child trafficking in Ukraine. In fact, Ukraine became the first former Soviet country to criminalise human trafficking in 1998 when amendments to the *Code on Marriage and Family* required amendments to the *Criminal Code* to accommodate new penalties for illegal actions related to adoption and human trafficking (Art. 124(1)).

Ukraine became a signatory to the Trafficking Protocol on 15 November 2001 and ratified it on 21 May 2004. The *Criminal Code* 2001 was subsequently amended several times since to bring the definition of trafficking into alignment with the Trafficking Protocol. Ukraine's anti-trafficking legislation includes the traffic of both men and women. In fact, Ukraine has had notable success – as reflected in the sex-disaggregated data from trafficking databases and field research – in ensuring that stakeholders understand that trafficking affects both men and women.

In 2011, the Verkhovna Rada (Ukrainian Parliament) Committee on Fighting Organised Crime and Corruption issued copies of a new anti-trafficking law which went into effect on 15 October 2011, the *Law of Ukraine on Combating Trafficking in Human Beings*. The amended law defines trafficking in terms even more closely aligned with the Trafficking Protocol:

> trafficking in human beings – settlement of an illegal agreement, the object of which is a human being, as well as recruitment, transportation, harbouring, transfer or receipt of a human being for purpose of his/her exploitation, including sexual, by means of deception, fraud, blackmail, abuse of a person's position of vulnerability or by use of force or threat of use of force, with abuse of power or economic or other dependence of the victim on another person, which is considered a crime under the Criminal Code of Ukraine (official English translation).

Various undefined and confusing references that existed under previous legislation, such as 'porno business' [9] are no longer included in the new law. The new provisions largely focus on cooperation in the fight against human trafficking. However, trafficking in Ukraine has been frequently prosecuted under other laws, including Articles 302 (creating or running brothels and trading in prostitution) and Article 303 (prostitution or compelling to and engaging in prostitution) of the *Criminal Code*, leading to an obvious bias towards prosecuting trafficking for sexual – as opposed to labour – exploitation. Depending on the elements of the crime, traffickers in Ukraine may also be prosecuted under Article 146 (unlawful imprisonment); Article 169 (concerning unlawful adoption); Article 190 (fraud, in terms of taking documentation by deceit); or Article 332 (illegal movement of persons across the state border of Ukraine) of the *Criminal Code*. While several presidential decrees exist on migration, including a Regulation of the Cabinet of Ministers of Ukraine 'On approval of the Concept of a State Programme of Cooperation with Ukrainians Living Abroad for the period up to 2015', none refer to exploitation.

Sex work is not legal in Ukraine. Under the Ukrainian *Criminal Code*, a number of parties are subject to penalties in relation to sex work, which range from a fine to imprisonment. Sex workers are subject to non-criminal penalties for engaging in prostitution, with liability limited to a fine or community service (Article 303(1)). Previously, providing sexual services was a criminal offence, with these new provisions aimed at protecting victims from blackmail and threats

---

9   'використання в порнобізнесі'/ 'vykorystannya v pornobiznesi'.

for testifying (see Law No. 3316-IV, 2006). Despite these penalties, the European Network for HIV/STI Prevention and Health Promotion among Migrant Sex Workers (TAMPEP) reported in 2007 that there were close to 60,000 female sex workers in Ukraine, almost 25 per cent of whom are HIV positive (2007: 7), with Ukrainian sex workers, as in Vietnam, considered a 'social evil' (2007: 12).

Ghana

Trafficking in Ghana is regulated by the *Ghanaian Human Trafficking Act* 2005. Many of the Act's provisions mirror those of the Trafficking Protocol, while others broaden its scope. Of particular significance is Article 1(4), where the consent of the child, parents or guardian cannot be used as a defence in a trafficking prosecution. This reflects an adaptation to the Ghanaian context which takes into account the documented involvement of parents in the selling of their children, alongside a history of child fosterage, adoption and migration for school and work discussed elsewhere in this book. Article 3(1) for example reads that 'a person who provides another person for purposes of trafficking commits an offence even where the person is a parent'.

While the *Ghanaian Human Trafficking Act* 2005 broadly covers trafficking in all persons, the Minister responsible for the Act's implementation is the Ghanaian Minister for Women and Children's Affairs (Article 42). Although the traffic of adults is known to exist, the scope of the problem remains unclear and could not be adequately explained during my research by informants from the Ghana Police Anti-Human Trafficking Unit or the Ghana Immigration Services. Conflicting information was offered by different informants and in one case, by the same informant at different stages of the same interview.[10] In addition to an explicit focus on children in the law and in practice, a legal distinction between migration and trafficking is evident, whereby the *Immigration Act* 2000 makes no reference to the potential exploitation of migrants or the overlaps between the two concepts.

Prostitution is criminalised as an offence 'against public morals' in the Ghanaian *Criminal Code* 1960 (Act 29). This idea of 'public morality' could partially explain the lack of public debate on, or domestic academic analysis of, the question of trafficking of adult women – as opposed to children – with discussions about sexual exploitation largely silenced (Vijeyarasa, 2013a; Vijeyarasa, 2011a). There also appears to be a lack of clarity around the distinctions between sex work and trafficking for sexual exploitation and limited attention given to situations where a woman may voluntarily enter sex work but is later exploited. At present, the lack

---

10   The data provided to me by this informant from the Ghana Police Anti-Human Trafficking Unit were extracted from the National Trafficking Database. While the traffic of a number of Ghanaian women to Russia was mentioned by several different informants, including by this informant, Russia was not listed as a destination country in the data given, raising doubts as to the thoroughness of the informant's data and/or the National Trafficking Database.

of debate on the topic has resulted in only limited resources to document the scope of the problem. This, in turn, has led to further apathy towards the issue. Despite criminalisation, a UNAIDS-funded study, conducted by IOM in partnership with Management Strategies for Africa and the West African Programme to Combat AIDS and STIs noted that, while exact figures are unknown, the sex worker population in Ghana is estimated to be between 47,780 and 58,920 (IOM, 2012b).

Vietnam

The exclusion of male victims of trafficking was a stark omission in Vietnam's former *Penal Code* Articles 119 and 120, which criminalised trafficking in women and trading in, fraudulently exchanging, or appropriating children. Furthermore, Article 1 of the *Law on Child Protection, Care and Education* 2004 defines children as Vietnamese citizens below the age of 16, not those below the age of 18 as in international law (UN Convention on the Rights of the Child, Art. 1). Therefore, male children aged 16 to 18 were excluded altogether from the protection of the former Vietnamese law on trafficking.

As of January 2010, the same provisions were expanded to include trafficking of men. More importantly, however, a new draft law was proposed in January 2011 and adopted by the Vietnamese National Assembly (supported by 91.68 per cent of members) in March 2011. The law entered into force on 1 January 2012 and is an improvement on the previous approaches of the Government of Vietnam. It specifically calls for victims not to be stigmatised or discriminated against (Article 4(2). However, the law continues to group trafficking with 'other social vices' (Article 5(1)), including sex work, drug use and HIV, which is only a minimal improvement on the former language of 'social evils'. This approach reinforces and exacerbates the stigma already experienced by victims of trafficking (see Vijeyarasa, 2010b).

Vietnam currently lacks a law on migration of Vietnamese overseas, although a law exists on guest workers (*Guest Workers Act*). This Act sets out the rights and obligations of Vietnamese going overseas to work as well as the organisations sending them. Notably, it does make reference to the 'lawful rights and interests of guest workers' (Guest Workers Act, Article 4) and states that harassment of workers is prohibited (Article 7(11)). While these are important provisions, no stakeholder during the course of my field research made any reference to the *Guest Worker Act*, suggesting that it is considered largely irrelevant when it comes to trafficking. However, this type of legislation demonstrates the willingness of the government to promote the export of labour and, to a degree, its dependence on this type of movement. There has been increased recognition by the Ministry of Foreign Affairs in recent years of the inadequate support provided by the Vietnamese Government to Vietnamese migrants in host countries. The support itself has been described as 'limited, passive and slow', with some acknowledgement of the fact that comprehensive solutions are required to improve the quality and effectiveness of such overseas labour migration (Government of Vietnam, 2012: 38).

Sex work is criminalised in Vietnam under the Penal Code and the Ordinance on Prostitution Prevention and Combat. Sex work is designated as a 'social evil' (see generally Vijeyarasa, 2010b), with 'strong pejorative labelling of these groups of people considered to be morally corrupt or decadent' (Doussantousse and Tooke, 2002). Sex workers are channelled into government-run 're-education' centres, known as '05 centres' mainly for women (Vijeyarasa, 2010b: 94–5; De Lind van Wijngaarden, 2007, 43; Khuat 2007, 15). The State's approach to sex work as a 'social evil' and the naming of the Department of Social Evils Prevention (DSEP), a branch of the Ministry of Labour, Invalids and Social Affairs (MOLISA), as the responsible entity, has negatively influenced attitudes towards sex workers and victims of trafficking alike (Vijeyarasa, 2010b: 90).

MOLISA estimated that there were around 48,000 female sex workers across the country in 2004. The strategy of criminalisation and 're-education', which targets sex workers as opposed to clients, has resulted in limited access by sex workers to institutionalised health care and testing and treatment for HIV and other STIs, particularly given sex workers' fear of detention (Doussantousse and Tooke, 2002). Coupled with stigmatisation, the use of 're-education' centres by the government has also acted as a barrier for researchers to identify, contact and interview trafficked returnees, limiting what is known about the demographics of victims in Vietnam and raising questions about the extent to which victims of exploitation are incorrectly labelled as 'criminals' under Vietnamese law.

Conclusion

This chapter was designed to present the legal landscape as it specifically pertains to the mainstream trafficking framework. As we have seen, the current trend is for international and national laws on trafficking to encompass both sexual and labour exploitation and protect both men and women. Despite this, frequently laws and their implementation tend to target – either implicitly or explicitly – the narrower categories of trafficking of women and girls and trafficking for the purpose of sexual exploitation. This is evident in the language adopted internationally ('especially women and children') or made explicit, for example, in the case of the SAARC Convention, which defines trafficking only in terms of the victimisation of women and girls. What results is a gender bias in the legal discourse on trafficking that affects the broader discourse on trafficking as a whole and reinforces the mainstream trafficking framework presented in this book. It also heightens the stigma faced by victims and creates artificial barriers for male victims to self-identify, perpetuating the female victim archetype.

Global, regional and national laws contribute to this mainstream framework and reinforce a one-sided understanding of trafficking, including an emphasis on the coerced victim. Moreover, such laws at the international, regional and national levels promote many myths and misconceptions about trafficking, including through the naming of 'root causes', the conflation of trafficking and slavery and the labelling of sexual exploitation as the characteristic form of human trafficking, without evidentiary basis or disclaimer.

There is also considerable confusion emerging from global provisions that include such phrases as 'abuse of a position of vulnerability' which are subsequently transposed without revision into national laws, creating interpretative difficulties as evidenced in Ukraine. By contrast, both Ghana and Vietnam have national laws on trafficking that have been clearly moulded to the national context. This, too, has its own challenges, with the Ghanaian law evidencing a bias towards child trafficking and the Vietnamese law containing stigmatising language around 'social evils' and 'social vices'. At the national level, it is also telling that laws on migration are often dealt with in entirely separate pieces of legislation.

National-level repression of sex work can be directly tied to the priority accorded to trafficking for sexual exploitation by police, legal officers and the judiciary in many countries. This is evident in the tendency to prosecute internal trafficking using provisions targeting the creating or running of brothels, trading in prostitution and compelling engagement in prostitution in Ukraine, and the explicit references to sex work as a social evil in Vietnam's anti-trafficking laws. In Ghana, criminalisation and discomfort with the topic of sex work have resulted in a lack of public discourse on the trafficking of adults for sexual exploitation, with public policy and media attention focused on child victims.

In destination countries like the United States and Australia, there is persistent concern over the extent to which efforts to prevent trafficking and prosecute traffickers give adequate weight to victim protection. In addition, the laws of both these countries demonstrate the manner in which there are stark differences in national legal treatment of the issue of trafficking; in the United States, trafficking is the 'illicit enslavement of individuals' while Australia addresses slavery and trafficking in two separate pieces of criminal code legislation.

Together with my assessment of the identifiable agendas within trafficking discourse in the previous chapter, this analysis concludes my overview of the mainstream framework. In the next part of this book, I scrutinise the individual assumptions that together form the mainstream trafficking framework and assess their validity, drawing on evidence from the ground.

PART II
Dispelling the Myths and Misconceptions

Chapter 4
The Coerced Victim of Trafficking

[Y]ou go to Cambodia to work in the sex industry and your plan is to sleep with 4 men a day and it ends up being 12 men a day. If it is 4 men a day, you say, that is what I came to do and it is fine. If you end up being forced to have sex with 12 men, I am being forced to have sex with 8 more men than I wanted. I am now trafficked. That is where the complexity lies. It is the level of exploitation that is the most critical.

(A. Bruce, Former Chief of Mission, IOM Vietnam, 21 September 2009)

What I strongly believe is that no person voluntarily goes into slavery.[1] If a person knew what kind of slavery conditions they would be facing, I do not think that a person would ever take a decision to do so. With the whole of migration, there is a lot of uncertainty. Until you get there and get your job, there is uncertainty. But there are various successful examples and that inspires people to go overseas and try to make money. People believe they will be lucky.

(T. Ivanyuk, Counter-Trafficking Programme Specialist,
IOM Ukraine, 3 September 2009)

In Part II of this book, I discuss the four most dominant myths and misconceptions concerning the demographic of victims of trafficking. I begin with the first assumption: the image of the coerced victim. Despite a persistent emphasis on the enslaved, coerced, kidnapped, abducted or sold victim in both non-academic and academic writing on trafficking, the coerced victim of trafficking is atypical. Like others who condemn exaggerated portrayals of trafficking, I do not dispute that coercive trafficking takes place. As Ronald Weitzer notes in a piece that critiques sensationalist approaches to trafficking for sexual exploitation:

> We also know that there are victims of coercive or deceptive enticement into the sex trade: people are transported to locations where they are pressured into prostitution. Reports from around the world indicate that coercive sex trafficking is by no means fictional. (2010: 65)

---

1 This is a fairly contentious statement and there is quite a significant body of literature on the notion of voluntary slavery. See for example Stanley Engerman discussing the sale of children and adults to the wealthy as a question of survival (2007: 95–6) or Walter Block discussing the contradictory nature of voluntary slavery, using the example of a man willing to be enslaved to raise funds for his sick child (2003: 45–6).

However, in order for coercion to be an accurate representation of the *typicality* of trafficking, there would need to be *widespread* evidence of coercion. To the contrary, the evidence presented in this chapter suggests that coercive movement, at least in the initial stages of migration, is not the norm. Rather, decisions appear to be based on some process of reasoning, typically driven by deception or a false understanding of life in destination countries.

Yet the Trafficking Protocol fails to give weight to the voluntariness of victims, instead focusing on kidnapping, abduction and coercion. To the contrary, this chapter offers examples of voluntary movement and decision-making – a counter-point to the coerced victim archetype. The agency exercised by victims should be accorded weight if we are to refine the meaning given to human trafficking. At the same time, this emphasis on the voluntariness evident in the decision-making process that *leads* to the subsequent exploitation of the would-be victim does not diminish the gravity and scope of exploitation experienced in destination countries nor should it be used to deny victims their right to redress.

To test the typicality of this coerced victim image, it is important to first establish a definition of coercion. According to the UNODC Model Law, which is not definitive but was designed to help states implement the Trafficking Protocol (UNODC, 2009a: 11):

> 'Coercion' shall mean use of force or threat thereof, and some forms of non-violent or psychological use of force or threat thereof, including but not limited to:
> i.   Threats of harm or physical restraint of any person;
> ii. Any scheme, plan or pattern intended to cause a person to believe that failure to perform an act would result in serious harm to or physical restraint against any person;
> iii. Abuse or any threat linked to the legal status of a person;
> iv. Psychological pressure.

This definition, which draws on a range of international instruments,[2] identifies both physical and psychological acts involved in coercion. UNODC also offers an alternative definition for consideration, taken from Nigerian law, which adds the element of abuse of authority:

> Force or coercion includes obtaining or maintaining through acts of threat the labour, service or other activities of a person by physical, legal, psychological or mental coercion, or abuse of authority. (UNODC, 2009a: 11 citing the Nigerian Harmonised Trafficking in Persons (Prohibition) Law Enforcement and Administration Acts 2005, Article 64)

---

2   For example, Trafficking Protocol, Article 3 (d); Convention on the Rights of the Child, Article 1; and ILO Convention No. 182 on the Worst Forms of Child Labour, Article 2.

This chapter draws on these two definitions and argues that, although it is impossible from a social science perspective to determine with precision the number or extent to which cases fall or do not fall within this category, we would need to see widespread examples that meet the above definitions for coercion to be convincingly presented as representative of trafficking. To displace the notion of coercion, I draw on examples of trafficking cases and data that fall outside of the above definitions of physical, mental, legal and psychological coercion. At the very least, these examples represent a serious challenge to the coerced victim archetype.

Judith Vocks and Jan Nijboer's study (2000) on trafficking of women from Central and Eastern Europe to the Netherlands entitled *The Promised Land* offers a useful framework for analysing the factors that influence such non-coerced decisions. Vocks and Nijboer make use of rational choice theory, strain theory and social control theory in an attempt to find a more precise and reliable explanation for trafficking in the region (2000: 380–81). Rational choice theory[3] assumes that a migrant's personal context influences their decision-making by defining the opportunities and restraints for their behaviour; risk and trust are important considerations. Strain theory identifies a strong pressure to pursue certain cultural goals as the primary driver. This leads to conformity with whatever norms achieve that particular form of success, particularly monetary. Social control theory emphasises the role of the family in providing attachment and a social network (2000: 381), in this case preventing movement. In Vocks and Nijboer's words:

> Rational choice theory assumes that victims try to optimise the balance of (probable) losses and gains. Strain or anomie produces a pressure towards acceptance of a job offer abroad, whereas social bonds, especially to the family, act as an inhibition. Therefore, a lack of social bonds makes women[4] more vulnerable to entering the trap of traffickers. (2000: 381–2)

Alongside the definitions above of coercion and deception, these three theoretical perspectives are valuable analytical tools for assessing trafficking patterns. Rational choice theory highlights the significance of pre-planning, family involvement and the making of conscious decisions to leave destination countries. All three elements are compelling examples in any assessment of the validity of the coerced victim archetype. Strain theory points to the role of images of success abroad that, as we will see, are drivers of trafficking. Finally, social control theory

---

3   See also Elizabeth Wheaton, Edward Schauer and Thomas Galli (2010) who also apply rational choice theory to explain the social situations that shape relocation and working decisions of what they term 'vulnerable populations' as well as the impetus for being a trafficker and the decisions made by employers of trafficked individuals.

4   While left out of the authors' discussion, there is no reason to believe that social control theory does not equally apply to the movement of men. To suggest otherwise actually reinforces expectations of the nurturing, care-giving woman.

raises important questions about whether or not families are a sufficient 'safety' net to block departures into risky – and potentially exploitative – conditions. In particular, I question whether the family as an institution, in the context of trafficking or migration more broadly, reduces vulnerability to trafficking or furthers the desire of potential migrants to seek work abroad based on family need.

In this chapter, drawing on both quantitative and qualitative data from my field research, I deal first with the elements of the Trafficking Protocol that misrepresent victims' roles in their movement. I begin with cases of kidnapping or abduction and then turn to the issue of deception. I also address the minor, who by definition, cannot be deemed a voluntary victim and may form an exception to what this chapter finds to be a coerced victim stereotype. Second, I discuss examples of victim's roles in their own movement. I outline evidence of rationally-based decision-making including voluntary acceptance of risk and pre-planning, particularly in search of social and economic betterment. I also explore false or exaggerated images of success abroad and the role of this fairy-tale life in shaping victims' decisions and behaviours. I conclude by examining those so-called push factors that reflect diminished voluntariness and freedom of choice, particularly presumed links between domestic violence, lack of social bonds and human trafficking.

My aim in this chapter is to highlight the limited value – and, in fact, inaccuracy – of portraying trafficking, exploitation and women's movement with the image of naive or duped women. Such narratives de-legitimise women's choices and defer attention away from the exercise of autonomous decision-making by women in a process which ends in exploitation. The coerced victim image also defers attention away from the drivers of migratory decisions.

The examples in this chapter point to the rarity of cases that match the slavery scenario of capture, forcible detention and lack of freedom during at least the initial movement of these individuals. Overall, the discussion therefore permits a deeper analysis of the meaning of the phrase 'use of force, *coercion*, abduction, *fraud, deception*', usually cited from the Trafficking Protocol as a single catch-all concept, without paying adequate attention to the meaning of the individual terms. The chapter concludes with a definition of 'voluntariness' and the 'voluntary victim' based on the data presented. This forms the first step in defining alternative approaches to trafficking that challenge the mainstream one.

Dispelling the Coerced Victim Archetype: Kidnapping, Abduction and the Deception of Victims

The Trafficking Protocol emphasises the role of the trafficker in the forcible or coerced movement of the victim. Yet, such references to coerced movement by threats, force and the abduction of victims in not only the Trafficking Protocol, but also in academic discourse, films and popular literature, fail to adequately give weight to a victim's willingness to seek work abroad.

In this section, I look at the atypicality of kidnapping, abduction and other forms of coercive movement. I also look closely at what proves to be one of the most relevant elements of the Trafficking Protocol: the deception of victims. I discuss deception regarding both the nature and the conditions of work and also explore who it is that is deceiving victims. Finally, I turn to the question of minors, for whom any willingness is deemed in the law to be irrelevant. I explore such examples of child trafficking as the possible exception to the view that the coerced victim archetype is largely stereotypical.

Displacing Kidnapping as the Norm

Practical examples from the field illustrate that trafficking and trafficking-like experiences commonly begin with a rationally-based, voluntary journey. During my fieldwork in Vietnam, Ghana and Ukraine, women and men were seen as exercising some degree of free will in the process of movement. Examples of voluntary decision-making by victims were given in all three countries. Some of these stories are based on direct testimonies shared by victims and provided by NGOs and medical service providers directly involved in the reintegration of returned victims of trafficking. Others are anecdotal.

Within these conversations, kidnapping (a form of physical restraint as per the definition of coercion) was labelled as uncommon. I heard no first-hand stories of kidnapping and I have not been able to confirm, through secondary sources, the only kidnapping incident that was shared by a Ghanaian informant based on anecdotal evidence.

Several informants in Vietnam indicated that a shift in thinking had taken place about trafficking, away from the notion of physical coercion in the form of kidnapping, towards the exploitation of the economic migrant in destination countries. According to one informant from the Vietnamese NGO community, while '[f]ive or ten years ago, when we talked about trafficking, we only talked about kidnapping', people no longer believe in that idea. Rather, due to extensive migration from the village, 'exploitation often takes place at the destination, whereas before, exploitation took place at home and along the way'. In addition, practice in the field also shows a substantial departure from the legal definition under the Trafficking Protocol. 'Agents' who play a role in helping victims with their transfers were deemed by informants as 'not needed' in the process of moving from the point of origin to destination (P. Changmanee, Regional Programme Director, Regional Anti-Human Trafficking Programme, Oxfam Quebec, 16 October).

The contention that kidnapping, a form of physical coercion, is not the norm in the Asia region was supported by another informant from an inter-governmental organisation who noted that while 'there must be some kidnapping', trafficking is much more about 'migratory movement'. People are on the move looking for opportunities and end up in situations of exploitation. Moreover, 'many of them are fully aware of this when they set out on their adventure' (A. Bruce, former

Chief of Mission, IOM Vietnam; Head of Regional Office for Asia, IOM Bangkok, 21 September 2009).

My research in Ghana and Ukraine similarly found that cases of coercion are rare, with such cases named as 'one-off' examples. In Ghana, Dr Sackey, former ILO-IPEC Ghana National Programme Coordinator, Ex-Director at the Ministry of Information and former Executive Secretary of the Ghana National Commission on Children (GNCC), shared a violent story of abduction of a young girl chained to a Tro-Tro[5] who was being 'sent against her will' (Dr M. Sackey, 22 July 2010). Interestingly no other informant mentioned this story and I was unable to find any secondary data to verify that it occurred. No other example was shared with me in Ghana by any informant having knowledge of the movement of victims that amounted to kidnapping.

Stories of coerced movement were widely considered the exception in Ukraine. Informants made a concerted effort to dispel the image of the abducted and coerced victim, frequently portrayed in films, novels and popular press about trafficking from Eastern Europe.

> ... verge cases, such as kidnapping or someone being caught on the street in Ukraine, are very, very rare. They are usually people going to make money somewhere. It is later that [trafficking] happens, that it is not what they thought they were getting into. (T. Ivanyuk, Counter-Trafficking Programme Specialist, IOM Ukraine, 3 September 2009)

Similar findings are suggested by IOM Ukraine's database of its 2004 to 2006 caseload involving 1,939 victims. The database notes that only 0.5 per cent of cases involved kidnapping and 1.5 per cent of cases involved a victim being sold by their family. In 85 per cent of cases, victims were recruited through a personal contact (A. Nguyễn, Counter-Trafficking Coordinator, IOM Ukraine, 13 August 2009).

The large supply of migrant labour relative to demand also highlights the illogic of traffickers needing to depend on the coerced victim. A Ukrainian Legal Advisor with the US Embassy and the primary contributor to the Ukraine section of the annual US Department of State's *Trafficking in Persons Report* shared this view:

> From the point of [a] trafficker, why would I kidnap somebody if I can just offer a job to someone and they gladly agree and go with me? (O.L. Kustova, Legal Adviser, Law Enforcement Section, US Embassy to Ukraine, 2 September 2009)

Other informants similarly highlighted the limited justification or need for traffickers to seek coerced victims:

---

5   Tro-tros are a mode of transport involving vans that operate as a form of local mini-bus.

Recruiters in Ukraine [are] going out to villages. But with such a massive outflow, why spend money and why take the risk of doing it here when you can just wait for people at the bus stations or the train stations or at the ship docks? ... As a recruiter, they are just waiting there and saying, 'Hey, are you looking for a job?'. (A. Nguyễn, Counter-Trafficking Coordinator, IOM Ukraine, 13 August 2009)

The evidence – at least from these three countries – illustrates the atypicality of kidnapping. Moreover, the above discussion highlights the illogic of employers depending on coerced labour given the available supply of voluntary migrant labour, particularly into informal sector work, a reality often not noted in trafficking literature.

Deception and Raising of Victim's Expectations

A central concept in human trafficking is that of deception which to a certain – but limited – extent could overlap with the definition of coercion.[6] Deception better represents the typicality of trafficking than coercion. The UNODC Model Law offers two (related) definitions of deception (UNODC, 2009a: 11):

'Deception' shall mean any conduct that is intended to deceive a person;

or

'Deception' shall mean any deception by words or by conduct [as to fact or as to law], [as to]:
i.   The nature of work or services to be provided;
ii.   The conditions of work;
iii. The extent to which the person will be free to leave his or her place of residence; or
iv.   Other circumstances involving exploitation of the person.

In this section, I deal with two key aspects of deception. First, I address the question of the expectations of victims which are raised by potential traffickers with respect to points i–iv above regarding, for example, the nature of the industry into which people may migrate and/or the conditions of work they will face in that sector. Deceit and the unmet expectations of victims prove to be core elements in the experience of trafficking. Second, I address the false friend as one of the actors who may be engaged in such deception.

---

6   There may be some deception involved in part (ii) of the UNODC definition of coercion, that is, deception may be involved in the process of leading a person to believe that 'failure to perform an act would result in serious harm to or physical restraint against any person'.

Deception as to nature and conditions of work

A number of studies show that frequently victims know the nature of the industry in which they will work; the conditions of that work are the main point of deception. A study by Joanna Busza and Bettina Shunter based on 28 face-to-face interviews and focus group discussions with 72 Vietnamese migrants working in the Svay Pak district in Cambodia found that most of the women interviewed knew they would work in a brothel in Cambodia (Busza, Castle and Diarra, 2004). The motivations that they shared with interviewers included, among others, economic incentives, a desire for an independent lifestyle and dissatisfaction with their rural life (Busza, Castle and Diarra, 2004: 1370). Yet their status as exploited victims was evident. The study showed that among the 100 women who participated, many 'expressed dissatisfaction with their work conditions or stated that they had not fully appreciated the risks they would face, such as clients who refused to use condoms, coercion from brothel owners, and violence from both clients and local police' (Busza, Castle and Diarra, 2004: 1370).

Laura Agustín's study on the trafficking of women from the former Soviet Union, West Africa and Latin America for exploitative work in Spain, found that women 'migrants'[7] are 'often aware of the sexual nature of the work', and like other migrants are 'variably able to resist the economic, social and physical forms of compulsion they face' (2005: 98). Similarly, a study by Judith Vocks and Jan Nijboer found that 'few' of the 72 women who were interviewed in an investigation of trafficking from Eastern Europe to Holland were 'coercively trafficked'; a large number had previously worked as sex workers and 'more than 50 per cent knew they would have to work in the sex industry' (2000: 383–4).

These views can be contrasted with the findings from my fieldwork in Ghana. Many informants shared the view that victims were unaware that they would be forced to work as sex workers in destination countries. One of the stories most commonly cited by a wide cross-section of stakeholders in Ghana involved a woman who was recruited by friends and sold her catering business with plans to become a nanny abroad. According to my informants, two other Ghanaian women, both hairdressers, were also identified by the Ghanaian Police Anti-Human Trafficking Unit as having been trafficked to Russia in the same manner. As noted by the Counter-Trafficking Field Manager for IOM Ghana: 'They did not know where they were going. They were deceived into believing they were going to become nannies and waitresses in Australia and were told they would go to Russia first, [at which point] they were told they would have to become prostitutes' (E. Peasah, Counter-Trafficking Field Manager, IOM Ghana, 21 July 2010). The

---

7   Due to her particular concerns regarding the frequent conflation of trafficking and sex work, Agustín often uses the terms 'migration' and 'migrants' rather than 'trafficking' and 'victims of trafficking'. Given my criticisms of the mainstream trafficking framework, I am sympathetic to Agustín's concerns. However, this approach does leave readers to question where in the spectrum of migration the women being discussed actually sit. Gradients of exploitation are lost in Agustín's approach.

repeated mention of this story by six different informants might suggest that it was considered representative of trafficking from Ghana, although it may simply mean that all informants had been informed by the same source.

As is also suggested in the literature (e.g. Busza, 2004: 232), Eric Peasah, Counter-Trafficking Field Manager for IOM Ghana, went on to note that some of these women remain at their destination, highlighting the problem of ignoring the possibility that a seemingly voluntary choice may have been, at some point, coercive:

> For some of them, they think I have done it now. I can do this. I can earn money (through sex work) ... Some of their parents do not like that they are in prostitution. They do not want to know that they are doing it but in the end, they have to pay the debt. Sometimes they get tired and want to run away, but if they are obedient, they get some money, some tips. (E. Peasah, Counter-Trafficking Field Manager, IOM Ghana, 21 July 2010)

Similar comments were made by the Executive Director of the Ghanaian Legal Resource Centre when referring to his first-hand experience of talking to several Chinese women who were identified as trafficked *to* Ghana. When asked if these women knew they would work as sex workers, he noted: 'From the story told by them, that is not why they came to Ghana. They were supposed to work in a restaurant'. He went on to describe their case as 'very classic' suggesting that this lack of knowledge of the nature, and not just conditions, of work was the norm in Ghana (Tuniese Amuzu, Executive Director, Legal Resource Centre, 13 August 2010). Without first-hand testimony, however, an overarching challenge is discerning whether these women had any incentive to downplay their knowledge and voluntariness when giving their testimonies.

The view from Ghana that victims knew *neither* the nature nor conditions of work can be contrasted with the opinions of my informants in Vietnam. These informants were of the view that there are high levels of knowledge among women travelling from Vietnam to Phnom Penh that they will enter the entertainment or sex industry. Informants qualified this statement, however, by emphasising that many such women do not imagine the conditions they are likely to face in the destination country. The same comment was made about women from Ukraine, some of whom 'knew that there may be sexual exploitation, but not in the same way, [expecting that] they will have conditions like in the Red Light District in the Netherlands, where the clients come and they are able to choose one of them' (O. Horbunova, Deputy Coordinator of Counter-Trafficking Program, IOM Ukraine, 31 July 2009).

These findings reflect a divergence of views as to the nature of deception. Ghana may be an exception when compared to higher levels of knowledge among victims from other countries. At the same time, cultural values and norms may influence the testimony of victims and their willingness to concede varying degrees of knowledge. Moreover, it is difficult to draw more general conclusions, for example, that victims show a higher level of knowledge about the nature of the work in Asia and Eastern Europe than victims in West Africa, since the issue has not been analysed sufficiently in the academic literature. A common trend, however, seems to be lack of knowledge of the gravity of potential conditions at the destination.

Deception by the false friend
The image of the false friend – the acquaintance or someone otherwise known to the victim who lures them into a trafficking situation – is a frequent feature of trafficking imagery. In many respects, it affirms the centrality of deception to trafficking. The notion of the false friend was explained by a Program Officer working for an international organisation through an anecdotal story from Cha Vinh Province, Vietnam:

> [There are] two people in the family, one is the aunt and the other is the niece. The first person was told that she would be free to go to Malaysia for tourism and she went and was forced to work as a sex worker. Then, the trafficker asked her to go back to the family and to get another girl. Then her niece also went to Malaysia. (5 October 2009)

A similar – in this case 'hypothetical' – story was recounted by an informant from the ILO-International Programme on the Elimination of Child Labour [ILO-IPEC] also in Vietnam:

> I have a friend from the countryside who went to work in Hanoi. She had a good income in Hanoi and when she returned home, she invited some of her relatives and friends to work with her as a domestic labourer ... And maybe if we were lucky, we would find a good family but by accident, she introduced me to one family in particular. In that family, I will do the same work as she is doing but that family is a trafficking broker and so I have been sold. (Anon., Child Labour Specialist, ILO-IPEC, 21 October 2009)

However, the false friend image may prove to be as stereotypical as the kidnapped victim. In Vietnam, one informant offered an explanation as to why the picture of voluntary movement is rarely presented in the media, simultaneously debunking both the kidnapped victim and notion of the false friend:

> Vietnam is exporting the labour force ... They do not want anyone to see that the system is not completely legal. It is not working properly ... The border between legal and illegal is so thin. Most of them are illegal. They do not have contracts – in Vietnam and outside – so for sure, there [is] a lot more trafficking ... They are just focusing on kidnapping and the false friends. All campaigns are on this idea of the false friend: you want to work as a waitress in Malaysia and after you end up in a brothel. But these [are] only stereotypes. (E. Ferreras, Programme Director, Multilateral Cooperation and Gender, AECID, 9 October 2009)

False friend imagery was seen by this informant as a tool to minimise attention to the scope of the government's reliance on export labour and the exploitation experienced by some Vietnamese labour migrants during this process. She forcefully presented a view that this is the primary reason for lack of attention to this voluntary movement, reaffirming the importance of analysing trafficking imagery within the context of potential government agendas. This was, however, the only instance during my research where an informant questioned not only the typicality of coercive movement but also the legitimacy of the 'false friend' story.

The Trafficked Non-Consensual Minor

Child trafficking is a well-known and documented phenomenon and one given great weight in global and national responses to trafficking. There are high levels of demand for cheap and submissive child labour in both the informal and formal sectors: domestic work, the service industry (e.g., bars, restaurants, cleaning), construction (e.g., crushing stones, making bricks), agriculture, fishing and mines. In the Middle East, there is also demand for young boys who are sold and bought as 'camel jockeys' (Getu, 2006: 144).

The Trafficking Protocol treats child trafficking in a distinct manner by including an exception for cases involving children – defined in this instrument as anyone under the age of 18 years (Article 3(d)). It specifies that when children are involved, none of the means listed (such as threats, deception or abuse of power) need to be present for the case to be considered trafficking (Article 3(a)).

Simply put, the Trafficking Protocol relies on the idea that a child's consent, even if it were possible, is irrelevant when assessing whether a situation of trafficking has arisen. Therefore it appears unnecessary to discuss any autonomous or voluntary decision-making on the part of the child given such voluntariness is treated in law as irrelevant. In this section, I look at the notion of the 'evolving capacities of the child' and discuss the appropriateness of the Trafficking Protocol's approach to the movement of children. I look at particular cases that exemplify the complexities involved in trafficking of under 18 year olds.

The evolving capacities of the child

At the outset, it is important to note the limited legal autonomy of children to consent. In fact, society often deems adulthood (that is, attaining the age of 18 under many legal regimes) as a precursor to autonomous decision-making with respect to education, work, marriage and parenthood. When it comes to migration, national laws set limits around the decisions of children (or their parents on their behalf) regarding work or travel across borders alone or without legal permission.

Simultaneously, it is important to recognise the capacity of those under the age of 18 to make decisions regarding their own lives and well-being. In fact, a 2011 IOM study, which focused on child and youth migration and included trafficking within this scope, highlighted how, contrary to frequent portrayals of the coerced movement of children, independent child migration takes place and is not necessarily damaging or exploitative (IOM, 2011).

In this respect, many legal systems and leading scholars recognise that a child's capacity evolves over time. An important provision in the Convention on the Rights of the Child (CRC), Article 5, requires that:

> States parties shall respect the responsibilities, rights and duties of parents or, where applicable, the members of the extended family … or other persons legally responsible for the child, to provide, *in a manner* consistent *with the evolving capacities of the child*, appropriate direction and guidance in the exercise by the child of the rights recognised in the present Convention. (emphasis added)

At the same time, the Children's Rights Convention speaks specifically to the question of economic exploitation of children in Article 32(1):

> States Parties recognise the right of the child to be protected from economic exploitation and from performing any work that is likely to be hazardous or to interfere with the child's education, or to be harmful to the child's health or physical, mental, spiritual, moral or social development.

Adding to these considerations is the fact that in various countries, adulthood – as well as legal work – may begin earlier or later than 18 years and may be considered different for men and women.

Therefore, three factors foreground any discussion about child trafficking. First, the Trafficking Protocol notes that any movement for the purpose of exploitation of someone under the age of 18 years will be considered trafficking, regardless of consent. Second, and to the contrary, the global community recognises the evolving capacity of the child, which is particularly relevant to the autonomous decisions of children to migrate for work. Finally, within this context, children should still be protected from any form of exploitation, despite the voluntary or non-coerced nature of their decisions to enter into this work.

The complexities of child trafficking

Fosterage, child labour and exploitation: The practice of child trafficking has complicated cultural implications that can be linked, at least in part, to the historical practice of child fosterage and expectations on children to contribute to family incomes. A small but significant body of literature exists to describe such practices, particularly, across West Africa, although various terms are used (ranging from child labour, child slavery, to child exploitation etc.). According to Kari Hauge Rissøen, Anne Hatløy and Lise Bjerkan, child fosterage is a system that relocates children from one family to another (2004: 9). It may address demographic imbalance and therefore involve the movement of children from families with too many to families with too few (Rissøen, Hatløy and Bjerkan,

2004: 9). In other instances, it involves the relocation of children from rural to urban areas where it is perceived that there are more opportunities for school and, in the future, work (Rissøen, Hatløy and Bjerkan, 2004: 15; see also Page, 1989, quoted in Anarfi and Kwankye, 2003: 24).

Taking the example of Ghana, a major challenge exists in identifying where in the spectrum – from acceptable to exploitative – fosterage sits. Based on my field work in Ghana, some actors, including a UNICEF informant, consider fosterage and adoption to be distinct from trafficking, the former being an acceptable social and cultural practice. Others, including an IOM informant, linked fosterage with trafficking into the fishing industry and referred to the fostering of children as internal trafficking.

The internal movement of children, particularly during holiday seasons, also raises doubts about the appropriateness of the term trafficking. During the course of my fieldwork, there was extensive media coverage of the alleged traffic of a busload of '248 children aged between four and 15 and some adults' (*The Ghanaian Times*, 13 charged with child trafficking, 18 August 2010). One of my informants shared his doubt that this was a case of trafficking and noted the possibility that these children were simply – and legitimately – returning to their parents at the end of the school term (Tuniese Amuzu, Executive Director, Legal Resource Centre, 13 August 2010). My informant added a further element of complexity by referring to the possibility that some of these children were *escaping* situations of exploitation that they were facing under the care of a legal guardian while away from their parents.

Benjamin Lawrance also emphasises the need for a nuanced approach to the issue, particularly given that the work of children and their contribution to family incomes may be considered 'part and parcel of the fabric of Ghanaian society'. The global response to child labour/trafficking, Lawrance critiques, has spawned the 'industry-regulation' model, (2010: 73–4), which is epitomised in the regulation of the West African cocoa industry under the auspices of the International Cocoa Initiative. Consequently, in Ghana, 'children are routinely portrayed as victims. Parents are often unwilling accomplices. These tropes prevail in spite of evidence suggesting a more complex picture' (Lawrance, 2010: 74).

Other authors have also expressed doubt about the coerced nature of such movement. A study conducted by Sarah Castle and Aisse Diarra between 2000 and 2002 investigated the experiences of youth presumed to be at a high risk of trafficking from Mali to the cocoa plantations of Côte d'Ivoire, as well as those children who had been intercepted or repatriated as victims of trafficking (Busza, Castle and Diarra, 2004:1369). A survey of nearly 1000 of these youth found that only four fit within the classification of having been deceived, exploited, or not paid at all for their labour. The study's authors do not explain the definitions they apply. One possible explanation for these findings could be a very restrictive standard to reach the threshold of 'deception' or 'exploitation', especially in the context of trafficking of children or young adults. Yet these figures reveal the difficulty in understanding with precision the scope of child trafficking.

The challenge posed in balancing culturally-significant, historical practices of movement with how we understand human trafficking is furthered by a specific reference to the legal liability of parents for trafficking in the Ghanaian *Human Trafficking Act*. The law can therefore be seen as rejecting traditional, familial practices of child labour and fosterage. Notwithstanding, prosecution of parents might pose difficulties where children and other family or community members are required to provide testimonies. Moreover, in the particular Ghanaian context, we face substantial inconsistencies and gaps in data, making it impossible to know the scope of child trafficking.[8]

The sold daughter and coercive movement: The practice of family members 'selling' daughters into exploitative labour is reported in a number of trafficking studies. However, much of the literature is framed in sensationalist language; evidenced-based reasoning is often lacking.[9] Among empirical studies, the practice is documented primarily in the Asia region (e.g. Asia Watch, 1993; Long, 2004; Rushing, 2006; Derks, Henke and Ly, 2006). These studies report the selling of Burmese women and girls to brothels in Thailand (Asia Watch, 1993: 46); Vietnamese women who are tricked, lured or forced into selling sex based on parental decision-making or familial obligations (Rushing, 2006); and family and kinship relations that encourage or rationalise the trafficking of girls and women 'in times of stress and dislocation' (Long, 2005: 5).

Yet, deeper complexities are evident in these studies. Rosanne Rushing (2006) discusses internal migration from rural to urban areas in Vietnam. Of the 23 families interviewed by Rushing, nearly all of the parents reported making the decision for their daughters to migrate: 'The family's perception of daughters as a source of reliable remittances and community norms supporting youth migration contribute to promote the migration of daughters to the cities' (Rushing, 2006: 481). Yet, the extent to which daughters consent is unclear and probably differs from case to case, making it impossible to classify all such cases as internal trafficking.[10]

---

8   The Ghana Child Labour Survey of March 2003 estimated that there are 1 million to 1.4 million child labourers, measured according to the definition in the 1998 Children's Act (Lawrance 2010: 65). Between 2002 and 2009, IOM Ghana rescued 684 children from the fishing industry (IOM 2009). The National Trafficking Database recorded 1808 victims of trafficking as having been rescued between 1998 and 2010, with 77.7 per cent of the victims for whom age data was provided being less than 16 years of age (with no age data provided for 300 victims) (Kyei-Gyamfi 2010).

9   For example, Jeana Fowler and others note, '[e]ven more shocking is that in many cases, the families often sell their own relatives', and that 'unbelievably, even families of these young girls will sell their own daughters in order to make financial gains!' (Fowler, Che and Fowler, 2010: 1346).

10   Additionally, Rushing found that parents expected to receive more remittances from their daughters than from their sons (2006: 489). Rushing concluded that as parents 'expect their daughters to remain in the city indefinitely as a secure source of income', many women stay despite exploitative conditions and a desire to return home (2006: 489–90).

Joanna Busza's study of Vietnamese women undertaking commercial sex work in Cambodia also highlights the difficulties involved in discerning levels of consent and levels of autonomy and how to conceptualise the familial obligation. Busza cautions that the issue is more complex than simply a sense of familial responsibility. Severe poverty, often catalysed or accompanied by an illness in the family and a lack of other options, are the driving factors that result in families pushing their daughters into sex work (Busza, 2004: 238–9). Tellingly, most of the women involved in Busza's study stated that they were 'ashamed' of sex work and that it was 'bad work'. Yet these women also report pride in making a valuable contribution to their families' livelihoods in line with expectations of self-sacrifice and filial piety (Busza, 2004: 240–41).

During my own research, many of the testimonies of my informants that referred to the selling of girls appeared to be based on anecdote or rumours or the above-mentioned literature. One Vietnamese informant from an inter-governmental organisation made the claim that the selling of girls only happens in the south of Vietnam and not the north because unlike the north where 'in the villages you always see the pagoda and the common house that has hundreds of years of age ... the south was formed in the 1980s or 1970s only. Life there is more relaxed' (Anon., Senior Project Assistant: Counter-trafficking, international organisation, 12 October 2009). This informant went on to refer to a study written by French scholar Nicholas Lainez as the source of his information. Lainez's study, explores the cultural and economic reasons that push young Vietnamese women to emigrate and in his words, 'at worst, to fall into the clutches of human trafficking networks, leaving essential landmarks behind: family and village' (2009: 9). His analysis uses the Confucian concept of filial piety to explain the phenomenon of trafficking. The relationship Lainez attempts to establish between trafficking and Confucianism was strongly criticised by another anonymous informant:[11] ' ... there are always reasons for gender inequality ... the Catholic Church, here it is Confucianism. But do we really have strong analysis on Confucian ideology?'

It is somewhat unsurprising that there is a lack of scholarship by Confucian experts on the topic of trafficking. The existing literature that discusses filial piety

---

11   This informant shared the following view about Lainez and his research: 'When I was visiting AFESIP (*Agir pour les Femmes en Situation Precaire*/Acting for Women in Distressing Situations), and they would not let me visit the shelter, he was telling awful stories: girls, 9 years old, 10 years old and trafficked, pregnant at the end of the trip, the worst scenario. When someone does not know you and you visit the organisation, you should try to be more technical. Telling you the really worst stories – the obscene parts – it was voyeuristic. I did not like that. It did not leave a good impression on me'. Several of Lainez's studies (e.g. 2011a) adopt sensationalist language with limited – if any – methodological details provided for the data discussed. Much of Lainez's research on trafficking was conducted with AFESIP, an NGO founded by Somaly Mam. Mam – a once highly acclaimed and award winning anti-trafficking activist – was discredited in 2014 after both her own personal story about being trafficked and the stories of several victims in the AFESIP shelters, were found to be fabricated (Marks, 2014; Fuller, 2014).

has in fact been written by experts on trafficking, women's rights or development and not Confucian researchers (e.g. Rushing, 2006: 480; Knudsen, 2006: 144; Wells, 2005: 8; Fahey, 2002: 6–7; Rydstrøm, 2003: 686). This gap highlights the extent to which it is problematic that 'Confucianism' was regularly named as explaining both gender inequality and the traffic of women in Vietnam during my fieldwork.

The above examples show that in some cases, the label of child trafficking is justified; these examples should be understood as clear reflections of coercive and exploitative practices. My preliminary findings, however, suggest that when evidence exists, it is often anecdotal and premised upon an oft-quoted but small body of literature. Rather, as noted by author Rende Taylor, whose research focused on the traffic of ethnic Thai women and girls, 'this practice appears to be becoming less common as migratory networks grow and as girls and families learn the risks of such arrangements from awareness-raising programs' (2005: 416).

Studies such as those of Rushing and Busza reflect a more nuanced understanding of family goals, motivation and what appears to be a partial level of autonomous decision-making on behalf of some young women and girls. Moreover, the notion of the evolving capacities of the child also reflects that some people under the age of 18 years do engage in decision-making that more closely resembles the voluntary decision-making of adults. By framing all consent as irrelevant, the Trafficking Protocol lends itself to a conclusion that all such migratory movement of children should be prohibited. This ignores the complexities whereby such migration may be voluntary, beneficial, valued by children and their parents alike. Indeed, such movement may act to beneficially remove children from exploitative situations. There is a need for more vigorous data collection to better inform how we approach – theoretically as well as practically – issues of child trafficking, child labour and child migration.

The 'Voluntary Victim': Refining our Understanding of Human Trafficking

Numerous aspects of human trafficking reflect 'voluntary' or non-coerced decisions on the part of victims. The Trafficking Protocol, however, requires that the consent of an adult victim is ignored from a legal perspective when any of the means listed, such as force, abduction or abuse of power, are used in the victim's movement. As a result, the Trafficking Protocol defers attention away from those aspects of victim voluntariness that are central to human trafficking. This includes pre-migration planning, voluntary pursuit of opportunities for betterment abroad and voluntary acceptance of risk. Also relevant is the possibility that a victim may be voluntarily fleeing situations of abuse, exploitation or inequality at home.

Two main categories of victims can be identified: a migrant (i) who is coercively moved to the destination country which, as noted above, is a rarity; and (ii) those victims whose expectations of work and life abroad are unmet, either at the point of arrival in the destination country or at some stage while residing in the destination country, placing the victim in a situation of exploitation. The fact that a potential migrant has engaged in some process of self-determined migration based on expectations of work and life abroad should not be seen as a reason to deny their victimhood. That is, although I emphasise evidence of voluntary or consensual movement throughout this book, at no point do I contend that the men and women identified during my research are not victims of trafficking. To express this idea, I have coined the phrase 'voluntary victim'. This new concept aims to highlight evidence of non-coerced recruitment and/or transportation of victims during this stage of the trafficking process and provide a vivid image in direct contrast to the kidnapped victim archetype.

The Decision to Depart

Evidence from the field reveals high levels of pre-planning among victims. Together with rational assessment of risks and opportunities, this picture contrasts sharply with both coerced movement and victim naivety. Here I draw on my field research in Ukraine involving 104 male and female returned victims of trafficking. Participants in this research were asked two questions specifically on this point: first, whether any of the relatives listed knew that they were about to depart from Ukraine (Annex 2, Question 23) and, secondly, whether any of the relatives listed actually assisted them in arranging their departure (Annex 2, Question 24). High levels of awareness of the pending departure were revealed, as noted in in Table 4.1.

Table 4.1   **Number of people aware about the respondent's decision to leave Ukraine**

Relation	Frequency	Percentage of total surveyed population
Mother	70	67.3
Father	33	31.7
Grandparents	15	14.4
Partner	26	25.0
Siblings	27	26.0
Aunt	6	5.8
Uncle	1	1.0
Cousins	6	5.8
Children	6	5.8
Friends	4	3.8
Nobody	5	4.8

Table 4.1 indicates that in 67.3 per cent of cases, the respondent's mother was aware of the decision to leave Ukraine. Further, in close to one-third of cases, fathers were aware of the impending departure. Siblings, partners and grandparents

also had knowledge in a considerable number of cases. In only 4.8 per cent of cases, no individual related or known to the victim was aware of the respondent's decision to leave Ukraine. Victim voluntariness is revealed in the high levels of pre-planning for this potential movement. This set of data leaves open the possibility of unexpected (and potentially coerced) movement for only 4.8 per cent of the respondents for whom no relation was aware of the impending departure.

In order to get a better insight into the meaning of these figures, these data should be compared with the responses to Question 24, regarding assistance in arranging the departure of victims. These findings are set out in Table 4.2.

Table 4.2   People involved in arranging the departure of the respondent from Ukraine

Relation	Frequency	Percentage of total surveyed population
Mother	6	5.8
Father	5	4.8
Partner (Husband/wife/boyfriend/girlfriend)	6	5.8
Siblings	2	1.9
Aunt	1	1.0
Cousins	1	1.0
Friends	11	10.6
Acquaintance	24	23.1
Unknown person	12	11.5
No one[12]	33	31.7
No response given	4	3.8
Other (abducted)	1	1.0

Levels of pre-planning and voluntariness – at least at a familial, if not individual level – are reflected by the high number of cases where the person who arranged the departure was a close family member of the respondents, including mothers (5.8 per cent), fathers (4.8 per cent), siblings (1.9 per cent), partners (5.8 per cent) and friends (10.6 per cent). Acquaintances assisted victims in 23.1 per cent of cases. While we could conjecture that their interests in the well-being of the victim would have been lower than family members and friends, this high number – almost one-quarter of cases – shows significant levels of pre-planning

---

12   In these cases, the respondents marked all of the listed relatives with the answer 'no' and under the category 'other', they did not identify any other people involved in arranging their departure. In 21 of these cases, they explicitly wrote 'no one'. See my comment on the five respondents who identified themselves as orphans on pp. 94–5, three of whom were among those who indicated that 'no one' was involved.

with people known to the victims. This does not, however, exclude the possibility that the victim was coerced by these family members, friends or acquaintances. It is important as well to note the exceptions. One returnee explicitly indicated that she had been 'abducted'. This not only reflects the reality that coercion in trafficking does occur, even if rare, but also the value of understanding trafficking as involving a range of experiences that sit on a migration spectrum.

With regards to other evidence of pre-planning on the part of victims, the use of tourist and also student visas was mentioned by several informants. This parallels the events that led to the prosecution of Wei Tang for slavery in Australia[13] as well as the more recent Australian prosecution of Keith Dobie.[14] I have discussed both extensively in an article that emphasises the importance of recognising the voluntariness of victims alongside their victimhood and right to legal redress (Vijeyarasa, 2010e).

The deliberate use of tourist visas for work was also noted by an informant working for the British High Commission in Ghana:

> From Ghana, the majority would go with a tourist visa and overstay that visa or sometimes people get someone else's passport and there is some kind of document abuse ... Obviously, once you get into mainland Europe it is very easy to move around ... It is not so easy in the UK, which is perhaps one of the reasons that the UK is not as popular a destination as Italy ... Almost exclusively they go because it is their own choice to go, but when they end up on that route – even before they get to Europe – they can find themselves in a position of vulnerability. (A. Fleming, 1st Sec. Migration Policy (West Africa), British High Commission, Ghana, 3 August 2010)

Fleming's mention of the UK and Italy also suggests high levels of knowledge and consideration of the opportunities and entry points available to potential migrants in destination countries. He provided evidence of the various ways in

---

13 The case against Victorian brothel owner Ms Wei Tang was the first jury conviction under the slavery offences in Australia's *Criminal Code* (Cth). This conviction was subsequently appealed (Court of Appeal of the Supreme Court of Victoria) and finally upheld by Australia's High Court in 2008. See *R v Tang* (2008); *R v Tang* (2007) and discussion in the previous chapter.

14 Keith Dobie was the first person to be convicted in Australia on charges of trafficking in persons pursuant to the *Criminal Code Amendment (Trafficking in Persons and Debt Bondage) Act* 2005 (Cth), which was introduced in Australia in July 2005 (Division 271), as well as on four counts of presenting false information to an immigration officer and one count of dealing in the proceeds of crime. The Court found that he deceived the first woman about how much work she would have to perform in Australia and the second woman about her work schedule. The facts clearly demonstrate that the women negotiated their expected terms and conditions for work in Australia prior to their departure. Based on these facts, the Supreme Court determined that the women's expectations were not met by Dobie. Dobie's appeal was dismissed by the Court of Appeal on 26 February 2010. This case was discussed in more detail in the previous chapter.

which 'trafficked' movement does not involve coercion. This does not dilute vulnerability to exploitation; by noting the illegality of, and victims' complicity in, the movement, Fleming highlights how vulnerability is aggravated under these circumstances, with evident risks of exploitation during movement as well as upon arrival in the destination country. This is particularly the case when threatened by the prospect that law enforcement may be informed of their illegal status.

Despite this reasoned decision-making that shapes the movement of victims, definitions of trafficking frequently fail to capture the role of the victim. Driven primarily towards law enforcement and criminal justice, when adopted outside of the law, definitions of trafficking give a one-sided perspective and fail to explore factors driving victim decision-making and expectations, shifting attention away from obvious links between migration, closed borders and trafficking.

Voluntary Risk-Taking and a Question of Luck

The Trafficking Protocol fails to reflect the high levels of voluntary acceptance of risk evident in trafficking. Despite the fact that not all informants during my fieldwork were specifically questioned about victims' awareness of the risk they were undertaking, seven informants – three from Ukraine and four from Vietnam – expressed in different ways the common idea that victims assume 'it will not happen to me'. IOM research similarly shows that although 80 per cent of people know about trafficking, they nonetheless believe trafficking will 'happen to someone else' (O. Horbunova, Deputy Coordinator of Counter-Trafficking Program, IOM Ukraine, 31 July 2009).

Informants from Vietnam noted that while a large number of victims generally understood the risks, many assumed that *they* were not at risk: 'Sometimes they refer to it happening to other people [who] are unlucky, […] they do not see themselves in those pictures' (Anon., Senior Project Assistant: Counter-trafficking, international organisation, 12 October 2009). One informant from Vietnam linked this to re-trafficking: 'They have heard of it. They know but they still want to try. Oh, it will not happen to me. They try again and again and they fail and keep doing it. They hope they will have luck next time. So there is a lot of re-trafficking' (P. Changmanee, Regional Programme Director, Oxfam Quebec, 16 October 2009).

Trafficking is frequently contrasted with 'successful migration' – the experience of the lucky migrant whose 'agent was honest and they were able to remit thousands of dollars back to their home' (Anon., Counter-Trafficking Coordinator, IOM Mission in Ukraine, 13 August 2009). Like 'luck', which brings to mind rational choice theory noted in the introduction of this chapter, of which risk is an important factor, the use of the term 'adventure' hints at more voluntary movement as opposed to coercion under physical or threatened restraint.

This language of 'adventure' was similar to that adopted by a Ghanaian informant when describing the trafficking of three Ghanaian women to Russia: 'The craze is for people to travel' (Anon., Ghanaian Police Anti-Human Trafficking

Unit, 27 August 2010). Andrew Bruce in Vietnam went on to compare what he sees as the reality for Vietnamese women with his perception of what occurs in Europe:

> To me, the trafficking of women into prostitution in Cambodia is the most interesting because it demonstrates the complexity of the situation. It is not a man, for example, an Albanian man who marries a woman and then sells her in Italy. It is [Vietnamese] women going to Cambodia and [...] they may even be aware that they are going into prostitution. (A. Bruce, IOM Head of Regional Office for Asia, 21 September 2009)

Besides the obvious value of the quote as one of several instances where informants debunked the stereotypes held about the country being studied, it is important to highlight a trend observed in several interviews: informants were ready to dismiss stereotypes of the country being discussed based on their first-hand knowledge, but they frequently drew upon stereotypical perceptions they held about other countries or regions when sharing their analysis of the global picture (in this case, the picture of the Albanian man).

There was substantially more diversity in the views offered by Ukrainian informants, arguably a product of its history. Discussing deception concerning conditions of work, one Ukrainian suggested the following reason:

> We receive a lot of women who believed that they would work as waitresses or models and it was very hard to believe they would be sexually abused ... Here – locally – people were cheated by the Government so many times, during the Soviet regime and after the Soviet regime breakdown. At the same time, when they go to another country – to North America, Europe, to a country with respect of human rights – they believe that they will be okay. (O. Horbunova, Deputy Coordinator of Counter-Trafficking Program, IOM Ukraine, 31 July 2009)

By comparison, a psychologist working in a rehabilitation centre felt that from her experiences of working in the field of victim reintegration and rehabilitation, awareness of risk when travelling to Russia is low due to the close historical ties between Ukraine and Russia:

> During Soviet times, we were brought up helping each other: 'We have to help each other'. They were called sisters and brothers. It is still in our blood. That is why, when people were trafficked to Russia, people thought, 'How can they do it to us? ... It is our brothers and sisters, so nothing will happen there'. (Dr I. Lysenko, Psychologist, IOM Rehabilitation Centre, Kyiv, 20 August 2009)

A US embassy official linked awareness of risk to a 'Soviet mentality'. She reasoned that 'Soviet people have a special mentality. If something is printed in the newspaper, people are inclined to believe in it. They are not inclined to check this information. Americans say, "Trust but verify" but for Soviet people, this is not normal' (Olena Kustova, Law Enforcement Section, US Embassy to Ukraine, 2 September 2009). These three informants give various justifications for why Ukrainian victims are more vulnerable to deception: either because of expectations of respect for human rights in North America and Europe in comparison with the Soviet regime; trust of Russians as their 'brothers and sisters'; or a natural inclination to trust what is printed as true. These diverging, and potentially contradictory, views can be explained in part by the difference of opinions among Ukrainian citizens on the Soviet transition. While these arguments suggest contradictory push factors, all three arguments highlight the voluntary and at times rational reasoning driving decisions.

Voluntary Pursuit of the Fairy-Tale Life Abroad

Contrary to typical depictions, the pursuit of monetary and social goals is central to trafficking. Images of successful migration abroad play a particularly motivating role in migration. The false or exaggerated nature of the expectations formed on this basis, when coupled with desires for a better life, raise the question of whether they can be deemed truly 'voluntary' acts. While the autonomy of these decisions may remain in doubt, what is clear is that the findings discussed below indicate the typicality of an initially voluntary process of movement that falls outside of the framework of coercion.

In Ukraine, Vietnam and Ghana, informants shared various examples of victims' false expectations in their search for economic and social betterment, although the term 'desperation' was most frequently used to describe irregular migration from Ghana. As one informant noted, '[t]here is a real desperation among Ghanaians to go to these countries and they will do anything if they are going. The opportunity to exploit people who migrate irregularly increases as governments introduce measures to make it more and more difficult to live as an irregular migrant in the destination country' (Mr A. Fleming, British High Commission, Ghana, 3 August 2010). Another Ghanaian informant emphasised how 'they thought that they will be better off than where they are. They are told that there is potential out there' (Dr M. Sackey, Former ILO-IPEC Ghana National Programme Coordinator, 22 July 2010).

The strength of such desires undermines the success of anti-trafficking programmes: 'The problem is because they are being deceived, no matter what you tell them beforehand, they think that you do not like them to prosper. You are seen as someone blocking their way' (E. Peasah, Counter-Trafficking Field Manager, IOM Ghana, 21 July 2010). At a later stage in the interview, the same informant referred to the 'dreams' of Ghanaians to make a life abroad, comments that were not only very telling of the initial voluntariness of migrants' departures, but perhaps also the stories (whether true or false) shared by returning migrants who perpetuate this belief in success abroad:

Most people believe that the only way you can make it in Ghana or Africa is to travel to Europe or abroad and this is all around the continent. So everyone's dream is to go abroad, to start making a life, to make ends meet. And a few people who went initially came back with a lot of property and made it work. So even if you are poor, you will help your child go to Europe as you believe your situation will change because your child is abroad ... That is why you have Ghanaians, African migrants walking from Africa, Ghana and Niger towards Libya. Walking and then crossing the ocean to get to Italy, Spain or Morocco. (21 July 2010)

It is important to note how myths concerning the opportunities offered by life abroad were common to all three countries, with many informants identifying these myths as a core part of the problem. In the case of Ukraine, the role of success stories was labelled by one informant as the 'Cinderella syndrome': 'These girls hear a success story and it only takes one or two success stories that they hear anecdotally to make them think: "You know what, I think that is the way". And the situation they are living in is so bad, so why not do it?' (A. Nguyễn, IOM Ukraine, 13 August 2009; see also Vijeyarasa, 2012a in which I discuss the 'Cinderella syndrome' in greater depth). The informant continued by noting how migrants would 'come back and parade around their village as a success story', or if able to remit money home, provide enough success stories to motivate others to go abroad.

Adding to this are the 'endless soap operas from Brazil ... People expect it is a very rich country because of what they observe in the soap operas. They see expensive villas, expensive houses and they think in Brazil everybody is living like this, which is not true' (O. Horbunova, Deputy Coordinator of Counter-Trafficking Program, IOM Ukraine, 31 July 2009).[15] Others in Ukraine made reference to these 'nice stories and fairy-tales about the excellent life abroad' (S. Lytvyn, consultant and former coordinator ILO Anti-Trafficking Programme, Ukraine, 8 September 2009).

Not all informants placed the primary responsibility on misleading images of success. Ukrainian informant Lysenko in fact indicated that these images are beginning to be questioned. She added, however, that people continue to seek work abroad, despite greater awareness of the reality and risks. She saw this as a sign of their level of desperation:

---

15 According to another informant, whom I specifically asked about the role of Brazilian soap operas following my interview with Horbunova, these soap operas may have played a significant role in the past but they were discontinued several years ago. On the one hand, Horbunova could be wrong in drawing this correlation. On the other hand, soap operas in Ukraine could continue to remain an influencing factor even after their discontinuance, thereby demonstrating the significant role they played in shaping expectations. At the very least, they continue to be *perceived* as an influencing factor by one of the experts working in the field of trafficking.

> At the beginning, there was a legend that abroad is really like heaven ... Now
> the borders are quite open. People are somehow more realistic about what is
> happening in other countries. So they are going there because they really need to
> find a way out. They do not just go there blindly. They know that they can earn
> money. They just have to find work and they will get paid. (Dr I. Lysenko, IOM
> Rehabilitation Centre, Kyiv, 20 August 2009)

Similar views were shared in Ghana, with several examples given of images of
opportunities abroad and the parading of success. Literature on internal migration
in Ghana also points to the relevance of such myths in migratory and labour-
related decisions.[16]

Two informants in Ghana referred to the concept of the 'burger', a positive
term that was originally used to refer to Ghanaian migrants who had lived and
worked in Hamburg, Germany. It was later extended to all Ghanaians who had
temporarily migrated to Europe and North America for work (Awumbila, 2010:
4). One informant noted how having children living abroad is a 'status symbol',
with the mother of migrant children referred to as a 'burger mommy': 'So there
is status for her as a mother' (J. Dzokoto, Assistant Director of Migration, Ghana
Immigration Service, 17 November 2010). A personal story that was shared with me
also highlights the value placed by Ghanaians on Europe as a destination country:

> When we prepare obituaries, people will look to see how many people are
> coming from the outside. It will say, this person's children are coming from the
> US, from the UK, from Australia. That will tell you how big the funeral will
> be ... I always think about my father's funeral and the way they talked at that.
> My brother at the time was coming from Swaziland and people thought the
> notice in the newspaper said Switzerland.

Dzokoto did say however, as was also noted by my Ukrainian informants, that
some people are beginning to question this imagery: 'It is a status symbol for some
of them. However for those of us who understand, it is no more because we have
come across people who have lived out there, who were not working, who were
not making money'. Nonetheless, she noted that some continue 'dreaming ... not
questioning why their father is not remitting'. The fact that such images are being
questioned, but migrants continue to make decisions based on this imagery in both
Ghana and Ukraine, is indicative of the long-lasting impact of such images of

---

16   See for example Laurian Bowles for an interesting analysis of the origins of the
myth of one migrant woman – a porter – who was allegedly earning a 500,000 Cedis daily
wage and the varying levels of disbelief among other migrants concerning the nameless
porter's story and her 'comfortable life' (2009: 313–14). Following redenomination of the
currency in 2007, 500,000 Cedis is the equivalent of 50 Ghanaian Cedis or USD25. At the
time the myth was first started, this was closer to USD50.

success and perhaps also of the need to believe that there is an outlet for improving one's circumstances.

As in Ghana, the efforts made by victims to convey images of success have been discussed in other research (Bélanger, 2014: 101). This includes unsuccessful victims borrowing money to buy a scooter or renovate their house upon returning home to give the impression of successful migration abroad. In addition, informants in Vietnam frequently shared with me observations that 'people think that the grass on the other side is greener. Most of the people in Vietnam think that abroad is always a new horizon with a lot of opportunities' (Anon., Senior Project Assistant: Counter-trafficking, international organisation, 12 October 2009).

Two other informants in Vietnam made similar observations. One informant – when asked about the solution she saw to trafficking – identified 'economic disparities compared with nearby countries' as the reason people migrate, having 'seen what life is like in other countries' through 'the media and the internet' (P. Changmanee, Regional Programme Director, Oxfam Quebec, 16 October 2009). Another informant noted how 'television is a motivating factor because you see the world, a lot of goods' (E. Ferreras, Programme Director, Multilateral Cooperation and Gender, Spanish Agency for International Development Cooperation, 9 October 2009).

False or exaggerated imagery of success abroad was common to all three countries during my research, with informants noting this imagery as a central factor in migration. It is important to reiterate that I made no reference to this imagery in my questions but that it was instead raised spontaneously by informants. These stories offer an appreciation of the factors that influence rational decision-making. Concepts such as the 'burger', the 'burger mommy', Brazilian soap operas and Cinderella stories reflect upon the expectations of potential migrants from Ghana, Vietnam and Ukraine and how these expectations are formed through images of success.

Such images contribute to individual and perhaps family goals, particularly concerning monetary success and personal wealth that influence decision-making, including in instances where such opportunities are only attainable through irregular and unsafe migration. These factors that clearly play a role in pre-departure decision-making also further discredit the notion of physical, mental, legal and psychological coercion as defined above. Some degree of rational and voluntary decision-making is at play in the pre-departure process, even if the false or exaggerated nature of this imagery may lead us to question how truly autonomous these decisions may be.

Diminished Voluntariness as a Push Factor

Some evidence exists that limited freedom or lack of a social safety net may be a driver of voluntary movement. Naturally, we should recognise the diminished voluntariness at play in these situations and question the extent to which this can be framed as autonomous movement. We may be able to understand these inequalities at home as factors pushing victims to depart.

Domestic violence is one such factor assumed to be a push factor for trafficking, not only in the literature but also among my informants. However, methodologically sound evidence of a relationship between human trafficking and domestic violence remains weak globally, with the assertion often unsubstantiated with first-hand data (e.g. Warnath, 2007 or Zimmerman and Watts, 2003 arguing that women trafficked into sex work 'share the vulnerabilities' of women who experience domestic violence). La Strada contends on the basis of research in Belarus that domestic violence is 'one of the root causes of trafficking' (La Strada, 2008: 54).[17] This claim was also made by several informants in Ukraine, including one who argued that 'labour migration has a woman's face, as women not only seek to earn an income in order to be able to afford a separate dwelling and avoid abuse in this way, but also to avoid any future dependence on the part of their children' (Elvira Mruchkovska, Director, Suchasnyk (NGO in Chernivtsi, Ukraine), Email interview, 3 September 2009).

The same informant argued that women from rural areas of Ukraine face higher levels of gender inequality and noted that, in the experience of her NGO, 80 per cent to 90 per cent of rural women experience gender inequality and abuse in the family. She was one of several local NGO stakeholders in Ukraine to assert a link between domestic violence and trafficking. Ukraine was in fact the only country of the three where a relationship between the two phenomena – domestic violence and trafficking – was raised. For example, Olena Kustova, a lawyer and Program Manager in the Law Enforcement Section of the US Embassy to Ukraine, asserted that there are two major push factors for migration: the lack of economic opportunities for women, and domestic violence, which together act as a driver for women to leave their homes and travel abroad (2 September 2009).

One anonymous informant from an inter-governmental organisation offered a more nuanced approach:

> Domestic violence itself is not an isolated phenomenon and it is usually combined with other circumstances, such as economic depravity, acceptability of violent treatment (whether by the perpetrator, the victim, or the community) ... some of the factors that may lead to domestic violence may equally lead to susceptibility to trafficking. (Anon., Human Rights Project Officer, Inter-governmental organisation, 29 November 2010)

My findings revealed another example of lack of social bonds that may have a potential relationship with trafficking. When asked about pre-departure knowledge

---

17   The La Stada study states that: 'there is a high incidence of domestic violence among trafficked persons, indicating that this violence is one of the factors contributing to trafficking' (2008: 13) but does not offer more concrete information on the nature of that experience or prevalence of this link.

and assistance from family members, five victims indicated that they were orphans. While estimates of the number of Ukrainian orphans vary, according to UNICEF, there were approximately 65,000 to 80,000 Ukrainian children in residential institutions for orphaned and abandoned children in 2006 (Degen, 2007), less than 1 per cent of the then child population of 9 million children. Analysing my data in greater detail, three of the five respondents who indicated that they were orphans left Ukraine when they were still minors and were orphans when they migrated,[18] thereby fitting the definition of orphans used in the UNICEF study (children under the age of 18 years left without parents and/or otherwise under state care).

Of the two remaining cases of victims who migrated as adults, one of them indicated that she had attended boarding school, had been disabled from childhood,[19] left Ukraine and returned when aged 21 years. It is possible that she was also an orphan before adulthood and hence could also be compared with the UNICEF data. The fifth case involved a migrant who left Ukraine as an adult (aged 21) and completed the survey at aged 23. It is unclear, therefore, if she was an orphan in the sense of the UNICEF definition or if her parents died during her adult years.

A conservative reading of these data shows that four of my 104 questionnaire respondents (3.8 per cent) were orphans within the UNICEF definition, a rate that is proportionately high given the average for the broader child population and an important factor to note as a potential push factor.[20] Even if only three of the respondents fall within the UNICEF definition, the proportion of orphans among my respondents (2.9 per cent) is still relatively high. This provides support for the contention that lack of social bonds may play a role in trafficking, although a much larger sample size would be needed to confirm this connection.

These findings provide evidence of experiences of trafficking that do not fall within the definition of 'coercion' outlined above, that is, threats of harm or physical restraint or abuse of the legal status of the person, as the cause of movement. Yet, they highlight other factors that raise doubts about the autonomy of decision-making. The lack of social bonds or social networks for orphans could increase vulnerability to trafficking in the same way that domestic violence may be a driving factor.

---

18   Two of the respondents indicated that they had been 'orphaned' before departing Ukraine, with one adding that she had 'no place to live/ Сирота, негде жить' in response to the question, 'Where was your home before you left Ukraine?' (Question 13). The third respondent repeated that she was an orphan when she indicated that she had been attending boarding school (школа-інтернат) prior to departing Ukraine.

19   Будинок-інтернат (сирота, інвалід з дитинства 1 грп.)

20   I have not been able to identify any reasons to question the questionnaire participants' statements that they were orphans.

Conclusion

At the outset of this chapter, I laid out a framework centred on the concepts of coercion and deception to assess the accuracy of the coerced victim archetype. Existing data, including findings from my own field research in Ukraine, Vietnam and Ghana, suggest the atypical nature of physical, financial, legal or emotional coercion. The selling of young girls by their families in Vietnam may be an exception, with a large number of informants in the field believing that the selling of young girls takes place, although primarily on the basis of other existing secondary sources, many of which are now outdated. Additionally, the evolving capacity of these children raises doubt about a simplified approach that frames fosterage or child labour in Ghana, for example, as trafficking, without recognising the capacity of these youth to make decisions about their migration and labour.

As far as adults are concerned, rationality and voluntariness are widespread. The rationality is seen in (i) the (at least initially) voluntary movement of male and female victims; (ii) their awareness of risks, and processing and acceptance of these risks, as well as (iii) pre-planning, perhaps with the support of, but at the very least, with the knowledge of family members and friends. These victims can be collectively included in what I refer to as 'voluntary victims'.

However, the role of deception in their decisions should not be downplayed. Many of these victims are deceived at times broadly about the sector or industry – as was noted by my informants in Ghana – while in other cases deception may be in a more restricted manner, mainly relating to the conditions of work. In some instances, deceived victims may later accept the conditions of work offered to them. However, as this analysis focuses on the process by which victims enter into a situation of trafficking, it is the initial deception and its role in the process of rational and voluntary decision making that is under discussion.

This combination of reasoned decision-making – including assessment of risks and pre-planning – and potential deception should be placed at the heart of any framework created to explain patterns of movement in trafficking situations. The evidence presented here dispels coercion as the norm and demonstrates the existence of some degree of autonomy in the decisions of migrants, opening the door for an understanding of trafficking as involving the voluntary victim and their unmet expectations.

Finally, while some may view deception and autonomy as incompatible, I adopt the view that deception does not render the way in which women act as agents engaged in a search for a particular outcome as any less autonomous. Rather, deception opens the door to *invalidate* those decisions. The 'voluntary victim', although commonly deceived as to the nature or conditions of work and life abroad, either by the trafficker or through false or exaggerated imagery, nonetheless engages in a process of autonomous decision making that displaces the typicality of the coerced and kidnapped victim. This highlights the need for a more nuanced understanding of trafficking that sits within a spectrum of migratory experiences. Simultaneously, victimhood must be recognised and access to redress for these victims guaranteed.

Chapter 5

The Uneducated Victim of Trafficking

I think we all understand that there is a myth about education and unemployment as the common reasons for trafficking. In reality, it appears that people from the community with low education are more vulnerable to trafficking. It does not mean they are the only ones. They are just more vulnerable to trafficking. There are some people with good education who are also tricked. I think the underlying reason for people making such assumptions is that people come from low socio-economic backgrounds and people interpret this as low education.

(Anon., National Trafficking Project Coordinator,
UN agency Vietnam, 16 October 2009)

A widely-accepted assumption in trafficking discourse is that a relationship exists between levels of education and migratory decisions that lead to unsafe and exploitative work. Education presumably creates opportunities for potential migrants to access decent work[1] in the domestic market. If they choose to migrate in order to work abroad, better-educated people are more likely to leave under safer conditions than their less-educated peers. Low levels of education are therefore seen as a major factor limiting the ability of potential migrants to find work at home and/or migrate safely. Education is often also assumed to increase the capacity of victims to understand, process and appreciate the risks involved when entering into a transaction. Victims of trafficking are therefore presumed to have a lower capacity to assess the risks associated with the contracts in which they engage.

This chapter involves an analysis of the two-part assumption that education levels and trafficking are intimately connected and offers an alternative view of how to understand the relationship between the two. After analysing the uneducated victim archetype in greater depth, in the second section of this chapter, I discuss the absence of data connecting the levels of school completion of trafficked victims and their vulnerability to trafficking. There is in fact a surprising lack of empirical analysis of the assumed correlations between education and trafficking. In the course of my research, I have identified only one study involving primary research conducted in Thailand that focused solely on the interrelationship between education, child labour and sex work (Rende Taylor,

---

1 The International Labour Organisation defines decent work as work that is productive and delivers a fair income, security in the workplace and social protection for families, better prospects for personal development and social integration, freedom for people to express their concerns, organise and participate in the decisions that affect their lives and equality of opportunity and treatment for all women and men. For more, see Vosko, 2010: 85–7.

2005). I have not found any academic work that involves an in-depth study into the relationship between trafficking and education levels and nothing at all on the issue of comprehension of risk.[2]

To the contrary, I propose the possibility of an inverse relationship between trafficking and education levels; higher educated individuals may face greater vulnerability to trafficking and exploitation. I also examine the question of comprehension of risk, a factor which is rarely analysed in trafficking literature but which proved to be pertinent during my own field investigations in Ghana. I discuss its relevance to vulnerability to trafficking and analyse the views held by several of my informants that potential migrants suffer trafficking and trafficking-like conditions not necessarily because of the tactics of 'traffickers' but rather due to the naivety of the victims themselves, being from the 'village' and ignorant. I also look at other trafficking-related experiences and decisions that may relate to education levels, including the types of sectors into which victims are trafficked, willingness to report their exploitation and, finally, the geographic distance travelled. In the final section of this chapter, I look beyond the aggregate figures of school enrolment and completion and explore other education-related factors that may prove relevant when assessing vulnerability to trafficking, including the quality of education and cost of schooling.

The Archetypal Uneducated Victim and its Origins

Numerous authors assert that there are clear correlations between education levels and the risk of human trafficking. At times, authors described strong correlations; in other instances, reference is made to education as one of a multiplicity of causal factors.

---

2   The closest analysis I have identified on the topic is an article by Bridget Ogonor and Austin Osunde in which they argue that the right to education is violated for young girls who are trafficked from their homes to places within and outside of Nigeria for labour and sexual exploitation, thereby depriving the victims of education (2007). They examine the successes and shortcomings of a Universal Basic Education Programme for 130 repatriated victims (that is, analyse education as a reintegration tool as opposed to specifically looking at lack of education as a cause). Ironically, the programme appears to have been largely unsuccessful, the authors failing to see the patronising and stereotypical views that they themselves adopt. The authors find themselves unable to explain why the girls 'seek to be re-trafficked at the least opportunity', and blame the programme for making 'no attempt ... to change the values and attitudes of the students who are well positioned to positively influence members of the larger society toward sexual trafficking' (2007: 617). Referring to trafficking as a social vice and making no distinction between the various types of exploitation suffered by victims of trafficking, the authors argue that the curriculum content should 'equip pupils with the personal agency to probe anti-female cultural values' – not explaining what these 'anti-female' values entail – and 'dissuade female students from accepting to be trafficked' (Ogonor and Osunde, 2007: 617).

Writing on trafficking of Romanian women, Sebastian Lăzăroiu and Monica Alexandru argue that education is an important 'vulnerability' factor: 'In this context *it is obvious* that the higher the degree of education and the longer the period spent in school, the more education constitutes a protection factor against trafficking' (2003: 27, emphasis added). Describing the global picture of trafficking, Vidyamali Samarasinghe and Barbara Burton argue that the 'roots of trafficking are structural and systemic', including 'profound disadvantages for women in terms of poverty, education and wage employment' (2007: 54). They continue that '[i]ndividuals at risk are usually children and women, aged between 5 and 25 years, mostly rural, poor, and with little education' (Samarasinghe and Burton, 2007: 55).

In the Asia region, several authors make similar arguments. In a few instances, these are empirically-based, although reports often lack a transparent methodology to determine the basis for data collection. This includes studies focused on Vietnam (Duong and Khuat 2008: 205–6 whose 2005 sample of 213 female respondents was 'relatively un-educated') and Nepal (Poudel and Carryer, 2000: 74–5). Mary Crawford and Michelle Kaufman identify various inequalities facing Nepali women, including 'educational inequalities' that are 'rampant' (2008: 905–6). They conclude, '[a]ll these socio-cultural forces put Nepali girls and women at risk for sex trafficking' (Crawford and Kaufman, 2008: 905–6). Susan Tiefenbrun, too, argues that women are 'victims of poverty' and suffer because of 'the failure of some cultures and societies to place value on traditional women's work, and of the lack of education and employment opportunities for women in developing and transition countries' (2001: 208, with her position echoed by Trépanier, 2003: 48).

In the Africa region, a 2001 study by ILO-IPEC, involving fieldwork in Benin, Burkina Faso, Cameroon, Côte d'Ivoire, Gabon, Ghana, Mali, Nigeria and Togo, identified three key underlying 'causal' factors of trafficking: socio-cultural factors, such as the social acceptability of children working and historical patterns of illiteracy or low education; economic factors, such as the inequalities between rural and urban areas; and juridical and political factors, such as the absence of enforceable legislation (2001: 13–14, 27–9). In regard to Nigeria, Jeffrey Cole argues that '[l]ack of education and the common view that daughters are servants of family interests have worked to channel girls, especially poorer ones, into prostitution, both at home and abroad, from the late 1980s' (Cole, 2006: 222).

In contrast to the above literature, Lisa Rende Taylor's 14-month study in two villages in northern Thailand (2005) presents a far more complex picture. Rende Taylor explored the correlations, if any, that existed between parental investment in education and child labour, sex work and trafficking. Her study found that last-born children stay in school the longest and enter work, on average, the oldest. However, many of the last-born girls go directly from school to Bangkok or abroad, migrating and entering hazardous work. The last-born children, despite receiving higher levels of education than their siblings, enter hazardous labour first or more often. Rende Taylor goes on to note that these younger daughters do not know how to farm and after such significant investment in their education it is considered undesirable for families to see them working in the farm or a local market. As a result, there is a tendency for these girls, who have received *more* education than their older siblings, including their brothers, to be sent into riskier work situations (Rende Taylor, 2005: 422).

In general, the literature discussed above reflects a tendency globally – and particularly in the discourse on Africa and Asia – to draw direct links between low levels of education and/or incomplete schooling and vulnerability to trafficking. Frequently, this 'link' is presented as a fact, without any solid evidence to support such statements. Exceptions to this perspective, such as that of Rende Taylor, are rare. There are significant implications of this amplification of the assumed relationship between education levels and trafficking. Substantial resources, for example, are invested in reintegration programmes focused on educating victims.

This assumption is quite puzzling when it comes to Eastern European countries like Ukraine. Quite often Ukraine is presented as the country with the highest number of victims of trafficking in the world (UNODC, n.d.: 6). However, the generally high levels of literacy among the majority of Ukrainians are widely recognised. Prior to 1989, literacy was near-universal, with levels of education in Central and Eastern Europe and the former Soviet Union ranking above other countries with comparable levels of per capita income (Corrin, 2005: 545).

Authors writing on the topic of trafficking have also noted the importance of avoiding 'stereotypes on this issue, as many trafficked women are also highly educated but living in countries where law and order and the authority of central government have broken down so that conditions are ripe for their exploitation' (McSherry and Kneebone, 2008: 71). Many Eastern European countries from the former Soviet bloc and the Balkan region conform with this description. Like Bernadette McSherry and Susan Kneebone, Rebecca Surtees, who has also conducted research on the trafficking of men (2008), states that '[g]enerally, trafficking victims had low education levels' (2005: 13), but highlights various exceptions:

> ... a small number of victims from countries such as Ukraine, Moldova, Romania and Bulgaria had higher education levels, including university and college degrees. Indeed, many trafficking victims had education similar to, and even higher than, that of the general population in their home countries. This highlights that it is not only the poorly educated who are trafficked (2005: 13).

In summary, the uneducated victim archetype can be found across the existing literature. However, there are some clear regional discrepancies and certainly some noted exceptions regarding education levels of victims. Despite this, many sources, including academic analysis, fail to unpack in greater detail these inconsistencies and what they say about inadequate education as an assumed cause of trafficking.

Contesting the Uneducated Victim Archetype

An Inverse Relationship between Education and Trafficking

My research in Ukraine – including data collected from questionnaires completed by 104 trafficked returnees summarised in Table 5.1 – revealed possible correlations between education levels and human trafficking. Of the 104 respondents from Ukraine, all reported having attended school in Ukraine prior to their departure. The majority of respondents (55.8 per cent) attended school up to the age of 17 years, the age at which high school is usually completed in Ukraine, with some continuing on to further education. In addition, 26.0 per cent of the respondents attended school up to the age of 15 years and 13.5 per cent attended school up to the age of 16 years. The minimum and maximum duration of schooling for the 104 respondents were 6 years and 11 years respectively, not counting those students who went on to attend college or university.

Table 5.1   Age up to which the respondents attended school

Age at final year of schooling	Frequency	Percentage of total number of surveyed individuals
13	1	1.0
14	4	3.8
15	27	26.0
16	14	13.5
17	58	55.8

In terms of tertiary education, 17.3 per cent of these respondents, or 18 trafficked returnees, went on to attend college or university before leaving Ukraine. Among these 18 respondents, ten completed their college or university degree and attained the resulting qualification (nine female and one male respondent). Overall, the data indicates that among the 104 respondents, 58 had finished school, with a further 18 continuing on to tertiary education. One in ten of the respondents had completed college or university-level education. This sample of 104 returned victims of trafficking cannot be deemed uneducated based on these figures.

For a more definitive analysis, a comparison with the broader Ukrainian population is required. As noted above, like many other former Soviet Union countries, levels of literacy, school enrolment and school completion in Ukraine are relatively high. According to the UNDP National Human Development Report in 2002, universal education among Ukrainians was approaching the level of developed countries at 79 per cent (for comparison, the world average is 65 per cent; in developing states it is 61 per cent; in developed Organisation for Economic

Cooperation and Development (OECD) states 94 per cent; and in Eastern Europe and the Commonwealth of Independent States (CIS) 77 per cent). In 2004, this indicator for Ukraine reached 86 per cent (UNDP National Human Development Report, cited in Ministry of Economy of Ukraine, 2005: 19).

Set against the UNDP data, a significant finding of my research was that the trafficked individuals surveyed appeared more educated than the broader Ukrainian population as a whole. For the purpose of this analysis, I have relied on the UNDP Human Development Report from 2008 (UNDP, 2008). This particular UNDP report documents levels of education of individuals in Ukraine aged 25 to 70 years as of 2006.[3]

According to the UNDP, as of 2006, approximately 49.2 per cent of people aged 25 to 70 in Ukraine had completed only lower secondary education (2008: 80), that is, had left school by the age of 15 (see UNDP, 2008: 104 and UNESCO, 1997), the age at which compulsory education ends. By comparison, only five respondents, or 4.8 per cent of my survey sample had left school prior to reaching the age of 15 and only 32 of the returned victims of trafficking in total, or 30.8 per cent of all questionnaire respondents, had ended their education by the age of 15. This reflects a considerable difference with the UNDP data which show that almost 19 per cent more of the broader population of Ukraine had left school at or before the age of 15 when compared to my trafficked respondents. The sample of victims who completed my questionnaire was, on average, more educated than their peers.

An informant from an inter-governmental organisation in Ukraine shared the experience of a trafficked couple who accessed reintegration support from a partner organisation. The informant's aim in sharing this story was specifically to highlight the misconception that trafficked victims are uneducated:

> There was a couple living in Ternopil. The wife had a PhD. She is an economist. The husband was one of the few ISO9000 auditors [a global standard for third-party certification as an auditor] in Ukraine. They wanted to start a business, a

---

3   According to my survey data, 87 per cent of victims spent less than one year abroad prior to returning and accessing reintegration support. Many of the victims who had completed my questionnaire in July 2009 would therefore have left Ukraine towards the end of 2007 or around the first half of 2008, depending on how long they had been accessing reintegration support. The 2006 data from this UNDP report are the only reliable available data on education in Ukraine that I have identified that closely resemble the time period when the victims who completed my survey would have left Ukraine. Moreover, it indicates a wide age range allowing some comparability with the age of my survey respondents, who ranged from 17 to 50 years old. It is arguable that the least educated segment of the Ukrainian population could be found among those aged 50 to 70 years, which would skew this analysis. However, there is no evidence that this is the case, especially given the longer life expectancy of the better educated. See for example Corsini 2010, a Eurostat publication. Although it does not discuss Ukraine – a non-member – it discusses Estonia, another former Soviet country. The study notes that higher educated people live longer than lower educated people for both men and women.

consulting firm. They had at that time a 4-year old daughter and decided to leave her with her grandmother and go abroad to work in the factories in Portugal. Why? Because they wanted to make enough money to start their consulting business. They decided to go and they ended up in a factory and they were trafficked ... The woman was in the trafficker's house for domestic labour and she was also raped. They were separated for 6 or 7 months because he was in the factory and she was in the house. Their 4-year old kid was back here in Ukraine. [A] grandmother isn't really equipped to take care of a 4-year old. The factory gets raided and they are deported. (Anon., Counter-Trafficking expert, inter-governmental organisation, 13 August 2009)

The informant went on to note the irony that, after being deported and returning to Ukraine, the family was finally able to access the micro-credit they had been seeking through an NGO programme for reintegration of victims. Beyond the anecdotal element, there is a very interesting issue raised by the comment of this informant who adopted a somewhat dismissive tone towards the victims.[4] In the context of an initially voluntary departure, the informant described this story in the language of migration, referring to remittances and goal-setting regarding potential income-earning from the opportunity they found in Portugal. Simultaneously, the informant linked exploitation to this initially voluntary movement; the victimhood of the couple cannot be questioned. Furthermore, their very high levels of education did not reduce their vulnerability to exploitation and could even be seen, in part, a cause for their initial decision to migrate. This furthers some of the related findings discussed in the previous chapter and serves as an interesting example of how monetary need acts as a driving force.

Comments on education and its relationship with trafficking were also made by the then Chief of Mission at IOM Ukraine, who highlighted that Ukrainians are a highly educated population. He went on to note that, '[a] lot of victims of trafficking have finished high school' and 'there is also trafficking of people with higher education' (J. Labovitz, former Chief of Mission, IOM Ukraine, 27 August 2009). While arguing that there is in fact a relationship between education levels and trafficking, the former Chief of Mission went on to suggest that it is 'not as pronounced' as is often thought. He also made a reference to brain drain, as has been noted in the academic literature (Uehling, 2004), situating trafficking within this broader spectrum of migration. This latter reference highlights the greater likelihood of migration among the better-educated.

Another informant also noted the generally high levels of education among victims housed in the IOM Rehabilitation Centre in Kyiv. She noted only two exceptions during her time there as a psychologist. Both involved children from Roma families:

---

4   We could conjecture that this could be due to the informant's familiarity with such stories and therefore lack of emotion, the informant's criticism of the couple's pursuit of money, or perhaps because of the ironic end to their experience that the informant highlighted.

... we had only two victims who had not studied at all. It was one girl from a Roma family. She was 17 years old and she had never attended school. There was a boy of 10 years also from a Roma family who had never attended school. So the level of education is quite high and there is no specific relationship between trafficking and the levels of education of victims. (20 August 2009)

Outside of Ukraine, only one informant, Andrew Bruce, former Chief of Mission at IOM Vietnam, made explicitly reference to the possibility of an inverse relationship between education and trafficking:

... The migrants of the world are normally the brighter people and the trafficked victims of the world are the migrants. I do not think it is the highly intelligent migrant who does not get trafficked and the dumb migrant who does ... With the women in Cambodia working in a brothel, maybe some smart people find their way out of a situation of trafficking [but] I think the smart people are trying to get out and move. [It is] the smart people who are looking for jobs and once you are looking for a job, you are vulnerable to someone getting you into something you do not want to be in. (21 September 2009)

Although based on a limited sample size, we can conjecture the possibility of an inverse relationship between education levels and greater vulnerability to trafficking, contrary to the presumption of an uneducated victim. This alternative approach to understanding the relationship between trafficking and education levels is illustrated in Figure 5.1.

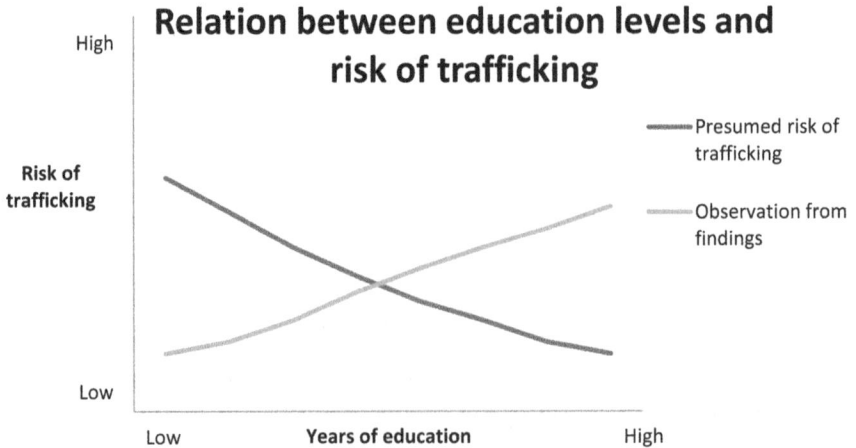

Figure 5.1   Observations on relationship between education and trafficking in Ukraine

Does Education Impact Trafficking in Other Ways?

Victims' Access to Shelters and Willingness to Report

It has been presumed that education levels impact not only vulnerability to trafficking but also the accessibility of reintegration centres. Based on an IOM study in Ukraine, in which the majority of women came into contact with rehabilitation support on their own initiative, Guri Tyldum and Anette Brunovskis concluded that women who initiate their own reintegration must be more educated than their peers:

> We may assume that having access to resources like education and social networks makes it easier to contact rehabilitation services and ask for help. We can thus expect that victims who contact NGOs for assistance and rehabilitation are systematically different from those who do not. (Tyldum and Brunovskis, 2005: 25)

I assessed the views of Tyldum and Brunovskis during my fieldwork to see if this reasoning could explain the high levels of school completion of my survey respondents, all of whom had accessed reintegration support. I specifically questioned informants about these claims and the extent to which they believed that victims staying in shelters and accessing reintegration services have higher levels of education than the broader population of trafficked individuals from that country. Contrary to the views of Tyldum and Brunovskis, informants noted that high levels of education may act as a deterrent for seeking help. One informant, Dr Lysenko of the IOM Rehabilitation Centre, noted:

> They had experiences in life. They were smart. They have studied so they are ashamed to ask for help. 'I am an educated person. I know about this. How did I fall for this offer to go abroad?' They usually never go to shelters because they are scared that everyone will know. The more educated a person is, the lower the person falls down after being trafficked because of the fall from where they have come. (Dr I. Lysenko, Psychologist, IOM Rehabilitation Centre, Kyiv, 20 August 2009, trans.)

Factors such as shame (or pride) appear to be excluded from Tyldum and Brunovskis' proposition that self-accessing shelter victims are likely to be more educated than their trafficked peers, an assumption that seems to be supported only by the intuition of the authors. Informants suggested shame was relevant in both instances of sexual and labour exploitation. A wide sample of victims – including both those accessing reintegration support through shelters and those who are in contact with researchers by other means – would be needed for verification.

Distance Travelled

No known studies of trafficking explore in depth the question of how education levels impact the distance travelled by the victim. Yet, several studies that are focused on migration more broadly address this issue. For example, a 2009 study on internal migration among French youth noted that the most highly-skilled youth do not receive a positive wage return from migration, demonstrating concomitantly that these young workers must instead contend with the national labour market. However, the opposite situation is observed for less-skilled young workers who obtain positive wage returns from migration (Lemistre and Magrini, 2009). Moreover, where a spouse similarly has a higher level of education, this may limit migration as movement may create conflict where there are separate career paths, suggesting that those with lower education and/or where their spouse similarly has a lower level of education may be more mobile.

In Ghana, there is also some evidence that education levels may influence the distance travelled by victims. Margaret Peil's 1995 study, although dated, presents data from a census conducted in the city of Madina (southern Ghana) in early 1993. The study involved interviews with 600 adults and included the migration history (both by regular and irregular means) of those returnees who were interviewed, as well as that of their siblings. It should be noted that no mention is made of the word trafficking or even exploitation.

Among those surveyed, nearly half of the returnees interviewed in Madina had been away more than five years, yet they eventually returned home, usually while still under the age of 40. Interestingly Peil found that among regular and irregular migrants from Medina, men and women with primary or no schooling were somewhat more likely to emigrate than those with middle, secondary and vocational schooling. However, almost all remained in West Africa. Those who left after middle school occasionally migrated long distances, as far as North America and Europe.[5] Given the study's inclusion of both regular and irregular migrants and the fact that the study covered a significant number of migrations that took place in the eighties and hence may not correspond to current patterns, it is almost impossible to extract accurate findings regarding the relationship between

---

5   Peil's study makes reference to sex-disaggregated data, but the poor wording of her research findings makes it very difficult to discern exact differences between the sexes. Peil writes: 'Men are more likely than women to emigrate at most distance and educational levels, though sometimes the differences are small. Gender balance is greatest for those with secondary, vocational or middle school education and least for university graduates. Men and women graduates reach Europe in almost equal proportions, but very few women go further' (1995: 353). It is unclear what Peil means by 'most distances' and 'gender balance is greatest' but she appears to suggest that differences in patterns of migration of men and women diminish as their levels of education rise. This is until they reach the level of tertiary education when an imbalance –with men travelling further than women – is once again evident.

education levels and trafficking, even using the proxy of migration.[6] The study would have been more useful for our purposes if it had captured such issues as exploitation abroad.

The education data from Peil's study reflect the data from a newer but much smaller study by the Centre for Migration Studies at the University of Ghana. This study suggests that it would be incorrect to say that those migrating for work abroad are uneducated, or even the lesser educated in the community. Of the 60 people interviewed in the study, 34 respondents (57 per cent) said they knew of the dangers of irregular migration but nonetheless undertook the journey. Twenty-three of these 34 respondents (67.6 per cent) had at least a basic level of education, eight had secondary school education or higher, including two who had post-secondary education (Awumbila, 2010: 10).

Any conclusions that we can draw on Ghana must be premised with a strong caution concerning the lack of first-hand demographic data on victims of trafficking from the country and the tendency for the existing data to be somewhat outdated and focused on male irregular migrants, without indications as to whether any of the participants in those studies would identify as a victim of trafficking. Nonetheless, the existing data suggest that it would be incorrect to assume that Ghanaian irregular migrants are generally uneducated.

Capacity to Comprehend Risk

There are no identifiable studies that link levels of education, capacity to comprehend risks and vulnerability to trafficking. Yet it is commonly assumed that victims have limited capacity to comprehend the risks associated with irregular migration or to discern deception in employment negotiations, leading to their exploitation. An IOM study of trafficking from Belarus, Bulgaria, Moldova, Romania and Ukraine, for example, found that many rural residents in all the countries studied had heard about cases of labour and sexual exploitation that happened in their surroundings but did not comprehend the probability that such exploitation may happen to them (IOM, 2006). The study therefore concluded that efforts need to be made to increase comprehension of risks. USAID programmes similarly assume low comprehension of risks and therefore invest heavily in mass media campaigns, particularly via MTV (USAID, 2008).

During the course of my own fieldwork in Ghana, many informants in the field held the view that potential migrants suffer trafficking and trafficking-like conditions not necessarily because of the tactics of 'traffickers' but, to the contrary, the naivety of the victims themselves. Informants went beyond questioning the extent to which victims had undertaken some form of due diligence to assess the nature of the work they were offered in destination countries – or in the instance

---

6   Peil's study explores migration at large. For example, she refers to the large number of Ghanaians studying in Britain and 'African professionals' in the US.

of child trafficking, within Ghana – to actually describing these victims as naive, from the 'village' or ignorant.[7]

Referring to the role of parents in child labour exploitation, one informant commented:

> Some of these people have lived in a village and do not have any degree of real or formal education. Maybe they have been educated to primary education. For some of these parents, this is simply how they are. You give them 50 Cedis or 100 Cedis[8] and they have no idea. (Anon.)

Another also referred to the 'ignorance of parents' as a 'key cause' (Anon.). Two informants referred to the easy ability of people to succumb to the 'vehicles, the clothes that they wear' and other items that successful migrants 'show off' (Anon., Government of Ghana). In the view of these informants, 'these people assume that all that glitters is gold' (Anon., international organisation; see also earlier discussion in Chapter 4 on the fairy-tale life abroad).

These comments can be contrasted with the perspective of an anonymous informant from the University of Ghana's Centre for Migration Studies, who was acutely aware of the grave risks faced by irregular migrants when travelling from Ghana to destination countries. His comments are affirmed by the study conducted by the Centre for Migration Studies cited earlier, which was officially released during the course of my research. Although addressing only a small sample of 120 informants composed of 60 returned individual irregular migrants and 60 households questioned in the Brong Ahafo Region,[9] the research has important findings when set against the comments above. Although the report notes migrant ignorance, it also shows fairly calculated decisions regarding the migration itself. This included the measures taken by potential migrants to raise the funds needed to acquire various documents (Awumbila, 2010: 5) and the rationale behind the decisions of these migrants to follow particular routes in order to gain the easiest access to Europe (in this case, Spain via Libya) (Awumbila, 2010:7). The study reminds readers not to underestimate the extent to which migratory movement is a calculated exercise.

---

7   Although not deliberate, many of these comments expressed a patronising tone. In these instances, I have chosen to quote my informants anonymously.

8   This is the equivalent of around 30 to 60 USD.

9   The report also notes that 29 in-depth interviews, 11 key informant interviews and 3 focus group discussion were undertaken in Dormaa, Nkoranza and Accra, although these do not appear to be the source of the findings discussed in the report. The report also fails to discuss transparently and in depth the entire methodological approach.

Other Variables in the Education Systems

Levels of school completion thus appear to play a more limited role than assumed in shaping the risks and vulnerabilities facing potential migrants. If this is the case, it is arguable that other education-related variables may play a role. In this final section, I discuss a number of other potential interlinkages between education levels and vulnerability to trafficking. This includes the quality of education and the cost of schooling.

Quality and Not Quantity?

As can be seen from the above, most analyses on trafficking focus on years of education completed by trafficking victims. Factors such as the quality of that education are given limited, if any, attention. However, this aspect is worth exploring as there are sufficient indicators that suggest other dimensions of education may be linked to trafficking. Vietnam and Ukraine are used as examples.

It is widely acknowledged that Vietnam has a relatively 'impressive record' in terms of access to education. Despite the system's reliance on fees, the World Bank has recognised how gaps in school enrolment between rich and poor remain narrow (World Bank, 2006: 93). According to UN Statistics Division (2011), Vietnam claimed a net enrolment rate for primary education for boys of 97 per cent in 2001 and 91.9 per cent for girls in the same year. No further data are given by the Government of Vietnam for any other year between 1991 and 2009. If victims of trafficking are in fact poorly educated, does this mean that victims come from the three to eight per cent who are not reaching higher levels of school completion or are other factors at play?

While acknowledging the high rates of school enrolment, the World Bank has noted, as seen below, that the actual quality of that education remains a concern in Vietnam. We could therefore contend that while the broader Vietnamese population, on paper, has high rates of school enrolment when compared to their global peers, the issue is in fact the quality of that education. This could explain the number of victims who are found to have high or higher levels of school completion than assumed.

According to the World Bank, while secondary education in Vietnam is sustained by well-trained and prepared staff, reasonable teaching aids and basic equipment, the issue is the length of the school day, with most days being organised on a half-day basis. While the Government has introduced a full-day of schooling for primary schools, this is not Government-financed, putting 'children from poorer families at a disadvantage in accessing quality education' (World Bank, 2006: 94). The World Bank notes that about one-quarter of students in the poorest quintile attend extra privately-funded classes, whereas nearly three-quarters of students in the richest quintile do so. The rate of attendance for additional classes is higher for females than males across all quintiles.

The difference is significant, there being 23 periods of instruction per week at the half-day rates compared to 35 periods of instruction in a full-day schooling week (World Bank, 2006: 94). This means that while over 90 per cent of Vietnamese children are enrolled in school, a large proportion are in fact attending school only two-thirds of the time that students attend schools in other countries around the globe (or when compared to wealthier Vietnamese). Whether or not Vietnamese victims are among the more or less educated, they still may on average be less educated than non-Vietnamese populations or more wealthy Vietnamese, simply because they have a significantly shorter schooling day. This raises the question of whether relative poverty is a characteristic of trafficking, an issue addressed in the next chapter. Therefore, even where Vietnamese victims prove to be relatively well educated, they may be 'under-educated'; education levels may in fact correlate with vulnerability to human trafficking, particularly for the poor.

Turning to Ukraine, UNICEF has highlighted the lack of data available from the Ministry of Education and Science to assess adequately the quality of education (UNICEF, n.d.: 2). However, there are indications of weaknesses in the Ukrainian education system. Concerns about quality range from lack of teaching and learning resources, particularly in rural areas (UNICEF, n.d.: 2) to out-dated curricula and, in the case of vocational schools, a tendency for students to be trained in fields that do not match the job market (UNICEF, n.d.: 3). This study may help to explain the relatively high levels of education among Ukrainian victims and yet the challenges faced in accessing work that could be identified as a push factor for trafficking.

While an assessment of the quality (particularly with regard to number of hours of schooling) may seem a diversion in the context of this chapter, it is actually central to this analysis. While we are unable to establish definitively the hours and quality of schooling attended by Vietnamese victims, these issues demand a more disaggregated analysis of the education experiences of victims in order to discern whether a relatively shorter school day is a factor. In the case of Ukraine, problems with the quality of the education system and particularly, the applicability of the curricula to the demands of the market could be a factor in explaining the apparent contradiction behind Ukraine's well-recognised, very educated population and yet the global picture that Ukraine remains one of the biggest source countries in the world.

The Cost of Schooling

As has been identified in extensive secondary research, it is a widely-held view that girls are often removed from school due to high costs of education, with limited family income being used to educate boys instead. In the following section, I address the possibility of a correlation between costs of schooling and increased vulnerability to trafficking. Thailand and Vietnam are used as examples.

In Rosanne Rushing's study on sex work and migration in Vietnam, school fees were noted as being too taxing on the family income and were one of the main reasons given for children leaving school (Rushing, 2006: 477). An earlier

2001 study by Jianye Liu noted the various 'opportunity costs' for parents sending children to school, particularly the girl child. Liu argued, 'The expected return to a son's education is higher than the return on investment in a daughter's human capital, which is lost upon marriage' (Liu, 2001: 389). Liu also notes how time spent travelling to and from school is a further consideration, with safety being a factor for parents with daughters (2001: 389). If we reflect upon the findings of Rende Taylor's 14-month study of Thailand (2005), the opportunity cost of educating children is clearly important. In this study, parents were found to invest in boys rather than in girls and, when girls were educated, parents sought a return on the investment in their daughter's education through encouraging their employment in risky, high-earning jobs.

The cost of schooling was observed to be significant in the Vietnamese context during my field work. One informant referred to the transition from government-provided social services to the increasingly privatised system today:

> [Q]uality was higher, especially regarding education or medical [services]. If you look at the number of doctors ... they were higher in the past but today, the number of medical facilities remains the same. Also, in the past, education was free but now it is a burden. (Anon., Senior Project Assistant: Counter-trafficking, international organisation, 12 October 2009)

This informant's comments refer to the traditional system of social protection in Vietnam. Prior to the transition, the Government of Vietnam was the primary employer of the national labour force and the only provider of what were then public services (Duong and Khuat, 2008: 60). Stark inequalities therefore resulted from *Đổi Mới*, or economic 'renovation' and are reflected in school enrolment, healthcare, child nutrition, life expectancy, employment and basic sanitation (Duong and Khuat, 2008: 62–3). Although primary education is free in principle, education can be expensive in reality and parents are expected to contribute towards improvements in school facilities and teachers' salaries (Liu, 2001: 389).

Similar contentions were shared by an education specialist with the UN in Vietnam. This informant expressed the view that a number of financial issues restrict the participation of girls from poor, remote and ethnic minority areas:

> While tuition is free at the primary level, additional fees for school construction and maintenance, school materials, uniform ... and other costs must be paid by individual families and are a heavy burden on household budgets of the poor. (Anon., Education Specialist, UNICEF Vietnam, 14 June 2010)

Sharing some of the sentiments of Rushing and Liu noted above, the informant from UNICEF described five key barriers to girls' education in Vietnam: economic and financial barriers and the need to work; the poor quality of teaching and learning in schools; inadequate school infrastructure; distance from home to school; and, finally, parents' and girls' perceptions of the value of educating girls. Like the

World Bank's recognition of visible gender disparities in higher education, which 'can lead to diverging opportunities between men and women in the labor market' (World Bank, 2008: 19), this informant also referred to the segregation of women in 'traditionally female' areas of study and how little has been done to facilitate women's admission to more technical disciplines (Anon., Education Specialist, UNICEF Vietnam, 14 June 2010).

Moreover, the UNICEF informant noted that 65 per cent of public spending in education goes to higher education, which favours students from middle and high income families, as only 30 per cent of the poor advance beyond primary school. Combined with the previous discussion, this analysis introduces important considerations, not only the length of schooling and its applicability to the job market but also the cost relative to household income, which may be relevant to vulnerability to trafficking. These examples – from Thailand, Vietnam and Ukraine – raise questions that may be equally relevant to other source countries where high rates of trafficking sit alongside seemingly high rates of education.

Conclusion

At the outset of this analysis, I set out the common assumption concerning the uneducated and naive victim. If proven, education and the risk of experiencing trafficking-like conditions would show a relationship of reverse-causality, that is, the lower the levels of education, the higher the risk of trafficking and vice versa. Lack of education would be shown to undermine the capability of individuals to achieve unhindered decision-making, to access decent work domestically and abroad and to comprehend risks involved in migration-related opportunities when compared with their more educated peers. The logical conclusion drawn from this model would be that most victims of trafficking exercise limited autonomy in their decision making.

In contrast, this chapter presents an alternative model, the educated victim as a risk-taker. In this model, education and trafficking are directly, rather than inversely, related. That is, the more educated a person, the more likely it is that they migrate, even by risky and irregular means, and, hence, the more exposed they are to exploitation and trafficking. The conclusion in this case would be that victims show a high degree of autonomy in the decision-making process, their education levels being one marker of this autonomy. Their movement is not driven by naivety but rather by the empowerment derived from higher levels of education than their peers.

As noted at the beginning of the chapter, most of the literature, as well as policy-makers and civil society actors, assume that the majority of trafficking victims are non-autonomous or partially autonomous due to low levels of education. From my findings, this is questionable. To the contrary, given barriers to legal migration, higher levels of education may in fact lead to higher levels of irregular, unsafe migration for those pursuing opportunities abroad. However, even this fails to capture other complexities such as how the distance travelled by victims is impacted by levels of education; whether other education variables – like quality and cost of schooling – impact vulnerability; and whether other considerations like return on investment drive migratory decisions. What has emerged from this discussion is a far more complex relationship between education, movement and exploitation than that which is generally conceded or portrayed in mainstream literature or analysis and certainly one that challenges a simplistic and linear relationship between low levels of education and vulnerability to trafficking.

Chapter 6

The Poor Victim of Trafficking

The push and pull factors are economic. That is the primary one globally. When I arrived [in Ukraine], the average income was less than USD100/month. It has gone up considerably and is probably adjusting as a result of the financial crisis. Opportunities were just not available for individuals. Ukrainians as a people – Moldovans are the same, Belarusians are the same – went outside, probably as much as 10% of the population here in Ukraine and in Moldova, around 30%. But they do not have legal opportunities for migration … So we are stuck in this Catch-22 where there are no legal opportunities to go abroad but there is a need.

(J. Labovitz, former Chief of Mission, IOM Ukraine, 27 August 2009)

A widely-held assumption concerning victims of trafficking is that both poverty and lack of livelihood opportunities in the domestic labour market increase vulnerability to exploitative work abroad. A comment by Pierre Sané, Assistant Director-General for the Social and Human Sciences Sector of UNESCO, in a preface to a 2006 report, *Poverty, gender and human trafficking in Sub-Saharan Africa: Rethinking best practices in migration management*, illustrates the assumption that links trafficking and poverty. Sané in fact goes beyond the assumption and argues that there is a vicious cycle of 'poverty – human trafficking – poverty' involved:

> Human trafficking, often qualified as the 'modern day slavery', is caused by human rights violations embodied in poverty while it also contributes to increased deprivation. In other words, poverty is one of the main factors leading people, especially women and children to fall preys [sic] to the traffickers. In turn, human trafficking locks up the trafficked persons in poverty through exploitation. This vicious circle 'poverty – human trafficking – poverty' denies individuals the basic right to education and information, the right to health, the right to decent work, the right to security and justice … Poverty and human trafficking will only cease when they are adequately addressed as two intermingled issues, which nurture each other and plunge vulnerable persons into deep deprivation and exploitation (Truong, 2006: 7).

Only a few studies question this link made between poverty and trafficking. Even then, the analysis that has challenged this picture has largely been in the context of the movement of children and not adults.[1]

---

1 Several studies address the relationship between household circumstances, child labour and migration. See for example Rende Taylor, 2005. See also Mills 1999, and

Even in instances when extreme poverty is not assumed to be a cause of trafficking, studies link trafficking directly with a somewhat desperate search for work abroad in an effort to fill a gap in the opportunities available at home. Frank Lazco and Marco Gramegna, referring to a database of victims from South Eastern Europe, write that '[i]n most cases (over 75 per cent), the recruiter offered the possibility of finding work abroad' (2003: 189). Vocks and Nijboer note about Central and Eastern European women that '[t]hey mainly chose to work abroad out of economic necessity, having an income equal or even lower than the minimum for existence' (2000: 386). Discussing Ukrainian victims, Donna Hughes and Tatyana Denisova write, '[i]n agricultural areas, often there are no wages at all' (2002: 44), with the result that 'the recruiters are moving into the countryside to small towns and villages to recruit women for work abroad' (2002: 43). Alexis Aronowtiz similarly argues about trafficking and smuggling that '[m]any who fall prey to smugglers and traffickers are usually those most disadvantaged in their own countries: those with poor job skills or little chance of successful employment at home. They are often women and children' (2001: 167).

If we understand trafficking as sitting within a spectrum of migratory experiences and recognise the voluntariness often exercised by victims at the departure stage, a connection between labour market barriers and trafficking is logical. When compared to the other myths and misconceptions analysed in this book, it is unsurprising that there may be some connection between income levels, labour market experiences at home and trafficking into exploitative work abroad. Yet, despite the logical and the frequent associations made in the literature between trafficking and the pursuit of work, no known studies exist that explore the labour market situation of victims of trafficking *prior* to their being trafficked. That is, there are no known studies that analyse whether or not victims faced barriers to the domestic labour market or sub-standard conditions of work before their departure and the extent to which either or both were factors that pushed them to seek opportunities abroad. By filling this gap, this chapter aims to make an important contribution to the current body of knowledge.

If we accept the assumptions outlined above, we could imagine two groups of individuals who are vulnerable to trafficking. First, it may be that people attempt to escape poverty and through that process find themselves in a situation of trafficking or trafficking-like conditions. Second, it may be that people are not satisfied with their work situation at home and pursue alternative employment abroad.

In terms of the autonomy associated with those decisions, there are clear differences between these two scenarios. Theoretically, the latter involves a higher degree of autonomy when compared to the decisions of those living in extreme poverty. In simple terms, the first group of potential victims seek work abroad as a question of survival and hence their real options are severely limited. We can define this as absolute poverty. According to the World Bank, absolute poverty is

---

Muecke 1992, both of whom, like Rende Taylor, shed doubt on the view that children are sent to work abroad simply as a question of economic survival.

understood to mean the absolute standard of what households should be able to count on in order to meet their basic food and non-food needs in order to survive.

The second group of victims, on the other hand, could be better described as 'pursuing a more satisfying life'. This may be captured in the phrase relative poverty, a measure which looks at income inequality in comparative terms rather than absolute material deprivation or hardship. The mainstream trafficking framework, as it is normally presented, refers more often to the former group, commonly using the language of 'desperation' to describe 'immense poverty and desire for survival' (Nadaswaran, 2012), this 'economic desperation' and poverty 'facilitating' the recruitment of women (Raymond and Hughes, 2001: 10).

In this chapter, I first explore the extent to which poverty appears to drive human trafficking. Secondly, I turn to the question of individual livelihoods and the extent to which a search for individual betterment, when compared to fellow countrymen and women and/or citizens living abroad, constitutes a push factor in migration and the willingness of victims to risk exploitative work abroad. The particular vulnerability of youth and the impact of gender-segregated domestic labour markets are discussed at length.

My findings suggest that rather than being desperate or deprived non-autonomous individuals, victims are often searching for an opportunity abroad that they believe will offer them *more* than the opportunities available at home, aligning with the second category described above. That is, although relatively poor, victims of trafficking are not among the poorest in their communities. This chapter therefore highlights the relevance of relative poverty to understanding trafficking. In reality, there is a range of scenarios that fall in between these two neat abstract categories.

Throughout this chapter, I use the language of 'irregular' migration rather than trafficking and I draw extensively on literature addressing irregular migration broadly as well as trafficking specifically. This chapter focuses on the pre-departure situation of victims and the extent to which domestic labour market conditions act as a push factor. At the pre-departure stage, what is revealed by my findings are the ways in which the pre-migration experience of victim of trafficking is largely indistinguishable from the broader category of irregular migrants. This accords with earlier arguments that, at the pre-departure stage, all potential 'voluntary' migrants fall within one large pool. These individuals have not yet become victims of trafficking, nor can any of these individuals be classified as actual migrants. They are all potential migrants and/or victims.

A further factor in choosing to engage with the broader literature on *irregular* migration (although not migration at large), is the inherent heightened risk of *unsafe* migration when the movement is undertaken through irregular means. As this type of migration frequently involves the status of undocumented or illegal in the destination country (Bogusz, Cholewinski, Cygan and Szyszczak, 2004: 324–5; Kelly, 2002; Cholewinski, 2005: 20), we often seen a relationship with trafficking identified in the literature (Saari, 2006; Uehling, 2004; Webber and Shirk, 2005).[2] Finally, before continuing, it should also be noted that the majority of trafficking literature that links poverty and trafficking focuses on income poverty, despite the fact that the development community increasingly adopts a broader definition of poverty that extends beyond the question of income levels.[3] An income-poverty focused definition has similarly been applied in this chapter.

Defining Absolute Poverty's Relationship with Trafficking

Are Victims of Human Trafficking the Poorest Citizens?

In this section, I address the links, if any, between absolute poverty and human trafficking. To what extent are the poorest of society most vulnerable to trafficking and exploitative labour abroad? Despite what is frequently a lack of solid evidence of a relationship between the two, a connection is often assumed and anti-trafficking initiatives are regularly designed on this basis:

> Poverty and human trafficking will only cease when they are adequately addressed as two intermingled issues, which nurture each other and plunge vulnerable persons into deep deprivation and exploitation. (Pierre Sané cited in Truong, 2006: 7)

My own field experience suggests that poverty continues to be perceived as a driver of human trafficking by many stakeholders working in the field. This was most evident in Ghana, perhaps unsurprising given its level of development compared to Vietnam and Ukraine. Ghana ranked 135th on the 2013 UNDP Human Development Index,[4] as compared to Vietnam which ranked slightly higher at 127 and Ukraine at 78 (UNDP, 2013).

My Ghanaian informants saw poverty as not necessarily linked to the trafficking of adults but rather as a driver of child trafficking. Several informants argued that the selling of children is a consequence of both 'poverty resulting from lack of employment and ignorance on the part of families' (Dr M. Sackey, Former ILO-IPEC, Ghana, 22 July 2010). Two different informants, one representing a

---

2   As noted earlier, however, trafficking can result from regular migration.

3   For example, the Swedish policy document for poverty reduction, *The Rights of the Poor – Our Common Responsibility*, describes poverty as a multi-faceted phenomenon. Poverty is not just a matter of income; to live in poverty is also to lack political influence, security, opportunities for social participation and access to health care, education and other social services (Government of Sweden, 1997: 12–13).

4   The Human Development Index (HDI) is a composite statistic used to rank countries by their level of 'human development' by comparing data on life expectancy, literacy, education and standards of living.

faith-based NGO and the other, the Ghanaian Ministry of Employment and Social Welfare, made similar comments connecting the sale of children by parents with both poverty and the need to supplement family income. An officer from a faith-based NGO argued that parents are frequently coerced into selling their children into the fishing sector because 'they are not really told what the children will do', 'they are poor' and perceive this as 'someone helping them'. Mawutor Ablo, Deputy Director of Policy, Planning, Monitoring and Evaluation at the Ministry of Employment and Social Welfare, in similar terms argued: ' ... the underlying issue here is poverty. This is what is normally the cause. People are poor. They want to supplement the family income with children's labour'. He went on to note the efforts of the Ghanaian Ministry of Agriculture to support families involved in farming through the development of services that help create some type of wage labour for parents.

The apparent role of extreme poverty in the migratory movement of Ghanaians is also supported by the secondary data (although recent literature is limited). The World Bank *Voices of the Poor* report argues that young urban and rural Ghanaians feel they have no choice but to leave home in search of work, since successful generation of remittances is likely to make the difference between food security and lack of it for their families (Kunfaa, 1999: 36), although the comment refers largely to internal migration. Discussing regular and irregular migration and the role of remittances, a later study (Higazi, 2005) similarly referred to remittances as a household support strategy. According to this report, '[w]omen were more likely than men to have been influenced by their families in their decision to migrate. Remittances were usually expected by the family and were a key reason for the initial migration decision of family-induced migrants' (Higazi, 2005: 12).

Some Ukrainian informants similarly referred to grave economic circumstances in Ukraine as a driver and described the search for work abroad as being more than a search for a better life. For example, Dr Lysenko, psychologist at the IOM Rehabilitation Centre in Kyiv, contended that it is not education levels that correlate with trafficking but rather 'economic reasons why people are going abroad'. She noted how 'young girls go abroad looking for work and are somehow involved in sexual exploitation'. She referred to the 'economic hole in their families' that girls feel compelled to fill (20 August 2009). Lysenko further noted the difference between those citizens residing in the capital, Kyiv, where the economic situation 'is best', from where they 'do not really have victims [...] because you can find jobs', and other parts of Ukraine. Her view contradicted that of other informants who instead suggested that trafficking results simply when 'people are not satisfied with their standards of living' (T. Ivanyuk, Counter-Trafficking Programme Specialist, IOM Ukraine, 3 September 2009). According to Lysenko, '[i]f there is a possibility to find a job in Ukraine, which is enough for them – ordinary things, money for food and to live – they will not go' (20 August 2009).

Referring to the economic crisis following Ukraine's independence, Lilia Koveshnikova, director of the NGO Women of Donbass located in the Lugansk

Oblast in the country's east, also framed trafficking as involving a response to the most extreme living conditions:

> The economic crisis that hit Ukraine immediately after the breakup of the Soviet Union was undoubtedly one of the primary factors for the proliferation of trafficking in women and children. Massive unemployment affected women, savings were lost to hyperinflation and those who had a job received minuscule wages, far below the cost of living and often after months of delay. All this led to impoverishment of the vast majority of people. (Trans., Email comm., 29 July 2009)

Her view is clearly supported by the secondary literature which indicates how following the transition, various factors, including hyperinflation and dramatically reduced economic output, lowered living standards in Central and Eastern Europe (Corrin, 2005: 545–6). As a result, feminisation of unemployment and poverty emerged (Malynovska, 2006). The increased cost of social services, deterioration in the quality of medical care and commercialisation of education also placed additional social responsibilities on women (Zhurzhenko, 2001: 37).

Consequently, by 1992, a sense of 'nostalgia' emerged among the poor and working poor of Central and Eastern Europe for the state subsidies lost during the early 1990s, with women's hard work no longer rewarded by 'the institutional services and benefits that they had come to see as their entitlements under socialism' (Gal and Kligman, 2000: 116). It is therefore unsurprising that some Ukrainian informants noted a link between trafficking and 'living in an economically depressed region, rural area or a small town … living in conditions of extreme poverty (literally, with no money to purchase food, clothing, personal hygiene items, medicine or pay for other family members' expenses)' (Victoria Ostapchuk, Director, Avenir (NGO), Zhytomyr Oblast, Trans., Email comm., 13 August 2009; see also Vijeyarasa, 2012a: 55).

With these comments in mind, we can reflect upon the data I collected regarding household size prior to the departure of victims. These data were collected with the goal of assessing the extent to which large household sizes related to questionnaire respondents' views that their household income was insufficient to cover their own expenses and those of the household. In response to my question concerning the number of people living with the victim prior to their departure (Question 17), more than half of the respondents were living with two (31.7 per cent) or three (21.2 per cent) other household members. The detailed description of the number of members living with each respondent, shown in Table 6.1, indicates that 15.4 per cent of respondents were living with 4 members, 13.5 per cent were living with 1 other member and only 3.8 per cent were living alone.

Table 6.1   Household structure of questionnaire respondents

Number of household members in addition to victim	Frequency	Percentage of questionnaire respondents
0	4	3.8
1	14	13.5
2	33	31.7
3	22	21.2
4	16	15.4
5	9	8.7
6	1	1.0
7	1	1.0
Victims living at boarding school	3	2.9
Missing data	1	1

The average household size, counting the victim, was 3.7 members. Interestingly, household sizes in Ukraine are on average relatively small – 2.5 persons according to the 2007 Demographic and Health Survey (Ukrainian Center for Social Reforms, State Statistical Committee of Ukraine and Macro International, 2008: 2). The possibility of a correlation between household poverty – deriving from higher household expenses that result from larger household sizes – and trafficking is raised by these data. Additionally, there were some particularly extreme cases within my sample, with 11 respondents living with five or more other individuals.

High household living expenses may explain why poverty was labelled a factor in Ukraine. There was, nonetheless, a distinct divide between my Ukrainian informants who, like the Vietnamese ones, saw trafficking as a result of a failed search for 'more' (whether better pay or working conditions) and Ukrainian informants such as Lysenko who identified the process of irregular migration into trafficking-like conditions as involving only those who could not even obtain a basic income in Ukraine needed for survival and therefore migrated out of economic desperation.

The Costs of Migration

While links are frequently drawn between absolute poverty and trafficking in the literature, there is some recognition that 'victims of trafficking are not always the poorest and most vulnerable' (Shelley, 2010: 292). From a practical perspective, the process by which people move abroad in many instances involves considerable expenses, especially to fund visas or transport. Such funds are only accessible in the global south to individuals with access to significant sources of income, whether their own or through their inner circles – mainly families. Some note that it is those who are affluent who may be able to pay smugglers to move them and their children, creating the risk of an exploitative end result (Shelley, 2010: 292). The inference is that the poorest are not able to engage in such movement.

On this basis, during the course of my research, one Ghanaian informant disputed the idea that poverty is connected with trafficking. The informant noted the scope of the resources – particularly financial – needed to support people's initial exit from Ghana:

> … The poor people, most of them, they want to go, but because of extreme poverty, they cannot afford the costs. Sometimes they use other means like connection men and they need to pay them. All of this involves money. So if you are extremely poor, I do not think you can afford the amount needed for travel. We assume that people who travel or migrate are not necessarily from a poor background. (Anon., Centre for Migration Studies, University of Ghana, Legon, 18 November 2010)

The *absence* of some of these costly requirements has been identified as a relevant factor in shaping migration in other countries. A Ukrainian study of 14 women *irregular* migrants from Ukraine to Poland indicated that the financial investment involved in obtaining a visa is in fact a risk factor considered by potential migrants (Kindler, 2008: 150). Beyond historical ties, the lack of visa requirements and ease of cross-border movement to Russia explained, in part, why Russia at the time was a major destination for Ukrainian irregular migrants. In the Ghanaian context, this might make other countries in West Africa similarly more appealing and certainly more accessible than Europe or the US. Income levels are thus likely to be a factor. Poor people migrate to different places on the basis of the costs of migration.

Similar arguments have been made by Leontina Hormel and Caleb Southworth in a study on labour migration from Ukraine, in which the authors argued that the heavy flow of migrant labour within the former Soviet Union, particularly to Russia, suggests that migrants do not choose destinations exclusively on the basis of the macro-economic conditions in the economy of the destination country. However, they added to the cost considerations discussed above other factors such as having contacts who pass on information about work opportunities and the ability to fit in through language and appearance (Hormel and Southworth, 2006: 615). These comments stress that pure economic need is not the sole or even decisive factor in the decision-making of potential migrants concerning their choice of destination.

Relative Poverty and Human Trafficking

The Search for Economic Betterment as the Primary Driver

While poverty continues to be perceived as a cause of trafficking, we cannot discount the reality that potential migrants will be driven to seek work abroad in instances where destination countries appear to offer their citizens relatively higher standards of living and apparently better conditions of, at least, pay and sometimes work. This notion explains known patterns of movement in migration literature such as the high rates of trafficking from Eastern to Western Europe (Kligman and Limoncelli, 2005: 119). Thus Elizabeth Kelly (2005: 240), along with Gail Kligman and Stephanie Limoncelli (2005: 126) recognise that the patterns of trafficking in Europe echo the globalisation of labour migration, heightened by stronger immigration controls following EU accession. It also explains, for example, the incidence of trafficking of Ghanaians and Nigerians to the Netherlands (Altink, 1995), of Nigerians to Italy, Belgium and the Netherlands (Elabor-Idemudia, 2003) and from Mozambique to South Africa (Vines, 1991; McKibbon, 1992).

In Vietnam, one informant offered an interesting analysis of poverty as a causal factor. While labelling poverty 'the root' cause in most cases, the informant's perspective was clearly one of *relative* poverty. Informants tended to describe migration to countries that are considered less poor and that potentially offer better income and employment:

> If you talk about the very specific causes for Vietnam of human trafficking, I think it is poverty. The root of the problem is poverty because people want to get a better income. They want to get a better job. They want to get a better life. They want more money, so they think about moving out of their place of origin, their community or their district and put themselves in a very vulnerable situation. For example, women from the Mekong Delta talk about getting out of the situation in their Commune. (Anon., Program Officer, International organisation, 5 October 2009)

This latter reference to escaping life in the commune also hints at the relevance of gender inequality discussed in the next chapter.

This 'want' or desire for more, in the views of my informants, is combined with other push factors. Panadda Changmanee, then Director for the Regional Anti-Human Trafficking Programme at International NGO Oxfam Quebec, noted a connection between this desire or want, education levels as discussed earlier and marriage:

> With low levels of education, they do not have the opportunity to get a better job in the country. There is a quick way of getting work abroad and with a better income than in Vietnam. This is a pull factor ... Their neighbour is going well when they come back; they have married the Korean man and are doing well. (16 October 2009)

Changmanee was the only informant who spontaneously raised the issue of 'marriage migration'. She continued by noting that as long as there are countries in the world that are better off than others, people will always seek to migrate:

'[Even] if you improve here, the other countries will always be better unless you have a sort of fair trade, where all countries share' (16 October). However, we cannot draw a clear distinction between absolute and relative poverty as a cause of trafficking. For instance, this same informant gave an additional example illustrative of a more extreme case of poverty:

> A family will never stop begging. To think that in one hour [of begging], they can get USD10. In a day, they can get USD100 if the baby is very vulnerable. There is no comparison ... I am not saying that poverty is the root cause. It is one of the main causes. (16 October)

Although Ukraine is a relatively more developed country than Ghana and Vietnam, Oksana Horbunova, Deputy Coordinator of IOM Ukraine's Counter-Trafficking Program, named poverty as one of the most important push factors, along with lack of employment. She went so far as to say that, '[f]rom my point of view, it is the main push factor' (31 July 2009). As was noted above with Vietnam, the concept of poverty in Ukraine is certainly less about starvation and the need to supplement income for survival and more related to desires for a higher standard of living than that offered by the Ukrainian economy to citizens. Informants tended to deem this search for 'more' as falling within the concept of poverty. At the same time, this is not to suggest that there is no extreme poverty in Ukraine. As Horbunova continued, 'people are looking for a possibility to change their life, to make their life better' and therefore do not 'just go and stay for a long time'. Rather they want to 'just make money and to get back' (O. Horbunova, Deputy Coordinator of Counter-Trafficking Program, IOM Ukraine, 31 July 2009).

This understanding of poverty was also explicit in the comments of Tatiana Ivanyuk, a counter-trafficking specialist with IOM. When asked to comment on the key causes of trafficking from Ukraine she responded, 'people are not satisfied with the amount of compensation they get for their work. People are not satisfied with professional opportunities, so those socio-economic weaknesses would be the most pertinent for Ukraine' (3 September 2009). This definition fits within the notion of limited economic opportunities but clearly does not amount to extreme poverty.

The Inadequacies of the Domestic Market

Having established the relevance of relative poverty, in the following section, I discuss the extent to which the search for work abroad appears to result from either lack of access to the domestic labour market (that is, the inability to find a job at home) or conditions of work that are considered sub-standard or below the expectations of individuals. First, I discuss barriers to finding work at home and focus particularly on youth and subsequently women. Here my own questionnaire and key informant research revealed particular findings regarding school-leavers and their search for work abroad. Second, I turn to conditions of work, with a focus on pay. Lower incomes than desired are unsurprisingly revealed to be a push factor in trafficking.

Youth access to the domestic labour market

On a global scale, there is substantial evidence of the heightened susceptibility of youth to exploitation abroad. This was particularly evident in my own research in Ukraine. Forty of the 104 participants in my research indicated that they were not earning an income prior to leaving Ukraine. This finding opens the door to two possible scenarios. On the one hand, questionnaire respondents may have lost their jobs prior to departing Ukraine, this having been a push factor. Alternatively, respondents may never have entered the domestic labour market. In this instance, respondents may have attempted to enter the labour market (that is, after finishing school, while at college/university or having finished college/university) and been unsuccessful. Alternatively, such respondents may not have even attempted to access employment in the domestic labour market.

Of the 40 respondents, the average age at the time of completing the survey was 23.4 years (Question 2), while the average age at the time the respondent left Ukraine was 21.5 years (Question 15).[5] Given that the average age (at the time of completing the questionnaire) of the total sample of 104 respondents was 25.4 years, it is clear that those who were not earning an income before leaving Ukraine were at the younger end of my sample.

Moreover, when these data are collated with my data on primary, secondary and tertiary education, as set out in Table 6.2, we can roughly conjecture that one of these 40 respondents interrupted their high school education to leave Ukraine at the age of 15, the age at which compulsory education ends in Ukraine; seven of the 40 left Ukraine straight from high school; four interrupted college/university (that is, did not complete the degree as per Question 11) and went abroad directly from being enrolled at college/university; and finally, assuming a college or university degree is no less than 3 years, three of these respondents went abroad immediately after completing their college or university degree. It is undeterminable whether any of these 15 respondents ever tried to access the domestic labour market, but it is surprising that the survey shows 15 Ukrainians went straight from being in an educational institution in Ukraine to leaving the country. From this construction of the data we could say that 14.4 per cent of all questionnaire respondents – assuming that they exercised some degree of autonomy in their movement abroad – when faced with the choice of entering the labour market for the first time, considered the prospects for their lives better outside than inside Ukraine.

In addition, a further 25 respondents were similarly not earning an income prior to departing Ukraine and had left their educational institution more than 1 year before leaving Ukraine. We can conjecture that from the time of leaving school or their tertiary education to the date of departure from Ukraine, these

---

5   Note that one respondent left this question blank. The average age for this question was therefore calculated on the basis of 39 respondents, not 40.

victims may have tried but failed to sustain an income in the domestic labour market. Overall, for these relatively young individuals, the lack of any income may have been the push factor.

Table 6.2   Portion of respondents not earning an income prior to departing Ukraine who left during or immediately after school, college or university completion

	Frequency	Percentage of non-income earners
Interrupted schooling	1	2.5
Departed immediately after completing high school	7	17.5
Interrupted college/university	4	10.0
Departed immediately after completing college or university	3	7.5
Total	15	37.5

These figures suggest the particular susceptibility of Ukrainian youth to irregular and unsafe migration. A reference was similarly made to the higher susceptibility of youth in Ghana during my research, with one informant linking this to lack of opportunities for youth and school leavers. One informant noted how '[o]nly about half of children have an outlet for progression or career development when they leave school, there is only work for around 50 per cent'. The problem appears even graver than this if one considers existing government data. For example, the 2008 Demographic and Health Survey reported an unemployment rate of 64.2 per cent among economically active female youth aged 15–19 and 60.1 per cent for males. For youth aged 20–24 years, the rate of unemployment was 25.9 per cent and 24.4 per cent for women and men respectively (Ghana Statistical Service and Ghana Health Service, 2009: 40–41). By contrast, the national unemployment rate for those aged 15–49 years was significantly lower, at 22.2 per cent for females and 19.3 per cent for their male counterparts (Ghana Statistical Service and Ghana Health Service 2009: 40–41). Other earlier sources suggest that of the 230,000 new Ghanaian job seekers who enter the market each year, only about 2 per cent find work in the formal sector (Boateng and Ofori-Sarpong, 2002: 7)

The lack of satisfaction of youth with traditional paths was also expressed by an anonymous informant from Vietnam:

> … There are young people in the cities or urban areas who are not interested in working in traditional fields so they are trying to get out of the family and are vulnerable to being trafficked. (Anon., National Trafficking Project Coordinator,

United Nations Inter-Agency Project on Human Trafficking, Vietnam, 16 October 2009)

The possible heightened vulnerability of youth highlights the need for sex- and age-disaggregated data to understand better the pre-migration situation of youths and particularly (i) the age at which victims leave; (ii) the extent to which their search for work at home failed; and (iii) the extent to which these youths perceived working life at home as offering satisfactory opportunities.

Women's access to the domestic labour market
The substantial differences between women's and men's access to the labour market is a globally recognised issue. Academics frequently identify a relationship between barriers facing women and heightened vulnerability to trafficking. This was evident during the course of my fieldwork, with occupational segregation raised as an issue by several informants. In Vietnam, for example, a gender expert with the UN commented:

> If you look at the formal labour market surveys and the Vietnam Living Standards Surveys, you can see the occupational segregation ... actual economic opportunities for women are pretty constrained. Even if you were to address the gender issues in education and skills development, what happens when women get out and into the market? ... Lack of economic opportunities is not just a pre-condition but a contributing factor for poor employment and life style choices. (Anon., Gender expert, UN Resident Coordinators Office, Vietnam, 20 October 2009)

This informant saw Vietnamese women as having two options as a result: either to accept the poor quality of the work available in the informal economy, such as selling goods in markets, or to migrate abroad. Labour market discrimination was also raised by a Vietnamese informant from UNICEF Vietnam: 'Job recruitment and promotion practices discriminate against women in the labour market and limit women's access to technical and non-traditional occupations and higher positions' (Anon., Education Specialist, UNICEF Vietnam, 14 June 2010). An extensive body of secondary literature exists to support these contentions (Wells, 2005: iii; World Bank, 2006: 19; Pham and Reilly, 2009; Pham and Reilly, 2007).

According to a senior economist working with a development bank in Vietnam, women were particularly hard hit by the financial downturn that affected industries such as tourism and retail around 2007 to 2008. The informant noted that the qualitative data that exist – Vietnam at the time of my research lacked systems to collect quantitative data on a monthly, quarterly or even annual basis – shows that women were affected more than men. The informant further noted: 'When the government tries to generate public works, it tends to be in construction, but that tends to be predominantly male orientated' (Anon., Senior Economist, Development Bank, 13 October 2009). The informant did not draw a link between the economic downturn and trafficking but emphasised Vietnamese women's dominance in the informal *domestic* labour market.

Occupational segregation and labour market discrimination against women were also issues raised by my informants in Ukraine, with links made to human trafficking:

> ... You can see the main push factors, like high unemployment, very low wages, even for qualified work and very poor social benefits for single mothers. If the person cannot compensate these low social benefits, they will look for work in other countries. (Sofia Lytvyn, Former coordinator of the ILO Anti-Trafficking Programme, Kyiv, Ukraine, 8 September 2009)

This informant had worked in migration and counter-trafficking in Ukraine for several years. She noted a clear change in perceptions of the underlying causes of trafficking, particularly among government officials. While trafficking was initially understood as 'a criminal issue, an issue of prostitution, an issue that should be under the responsibility of Ministry of Internal Affairs', she argued that it is now increasingly viewed as a 'labour migration issue, a labour market issue' (8 September 2009).

The labour market was also noted as the most prominent 'push factor' by other informants. For example, one Ukrainian informant contended that '[t]he combination of economic need and lack of opportunities for satisfying it would appear the most prominent', with the same informant also identifying as relevant a perception about the acceptability of poor conditions of work for women: 'Other contributing factors include perceived acceptance for women to work or perform services in sub-standard conditions' (Anon., Human Rights Project Officer, Inter-Governmental Organisation, Email comm., 29 October 2010). Particular to Ukraine, this includes even sectors of the population who have attained higher levels of education.

My informant added to this discussion the issue of layoffs related to macro-economic shifts. She noted, for example, how the metallurgical sector had suffered layoffs in the recent years prior to our interview, this sector being situated mostly in the eastern region of Ukraine, close to Russia (8 September 2009).[6] She also referred to the agricultural sector, which is particularly important in the western part of Ukraine, but which at the time was failing to produce a sufficient income for its workers, resulting in a perceived need to migrate to EU countries. She went on to distinguish two situations. Firstly, during times of economic boom, trafficking could be linked with low pay, where people are 'not satisfied with their

---

6   This type of scenario was reflected in a comment by one questionnaire respondent (female, age 27, from the Sumy Region of Ukraine) who had completed secondary school and a college/university degree. In response to Question 20, regarding how long she had been working as a secretary before leaving Ukraine, she wrote, 'I've been working for two years and then I got laid off'.

salaries and prefer to work abroad'. Secondly, outside of such times of prosperity – as she contended was the case at the time of my fieldwork – unemployment rather than low pay is the main factor, with Ukrainians 'forced to look for work and opportunities in other countries' (8 September 2009), thereby more closely resembling a picture of poverty. Her observations warn against drawing a sharp distinction between absolute and relatively poverty.

There were also some real and perceived barriers noted to small business ownership. As in the case of Vietnam, these findings are also well supported by the secondary literature on Ukrainian women's experience of the labour market (Aidis et al., 2007: 160; Ganson and Laux, 2004: 39; Van Klaveren, Hughie-Williams and Ramos Martin, 2010; Vijeyarasa, 2012a).

The comments above illustrate the difficulties facing women in accessing the formal labour market, which is likely to play a role in their migratory decisions. What is not clear from these comments, however, is exactly what these difficulties mean in practice. Rather than always leading to unemployment, at times it results in a perception of insufficient or unfair remuneration. A combination of factors – low wages, a desire for a better income or working conditions, along with perceived opportunities abroad – are at play in the migratory movement of these victims.

Poor Conditions at Home and the Booming Economies of Abroad

As indicated in the above analysis, we cannot ignore the pull of foreign countries experiencing times of (relative) economic boom. As one author notes referring to the rather unusual shift that Ghana underwent from a net immigration country to one of net emigration: 'While national mismanagement and associated economic and political problems provided the "push" for this unusual migration transition, the booming economies of neighbouring African countries and in Europe also constituted a "pull" for migration' (Anarfi and Kwankye, 2003: 19).

Sofia Lytvyn of Ukraine tied trafficking to potential pay abroad: 'The labour wages in other European countries [are] a pull factor. Doing the same job or less, you can earn a lot more than in Ukraine. This is a push [sic] factor for our people'. This finding is partially confirmed by my questionnaire data. More than half of the 104 questionnaire respondents (62.5 per cent) reported that they were earning an income prior to leaving Ukraine. The most popular occupations included working as salespersons (14 per cent), skilled workers (8.7 per cent), waitresses (7.7 per cent) and unskilled workers (7.7 per cent). The complete distribution of occupations in which the respondents were involved is shown in Table 6.3.

Given these figures, unemployment itself cannot be considered the primary factor. Along similar lines Iryna Babenko, President of the Women's Information and Advisory Centre in Zhytomyr Oblast in Ukraine explained that from her experience working on reintegration, many victims are employed but '[a]ll victims had an income of below 500 hryvnyas [around 65 USD] per month for the whole family' (trans., email comm., 12 August 2009).

Table 6.3   Occupation of the respondents prior to departure

	Frequency	Percentage of questionnaire respondents
Administrator	4	3.8
Bartender	2	1.9
Construction	2	1.9
Distributor	3	2.9
Farmer	5	4.8
Maid	3	2.9
Nurse	1	1.0
Sex worker	2	1.9
Salesperson	15	14.4
Skilled worker	9	8.7
Teacher	2	1.9
Unskilled worker	8	7.7
Waitress	8	7.7
Not earning an income	40	38.5

To understand this context better, during my fieldwork, questionnaire respondents were specifically asked whether their income prior to departure was sufficient to cover their own expenses and the contributions they made to family expenses. Only five of the questionnaire respondents said that their income was sufficient; their occupational groupings are noted in Table 6.4. However, there is a natural bias in this question where respondents feel the need to justify their decisions to go overseas by indicating that they were not earning a sufficient income to cover their basic living expenses.

Table 6.4   Occupational group and years of employment for individuals who considered income sufficient to cover their expenses and family contribution

	Occupation	Number of years in occupation
1	Laying asphalt	2
2	Administrator	1.5
3	Sex work	6
4	Sales person	5
5	Distributor	4

Nonetheless, these victims stand out as quite exceptional, being only five out of 104 who considered their incomes sufficient to cover their own expenses and their contributions to family expenses. The fact that these victims were earning an income that they believed to be sufficient and yet were still identified as trafficked outside of Ukraine raises doubts as to the extent to which their departures were planned and/or non-coerced. Indeed, for the first and fifth victims (exploited laying asphalt and as a distributor), no family member knew of their impending departure or assisted in their movement. This was the same for the third victim trafficked into sex work who identified as an orphan. For all three, there is a real possibility of coerced movement.[7]

From this evidence, we can extract two general findings. First, it seems clear that a neat line cannot be drawn between the category of those migrants unable to find work altogether and those who seek better conditions of work, particularly in light of rapid changes in a country's economy. Second, the actual conditions of work are certainly relevant in the decisions of victims to leave. The fact that some victims may consider their income prior to departure sufficient but nonetheless seek work abroad highlights expectations of relatively improved conditions and pay – for the same labour – as a factor potentially correlating to trafficking. Rather than a desperate attempt to meet basic food and non-food needs, some victims are seeking a relatively better income.

Conclusion

This chapter has shed doubt on the assumption that poverty and barriers to access the local labour markets are definitive push factors for trafficking. While many academics continue to perceive trafficking as linked to poverty, it appears that those who are trafficked are not the poorest in their communities. In this respect, the key element to assess the validity of this assumption may be adequately defining what we understand by 'poverty'. In general, studies and trafficking discourse fail to distinguish between absolute and relative poverty. My informants and the quantitative data collected during my own research provide support for the contention that trafficking has an identifiable relationship with the *perceptions* of migrants that 'abroad' could offer them better living conditions.

Consequently, the main conclusion we can derive is that trafficking may show a stronger correlation with relative poverty than with absolute poverty; it is the pursuit of improved economic (and social) circumstances rather than the need to address extreme hunger or desperation. Ghana may be the exception among the three countries where I conducted research. Given that Vietnam, Ghana and Ukraine

---

7 For the second victim (administrator), their partner knew of their impending movement. For the fourth victim (sales person), both their mother and partner knew. This evidence of pre-planning sheds doubt on the possibility of coerced movement as discussed in Chapter 5.

have all achieved different (and admittedly shifting) levels of development, it may be possible to see the relationship with trafficking similarly sitting on a spectrum from relative poverty to absolute poverty depending on where the sending country sits in the Human Development Index. Obviously the challenge here would be to define the terms for this comparison (i.e. if relative poverty should be understood as being poorer than other people in the victim's country of origin or poorer than the average perceived situation in the country of destination), as well as the threshold to distinguish between relative poverty and absolute poverty.

Second, barriers to accessing the domestic labour market and the quality of experiences in that labour market are evident drivers for victims. However, the role of subjective perceptions also needs to be recognised. From the data presented it may not be necessary for women or youth to actually suffer barriers to decent work; the mere perception of their existence may suffice. Whether it is because of failed attempts to access the domestic labour market or due to the perception that they will face discrimination or other difficulties when applying for work, as well as the possibility of poor work conditions (i.e. job insecurity, low pay), victims may seek labour opportunities abroad and often in the form of irregular migration.

The analysis in this chapter should lead us to question the indiscriminate link made between poverty and trafficking that we saw at the start of this chapter in Pierre Sané's oft-quoted remark, whereby poverty and trafficking are seen as caught in a vicious cycle. A more nuanced approach would be to highlight the importance of relative development between source and destination countries in terms of conditions of employment and access to existing jobs. It would also require reconsideration of what we mean by the term 'poor' and paying more attention to the profile of the exploited economic migrant, or as stated elsewhere in this book, the 'unlucky' migrant who is in search of better pay and work abroad. Moreover, when set against the broader body of literature on migration, the evidence presented in this chapter offers further justification as to why trafficking should be seen on a migration continuum. Many of the factors that drive migration on a global scale are the same factors that shape the decisions of individuals who face barriers to legal migration to seek better pay, conditions and opportunities and find that their only means is through irregular and often unsafe and risky migration.

Chapter 7

The Female Victim of Trafficking

You have couples involved in trafficking. But for me, there are some things in trafficking related to gender: less power, less access, less opportunity, less healthy life, less possibility of choice, the less. There is something about being less. So being less, there is a lot on gender. Even being a man. Maybe a lot of men trafficked also suffer from the less ... So I think it is really related to gender issues.

(E. Ferreras, Programme Director, Multilateral Cooperation and Gender, Spanish Agency for International Development and Cooperation, 9 October 2009)

Human trafficking is frequently described in 'gendered' terms, with women seen as 'easy targets' for traffickers (US TIP Report, 2009: 36) and as 'more vulnerable than men to being trafficked' (Mediterranean Institute of Gender Studies, 2007: 6). In many respects, this is an unsurprising assumption given the attention paid by international organisations, academics and the popular press to the 'feminisation of poverty' (e.g. Ansah, 2006: 101 on sex work and trafficking in Ghana) and the 'feminisation of migration' (e.g. Andrijasevic, 2004: 181; La Strada, 2008: 76, 82; Wijers and Lap-Chew, 1997: 43).

The assumption that females are most at risk of becoming victims draws upon the view that class, race, sexuality and culture intersect to reinforce women's marginalisation. First, women are seen as more vulnerable to trafficking simply because they are women, with gender inequality assumed to be a driver of trafficking. Second, and interlinked with this assumption, are the socio-cultural values, expectations and traditions that shape women's decision-making with regard to whether or not to migrate and what conditions of work to accept abroad.

Furthermore, the dynamics of trafficking themselves are presented in a gendered and stereotypical manner: women are pictured as victims who suffer at the hands of largely male perpetrators. Authors frequently emphasise the *male* perpetrator, or the *male* client in discussions on sex work. Donna Hughes, for example, writes that both trafficking and prostitution are 'highly gendered systems that result from structural inequality between women and men on a world scale'. She continues by noting how '[m]en create the demand and women are the supply' (2006: 10). Significantly less recognition is given in the academic literature to the female perpetrator. While it is a norm to hear references to the 'madam' in literature on sex work (e.g. Bernstein, 2007; Ward and Day, 2006; Dandona et al., 2006; Wahab, 2002), the female trafficker is often ignored.[1]

---

1 An interesting study by Bridget Anderson (2002) on migrant labour in the EU, which analyses why the increased demand for domestic workers is met by migrant women, highlights how the race and citizenship status of migrants distinguish them from their *female*

In this chapter, I explore this 'gendering' of trafficking. Unlike the uni-directional approach of authors such as Hughes and their unquestioning focus on the female victim, I use gender as a lens to explore various dimensions of the phenomenon of trafficking. I argue that trafficking *is*, in fact,gendered and I support a number of the contentions outlined above regarding a correlation between some aspects of gender inequality and heightened vulnerability to trafficking. However, my analysis also highlights the need for the mainstream trafficking framework to adopt a more nuanced approach to gender, one which moves beyond the simple dichotomy of male perpetrator and female victim.

First, I discuss the contention that trafficking is driven by gender inequality. After briefly setting out the literature, I examine the argument that traditional values imposed on women play a role in the process of human trafficking. Next, I turn to evidence from the field regarding the assumed role played by such factors as domestic violence, women's secondary status in the family, obligations to provide for one's family and Confucianism in the course of human trafficking.

I then turn to the 'non-gendering' of trafficking. Jeff Jearn and Linda McKie note, particularly in relation to domestic violence, that men are not usually gendered or mentioned as men (2008). The non-gendering of men, as Johanna Niemi points out, is also evident in research on sex work, when the 'buyers-abusers are invisible and nongendered' (2010: 161). That is, by comparison to the deliberate emphasis placed on the gender of *women* as *victims* of inequality or in this case trafficking, perpetrators are referred to as men, with no analysis of the significance of their gender. As will be discussed below, I add that little effort is made to assess whether perpetrators are or are not in reality typically male.

Throughout this chapter, I argue that when the mainstream trafficking discourse shifts beyond a focus on the 'female victim', trafficking becomes non-gendered, ignoring both male victims of trafficking but also unexpected or non-stereotypical gender roles evident in current patterns of human trafficking. I review data on male victims. I also analyse the gendered aspects of exploitation experienced by both male and female victims in destination countries. I subsequently turn to what can be considered a reversal of the female victim/male perpetrator dichotomy and examine the female trafficker. My discussion ends with an analysis of male and female victim stigma. I conclude by arguing that the failure of observers of human trafficking to see and deconstruct the gender of the phenomenon beyond the 'female victim' has contributed to the assumption that the typical victim is a woman trafficked into sexual exploitation.

For the purpose of this chapter, my definition of gender is broad, encompassing the biological sex of victims, gendered social inequalities, gender stereotypes, gendered labour and exploitation and finally, engendered stigma. I also touch briefly

---

employer. However, Anderson made little of the fact that it was largely the female member of the household who was seen as the employer rather than the male or both members of a hetereosexual couple.

on the issue of sexual orientation and gender identity.[2] Of the few authors to explore gender in the context of trafficking, Adriana Piscitelli and Marcia Vasconcelos critique the equating in trafficking literature of the term 'gender' with women (2008: 14).[3] This equation is in fact a common practice throughout the development and human rights sectors.[4] Drawing on the work of authors such as Judith Butler, Piscitelli and Vasconcelos urge us to look beyond gender as synonymous with women, or the view that gender relates simply to power relations between men and women. In this chapter, I concur with this view and use the term gender in the broader sense as a tool for better understanding the dynamics at play in trafficking.

Despite the need for a more nuanced approach to discussing the gendered nature of trafficking, it is nonetheless essential to recognise women-specific patterns of migration. Stringent standards for legal migration often leave men and women who wish to migrate few options other than to accept the social and economic vulnerabilities that arise with unsafe migration. When combined with cultural values that emphasise women's roles as mothers, wives and daughters and economic contributors to their households, alongside the possibility of accepting less than desirable work to fulfil these expectations, there is a 'female' gendered aspect of trafficking that involves specific push factors and experiences of trafficking that cannot be ignored. It is here that I begin my analysis.

'Gender' Inequality and the Traffic of Women and Girls

Gender Inequality as a Presumed 'Push Factor'

There is an array of literature that assumes a link between gender inequality, in terms of women's subordinate status, and human trafficking. At times, this is a passing reference; yet often it is the stated objective of the author to defend the existence of such a link. Policy-makers such as Noeleen Heyzer, former Executive Director of then UNIFEM (now amalgamated into UN Women), have argued that 'daughters are perceived as a liability by their families, who are obliged to marry them off well, ensure their pre-marital sexual purity, provide substantial marriage

---

2   One informant in Ukraine, academic Larysa Magdyuk, when asked whether people understand what gender equality means, responded, 'We had to work pretty intensively on explaining this to people, this *gender politica*, this *gender ideologica*. These are still new words' (4 August 2009). In reality, informants during my research may have attributed diverse meanings to the term 'gender'.

3   That is: 'gênero é freqüentemente tratado como sinônimo de "mulheres"'. The authors' interests lie primarily in the experiences of women and transvestites in the Brazil sex industry, as well as their experiences of working in Spain.

4   Gender inequality and gender mainstreaming, popularised by the development sector from around 1997 onwards, has come to signify inequalities facing women when compared to men and the mainstreaming of women's rights throughout development and human rights practice (Edwards, 2010: 35).

expenses and continue to offer material resources to the daughter's marital family on auspicious occasions' (2002: 9). As a result of these value systems, Heyzer argues that we see 'the sale of women and girls into marriage; willingness to marry off young girls to strangers who make no monetary demands, thus predisposing [these girls] to trafficking' (2002: 9). Heyzer adds that vulnerability caused by marital infidelity, alcoholism, domestic violence, desertion by husbands and divorce all increase the risk of women being trafficked (2002: 9).

Similar arguments have been made by the former UN Special Rapporteur on Violence against Women, Radhika Coomaraswamy, who argued in a 2000 report (pre-dating the Trafficking Protocol) that trafficking in women 'flourishes' precisely because of vulnerabilities arising from women's lack of access to resources, what she termed the 'women-specific character' of the human rights violations that underlie trafficking (2000: ¶ 1). In her view, poverty and gender discrimination are maintained through the collusion of the market, the state, the community and the family unit. Like Heyzer, Coomaraswamy argues that traditional family structures, sex roles and the unequal division of labour in the home support a system of trafficking. Coomaraswamy further notes that a 'push' factor of trafficking is a 'preference for male children and the culture of male privilege' which 'deprives girls and women of access to basic and higher education, and, consequently, illiteracy rates among women remain high' (2000: ¶ 57).

Academic writers have drawn similar links to the gendered nature of irregular migration. Sebastian Lăzăroiu and Monica Alexandru, writing specifically on Romanian women, argue that the demand for low-wage labour and the existence of gender-specific employment sectors generate a segmentation of the migration labour market, with labour opportunities more numerous and better regulated for male rather than female migrants. As a result, they contend, female migrants have to resort to unofficial channels. They further note that '[c]lassified ads seeking female labour often publish criteria that have less to do with professional skills, and much more or exclusively with the applicant's physical appearance or age' (Lăzăroiu and Alexandru, 2003: 21).

Patience Elabor-Idemudia, writing on the traffic of women and girls from Africa, states (without providing quantitative evidence) that the 'overwhelming majority of trafficked persons are women and girls', with trafficking presumed to be the 'result of discrimination on the basis of sex' (2003: 116). Elabor-Idemudia adds that inadequate attention has been paid to intersectional discrimination, with race-related gender inequality often ignored. She notes that if attention is paid to which women are trafficked, the link to racial and social marginalisation becomes evident. Race constitutes not only a 'risk factor' but possibly also determines 'the kind of treatment that women experience in destination countries' (Elabor-Idemudia 2003: 116).

Linking gender inequality and trafficking is particularly prominent in NGO reports and programmes. For example, La Strada, a European NGO network addressing trafficking in human beings within the region, particularly from central and eastern Europe, adopts the view that there is an indisputable and intimate link between gender inequality and human trafficking: 'It is generally known that women are disproportionally affected by the social and economic factors that are known to be root causes of trafficking, namely, poverty, discrimination, gender-based violence, armed conflict, unemployment and inequality and oppressive social structures' (2008: 7). Yet, there is a lack of empirical evidence of the links between specific manifestations of gender inequality and human trafficking. The evidence that emerged from my field research concerning the existence of a relationship, if any, with gender inequality, is discussed in more detail in the following section.

Confucianism, Communism and Post-Communist states

During the course of my research in Vietnam, Ukraine and Ghana, the lesser status of women when compared with men was evident. No informant disputed the existence of this inequality and none questioned gender inequality as a 'push factor' for trafficking. However, many informants reiterated the complexity of this relationship, with several questioning linear arguments. For example, Vietnamese informants expressed doubt about the supposed link between the secondary status Confucianism attributes to women when compared to men and the eventual exploitation of Vietnamese migrant women abroad. In Ukraine, while some informants emphasised domestic violence as a push factor, other informants noted a lack of substantial evidence to establish a direct connection between gender inequality, and domestic violence in post-Soviet Ukraine and trafficking. In Ghana, while cultural factors were noted as a central barrier to women's equality with men, no informant explained how such barriers relate to Ghanaian women's entry into situations of exploitation abroad.

Beginning with the question of Confucianism, this ideology has been 'blamed' for gender inequality in Vietnam[5] (Phan, 2005; Marr, 1976: 372; Ngô Thi, 2004: 71; Leung, 2003: 361). Peter Chan Phan, for example, argues that Confucianism as an ethic-religious system is still deeply influential among Vietnamese whose

---

5   There are numerous manifestations of gender inequality in Vietnam. The CEDAW Committee, for example, has expressed concern about the persistence of patriarchal attitudes and deep-rooted stereotypes regarding roles and responsibilities of women and men, as well as a preference for male offspring, with the resulting disadvantage for women taking both economic and political forms (2007: ¶ 12). The World Bank and others have expressed concerns specifically about ethnic minority women in particular, who have much lower literacy and education participation rates and experience significantly higher infant and maternal mortality. Twenty per cent of ethnic minority young women have never attended school (World Bank, 2006: 26, 29). Across the Vietnamese population, only 33 per cent of land use certificates are issued in the name of women or both spouses (World Bank, 2006: 43). Women work longer hours than men, reflecting their dual responsibility for productive work and care-giving (World Bank, 2006: 41; Lee, 2008: 13). A survey by, among others, the Ministry of Culture, Sports and Tourism, showed a prevalence of domestic violence in 21 per cent of couples (husband to wife and vice versa) (MOCST et al., 2008: 36). Violence is, however, overwhelming perpetrated by men against women (MOCST et al., 2008: 36).

'Confucian DNA' remains in spite of the political, social and religious changes of the last decades (2005: 40). In reports from the mid-90s and in more recent studies, pressure on potential women migrants to supplement family income has been attributed to Confucian values such as 'filial piety' (Rushing, 2006, 475; see also Siddiqi and Patrinos, 1995:7).

The notion that Confucianism has any relationship with trafficking was, however, firmly disputed by one informant, who spontaneously raised the issue:

> Trafficking is an economic issue. Trafficking of women for sex and marriage is a demographic issue and driven by the market. I think there are cultural factors that make trafficking more or less likely, but it would [have] more to do with how women see their roles and their economy and their duty to the family and therefore their sense of shame and honour ... Cambodian women are trafficked all the time and they are not Confucian. (Anon., Gender expert, UN Country Team, Vietnam 20 October 2009)

In a similar vein, another informant reflected on the centrality of familial obligation and women's perceptions of their roles. This informant labelled the family pressures on women as 'one cause' but not the main one. The informant continued by arguing that 'the pressure from the family, it is a very Asian thing. The woman always has to go out and do the work to support the families'. She further noted that 'women themselves "desire" to support their families' (P. Changmanee, Regional Programme Director, Regional Anti-Human Trafficking Programme, Oxfam Quebec, 16 October 2009).

The view that gender inequality is one cause but that '[i]t is always a complex of factors' was shared by another informant from an international NGO operating in Vietnam. This informant went on to share the experience of one victim that reveals a complex intersection of sex, gender identity and sexual orientation:

> One of the women in the cooperative [for trafficked returnees] had finished high school. She [had been] offered a job abroad, spoke Russian and was trafficked to Russia. She said: 'In my case, I do not have a poor academic background. I did not have enough money to receive a university degree, but I wanted a better life. I am not naive; I just wanted a better life'. She was forced into marrying a Russian and had to flee, leaving behind her child. She is actually a lesbian. She lives with this partner. She told me she wants to be called 'father' and I asked her why and she said: 'Men are powerful. I want to be labelled as a man'.

Analysing this story, the informant noted the pressures faced by women in rural societies that make them more vulnerable. Having worked previously in Bangladesh, she went as far as to contend that the greater freedoms offered to Vietnamese women when compared to Bangladeshi women in terms of work, dress and travel abroad, particularly following the transition, might make them *more* vulnerable: 'Freedom of movement is wonderful but perhaps it exposes you to something else' (12 October 2009).

Similarly offering a view on the question of the socialist transition, one informant in Vietnam argued that socialism gave priority to gender equality. Noting that this was a generalisation and not wanting to be 'an apologist' for any socialist regime, the informant contended that 'gender inequality becomes a kind of a protest against socialism' (Anon., Gender expert, UN Country Team, Vietnam 20 October 2009). This informant continued: '[w]omen are saying, "Well, we were better when there was public housing and the communal canteens". So I think women appreciated it, even though no one appreciated the extent of intervention in private lives'.

Nonetheless, a substantial body of literature highlights the inequality similarly suffered by women under socialist regimes. Alicia Leung describes the reproduction of patriarchy by male and female Communists in Marxist-Leninist-Maoist China despite their strong commitment to women's emancipation (Leung, 2003: 360, 363–4). In Susan Brownmiller's discussion of Vietnam's communist movement, she similarly notes the tendency for female Communist revolutionaries to join what became a side-lined Vietnam Women's Union (VWU), a mass organisation formed in 1930, the formation of which 'effectively shut women out of full participation of the main arena' (Brownmiller, 1994: 83).[6] If we were to accept the analysis of these authors, one could say that it is not the influence of Confucianism that is the key cultural factor for the imbalance of gender relations in Vietnam, but possibly the Communist system which created a separate entity for women and side-lined them from mainstream opportunities. This side-lining of the VWU has arguably persisted in modern-day politics in Vietnam.

Evidence from my informants suggests a regression in the level of equality experienced by Ukrainian women after the transition: 'While in the previous periods of society, women were more or less mandatorily represented in all sectors of life – public and economic – the transition brought a variety of different opportunities. Women have not been completely integrated in all of these opportunities' (Ilaria Carnevali, Equal Opportunities and Women's Rights Project Manager, UNDP, 11 August 2009). The important point to take away is

---

6   Still today the *de facto* national women's bureaucracy, the VWU is one of the largest women's mass organisations in the world, with an estimated 50 per cent of women over 18 years of age as members. With strong links to women at the village level and horizontally to trade unions, the VWU is a frequent partner for implementation of projects with the UN, international organisations and donors. However, it is an under-resourced entity that 'lacks mechanisms for coordinating policy with government units' (Goetz, 2003: 77). As one informant commented, the 'Women's Union does not exist to discuss emerging gender issues in the society of Vietnam. It exists to maintain the status quo' (Anon., Senior Economist, Development Bank, 13 October 2009; see also Vijeyarasa, 2010c: 94 for a more detailed analysis of the VWU).

that women in these three countries often experience less equality than may be presumed following transitions that were believed to enhance freedom for all.

Attention also needs to be given to women's own expectations and how this influences socio-economic decision-making. While this analysis is centred on a critique of gender inequality, one of my informants contended that for many Ukrainian women, 'it is enough to successfully get married and their husband [to be] the bread winner' (M. Alekseyenko, Women's Consortium of Ukraine, 31 July 2009). This view was supported by another informant, a Ukrainian academic who described the 'interesting dichotomy between traditions and stereotypes', referring to the position of the woman as housekeeper and housewife as a tradition that is widely promoted as a value to be maintained in Ukrainian society (L. Magdyuk, Independent gender expert, Ukraine, 4 August 2009). The academic explained her view that 'many women seriously *oppose* gender equality in this country', many of these being women who are 'closer to being able to make decisions'. Thus, in our interview, she referred several times to former Ukrainian female politician Yulia Tymoshenko and the reinforcement of traditional imagery particularly by political elites.[7]

From politics to the popular press, the promotion of the image of wife and mother in Ukraine was seen by my informants as a reflection of a lack of gender inequality but perhaps also a lack of desire for the type of equality that might be sought after by women in other countries. No informant, however, reflected upon what these images say about the woman migrant. We could in fact conjecture that this imagery of the quintessential 'good wife' presents a woman who stays at home rather than travels abroad, leaving the role of income earning to men. This inequality should therefore act as a *deterrent* for trafficking of women and not as a cause.

Despite general recognition of the inequalities emerging in the post-Soviet era in Ukraine,[8] one of the differences between the views of my informants in

---

7   Ukrainian academic Oksana Kis gives an analysis of the political career of Tymoshenko and how Tymoshenko constructed and used stereotypical women's images (including Mother of the Nation, National Heroine, Victim/Martyr, Faithful Christian, Fashionable Lady, Sexy Woman, and Businesswoman) 'which correspond with different stages of Tymoshenko's ascent up to the summit of Ukrainian politics' (2005b). Elsewhere Kis notes how the image of motherhood as women's God-given and only natural destiny suggests that the 'genuine Ukrainian woman' is one who is dedicated to the 'physical and cultural reproduction of the nation through appropriate nurturing of children' (Kis, 2005a: 109). Ukrainian feminist theorist Tatiana Zhurzhenko adds that, like the image of the housewife, the image of the Ukrainian business woman was an important sign of a successful transition: 'The image of the successful woman entrepreneur promulgated by the mass media fulfils the function of legitimization of the new market order, much like the image of the happy female Soviet worker in Communist propaganda was used in the past for legitimization of the Communist regime' (2001: 42; see also analysis in Vijeyarasa, 2012a: 58–9).

8   Ukraine has slipped back in the World Economic Forum's Gender Gap index, from a ranking of 47 in 2006 to 57 in 2007 (World Economic Forum, 2007: 7). Sex disaggregated

Vietnam and Ukraine was the clear association of the very specific inequalities Ukrainian women experience in the labour market with trafficking. These labour market barriers were identified as the most prominent manifestation of gender inequality having a direct relationship with trafficking. Such barriers were discussed extensively in the previous chapter. While similar factors were noted by informants from Vietnam, these were not as closely linked to trafficking.

Domestic Violence, Single-Motherhood and Lack of Decision-Making Capacity: Exploring the Link to Trafficking

Throughout the literature, several other manifestations of gender inequality have been linked to the traffic of women. One of the most prominent is domestic violence which was discussed in Chapter 4. One other aspect which is said to relate to trafficking is the consequences of sole-parenting. Single motherhood in Ukraine, for example, was noted as a vulnerability factor by several informants. Lilia Koveshnikova, Director of a local NGO, Women of Donbass in Lugansk Oblast, argued that Ukrainian victims are often single mothers: 'Women who were victims of abuse in the family, women who wanted to settle their personal issues by living abroad, complement the so-called profile of vulnerable women' (Trans., Email comm., 13 August 2009).

The high number of single mothers in Ukraine was noted by another informant: 'There are […] many single mother families in Ukraine and here the woman is the breadwinner, the housekeeper and everything together' (Larysa Magdyuk, Independent gender expert, Ukraine, 4 August 2009). The increased pressures for income generation, linked to barriers to income earning in Ukraine, was seen as leading to migration abroad. Oksana Horbunova, the Deputy Coordinator of Counter-Trafficking Program for IOM Ukraine also made reference to single mothers' higher vulnerability to trafficking, with the need to provide economic support for children as the driving force (31 July 2009).

An interesting phenomenon was observed specifically in Ghana where the unequal position of women in Ghanaian society is well documented.[9] First,

---

data is still scarce and unavailable among most Government ministries due to lack of skills and lack of resources (UNDP 2009, 12). Even in this context, the Government itself reports that the gender parity that is proclaimed in the Constitution of Ukraine is not practised, noting discrimination on the basis of family status and age, with single women, women with young children and women over 40 years of age vulnerable to discriminatory practices in public and private sector employment (Government of Ukraine, 2008: ¶ 50). In spite of *de jure* equal status of women and men, women are still discriminated against in the political field as a result of the lack of a consolidated women's and gender movement; absence of support for women politicians, the influence of stereotypes that 'politics is dirty' as well as a general lack of understanding of the importance of women's representation in politics (Women's Consortium of Ukraine 2008, 29).

9   Studies in Ghana have shown that Ghanaian women experience greater poverty than men and this has been identified as directly related to their lack of access to economic

however, it is important to recall the child trafficking framework that appeared to govern much of the discourse on trafficking in Ghana. Despite this narrow lens, a gendered perspective on trafficking emerged. A link was drawn between lack of access to family planning and control over decisions regarding reproduction and the traffic of Ghanaian children, that is, the former was said to result in very large family sizes to which 'trafficking' is seen as a solution.

By way of context, aggregate figures in Ghana indicate a fertility rate among women in rural areas of 4.9 children per woman, as against 3.1 in urban Ghana. However, the fertility rate is as high as 6.8 children per woman in northern Ghana and 5.4 in central Ghana when compared to 2.5 in Greater Accra (GSS and GHS, 2008; see also see Faria, 2008; Bankole, 1995 for discussions on the challenges Ghanaian women face in negotiating family sizes with their male partners). My informants described the selling of young children as a solution to 'too many mouths to feed'. In some instances, parents – most commonly mothers – were seen as accepting relatively easily offers of traffickers to take their children to be schooled elsewhere. In other instances, children were described as contributors to the family income and are trafficked into exploitative labour within Ghana as a result. Several informants from both the NGO and donor communities named patriarchy, culture and religion as drivers, with men in families determining the number of children that would be conceived and provision of care being deemed too difficult in family sizes that range from between five to ten children.

For example, James Kofi Annan, Executive Director of a local NGO Challenging Heights, while noting that the problem is multi-faceted, similarly referred to how family sizes at times range from between five and ten children, making care difficult: 'We know that one of the reasons children are sold is large family size' (17 August 2010). Another informant blamed patriarchy, culture and religion, arguing that men continue to control the household, including determining how many children they will have, exacerbated in non-Christian households where men marry 'as many as they want' (H. Afrifa, Projects Officer (Migration and Criminal Justice), British High Commission, Ghana, 3 August 2010). His colleague at the

---

resources, including credit, land ownership and inheritance, the absence of economic opportunities and autonomy, lack of access to education and support services and women's minimal participation in decision-making processes (Wrigley-Asante, 2011). One study focusing on women's economic empowerment through credit found that socio-cultural factors, including power relations in the household, continue to act as 'cages' for women (Wrigley-Asante, 2011). According to the report of the former Special Rapporteur on Violence against Women, Yakin Ertürk (mandate holder from August 2003 to July 2009) following a mission to Ghana, '[a]lthough social attitudes are gradually changing, especially in urban settings, women continue to occupy a subordinate position to men in virtually every domain of life' (2008, ¶ 17). Unequal gender relations are sustained by discriminatory marriage practices and marital relations. Early marriage persists. According to the 2006 Multiple Indicator Cluster Survey, more than one in four married women (25.9 per cent) were under 18 years of age when they married and 4.4 per cent were aged under 15.

British High Commission also noted that '[m]ost of the parents have five, six or seven children to feed and if someone offers them even a small amount of money to take their child away, they will take it' (A. Fleming, 1st Sec. Migration Policy (West Africa), British High Commission, Ghana, 3 August 2010).

Economic dependence on men and lack of power to negotiate was also raised as an issue. A programme manager for human rights, HIV and trafficking at a faith-based organisation directly linked family size with women's lack of autonomous control over their socio-economic situation and human trafficking, referring to the patriarchal society in which women have to operate. The informant continued by describing the absent father in these relationships:

> These people are not even looking after your children. They are mostly fisherman in the Kota communities. In the lean season they do not have work so they do not have money. So it is the mother's business to look after these children. When the traffickers come, they find a safe haven for their children so they give their children out. (18 August 2010)

These comments indicate the possibility that a number of markers of gender inequality in Ghana, including barriers to family planning, unplanned pregnancies and lack of negotiating power within relationships, correlate in some way with the traffic of children. These inequalities are also affirmed by the secondary literature. Strongly held norms exist in Ghana about male dominance in decision-making (Takyi, 2000). Intimate power relations between men and women, both married and unmarried, are said to be shaped by these traditional gender norms around reproductive roles and also by conservative Christian and Muslim beliefs (Faria, 2008). However, further research to address the absence of a sound evidence-base is needed. It should begin with interviews with mothers of trafficked children to determine the extent to which the pressures created by large family size are linked to their decision-making and how much awareness parents actually have of the conditions children are likely to face.

The above discussions indicate that gender inequality manifests itself in a number of ways. Some stakeholders view these manifestations as linked to trafficking. In Vietnam, the discussions were broad, suggesting that the general lack of power for Vietnamese women, particularly political and economic, leads to other forms of inequality, including women's increased involvement in work in the informal market and unsafe migration. In Ukraine, the assertions were much more specific, with links made by my informants between abuse in the home and the need to support families as a single mother and the solution to these problems being found in migration. In Ghana, while informants were able to note the inequalities experienced by women with regard to cultural values, lack of political participation and domestic violence, the link to trafficking was far less clear. However, the secondary literature supports the contention of high expectations on both Ghanaian *men and women* to supplement family income.

Seeking an Empirical Base for the Linkages between Trafficking and Gender Equality

The above discussions indicate that to a significant extent, markers of gender inequality are believed to figure in the dynamics of trafficking on a global scale. This inequality, and its assumed correlation to trafficking, manifests itself in different ways, and to different degrees. In Vietnam, it is Confucian values and filial piety; in Ukraine, domestic violence and labour market barriers; in Ghana, it is large family sizes and the impact this has on decisions regarding child labour, migration and trafficking.

What is also evident, however, is the lack of an empirically-based, comprehensive analysis behind the contention that 'gender inequality' drives trafficking. Given the existence of gender inequality in countries across the globe, a very careful analysis is needed to discern what aspects of such inequality correlate with trafficking and in what ways. Demographic studies of women returnees, which include questions concerning experiences of domestic violence prior to being trafficked, for example, are possible, although as noted above, such primary research is lacking.

In recognising the global nature of gender inequality, it is important to reflect on the impact that this has on women not only in source but also in destination countries. There is extensive literature on the unequal status of migrant women (even outside of the context of exploitative labour, e.g. Cranford, 2012 on unionising among Latina/o immigrant janitors in Los Angeles; Sun-Hee Park, 2011 on migrant women's lack of access to health care in the US or Moyer, et al., 2012 on the sexual and reproductive health status and knowledge of women migrant workers in China). One would assume, therefore, that whatever gender inequality is suffered by trafficked women before their departure, it is likely to be exacerbated by their situation in destination countries. If anything, we would assume that this would act as a push factor for their return home and a decision not to engage in irregular migration again (avoiding a situation of 're-trafficking'). To a certain extent, this undermines the intuition that there is a correlation between gender inequality and trafficking. This also brings to mind the image of the 'good woman' in Ukraine as the one who stays at home, which also undermines the idea of a correlation.

Human Trafficking and Male Victims

In the following section, I discuss the inadequate attention given to male victims. In recent times, there has been a growth in literature on trafficking of men. A few studies refer to the phenomenon, even if it is simply to emphasise its under-researched nature. A USAID report on the trafficking of men to Eurasia highlights the 'dearth of information available on trafficked men', partly as a result of underreporting (2010: v). The report emphasises the inability to profile victims who are this diverse: aged between 20 and 50, single and married, educated and uneducated. It does suggest, however, a tendency for men to be trafficked into construction and construction-related work and agriculture, as well as for work in factories, in food processing industries, on ships, in forestry and in oil extraction (2010: vi). The report's authors note that it is impossible to draw a distinction between trafficking for labour exploitation and forced labour, highlighting the need for a broader framework for analysis that includes exploited labour migrants at large, with less emphasis placed on the process by which such migrants find themselves in the situation of exploitation in the first place.

NGO Verité has also highlighted how '[l]ittle is known' about the trafficking of Filipino men (n.d.: 4). Verité's contention, similarly to that of USAID, that 'the operational definition of human trafficking is being slowly expanded to encompass various modes of exploitation of migrant workers, including the exploitation of workers migrating legally under their own will for legitimate forms of employment', (n.d.: 4) highlights the need to view trafficking as sitting within a spectrum of migration. These studies present an opportunity not only to expand the trafficking framework to include men, but also to comprehend the voluntariness (and even legality) of their initial entry into that situation (see also IOM, 2011: 4).[10]

One of the few studies that focus solely on male trafficking is that of Rebecca Surtees, based on data from Belarus and Ukraine in which male victims accounted for 28.3 per cent and 17.6 per cent of the IOM assisted caseload respectively between 2004 and 2006 i.e. around 685 trafficked men (2008a: 9).[11] The majority of Belarusian and Ukrainian trafficked men assisted in that period were adults aged between 18 and 44 years. This is consistent with the demographics of my own research in Ukraine, in which 14 of the 104 Ukrainian respondents to my questionnaire were men aged between 17 and 48 years.

This data on male victims in source countries can be compared with the figures we have from destination countries. The EU reported in May 2012 that, based on a set of consolidated data from EU member states from 2010, the majority of victims identified – 79 per cent – were female, with girls accounting for 9.5 per cent of the total number of victims (Scheerer, 2012). This can be compared to an article in the popular press, also from May 2012, in which the Salvation Army's trafficking coordinator for the UK was quoted as saying that 41 per cent of the victims they support are men, specifically identifying Eastern Europe and Africa as their place of origin (Evans, 2012). Not having access to the original databases, it is impossible to determine if there were other biases involved in the methods

---

10   This study discusses both the traffic of 63 Cambodian men into the Thai fishing industries that operate between Thailand, Malaysia and Indonesia and the traffic of Ukrainian, Bulgarian, Bangladeshi and Indian men to work in Iraq in the construction, domestic and services sectors.

11   Both Surtees and I draw our analysis from data collected from a similar group of male victims, that is, victims of trafficking who had been assisted upon their return. This in many respects may explain the similarities in our findings. It is also important to note that our findings cannot necessarily be extrapolated to non-assisted male victims of trafficking.

of data collection or their analysis. However, there is little reason to assume that male victims are more likely to be trafficked to the UK than other parts of Europe. Potential explanations could be differences in the criteria used for identification of victims or the definition of victim itself. Nonetheless, such distinctly different figures for the percentage of male victims identified as trafficked to Europe highlight the extent to which there are shortcomings in existing methods of data collection.

Generally speaking, an emphasis on female victims of trafficking was evident throughout my research in Vietnam, with the Ghanaian focus being on the child victim. Both of these countries can be contrasted with Ukraine, where there was an evident recognition of the traffic of men. Ukrainian informants spontaneously raised the issue of stereotypes about Ukrainian men. UNDP gender expert, Ilaria Carnevali blamed these gender norms for 'social degradation, alcoholism and vicious cycles leading to unemployment' in Ukraine (11 August 2009). She noted how certain stereotypes emerged during Ukraine's transition, including 'that a real man is the man with the big bucks and the big cars ... The ideal woman is the one who conforms to certain aesthetic stereotypes and requirements and is able to get the man with the big bucks'. In her view, these stereotypes 'have a deep impact on family life, social life, and how women and men work and live together' in Ukraine (11 August 2009).

Another informant noted that men are under similar 'gender' pressures as women, with Tatiana Ivanyuk suggesting that men may face even higher pressure to provide for their families than women:

> Throughout Ukraine, men are still very much under traditional gender pressures and the traditional gender expectations on men. Men should provide for their families. Families do not have an income so they keep pushing on men. In that way, there might be a bit more pressure on [men] but generally, the push factors are quite similar. (T. Ivanyuk, Counter-Trafficking Programme specialist, IOM Ukraine, 3 September 2009)

Men's migration-related decisions are not made as freely as is often assumed. We cannot presume, therefore, that it is a global commonality that the familial pressures facing women are any stronger (or any more of a push factor) than those facing men.

In regard to male victims in Vietnam, it became clear from my interviews that this is a 'new issue' (Anon., Counter-trafficking expert, international organisation, 12 October 2009), particularly given that the legislative reforms that involved the inclusion of men in the Vietnamese anti-trafficking provisions were relatively new. At the same time, recognition of this type of trafficking by the Government of Vietnam was a major impetus for the change in law. Despite the lack of a body of documented literature on the topic, one informant argued that '[internal] trafficking in men is more severe' and noted that Vietnamese men are trafficked into illegal mining [of bauxite particularly in the Central Highlands], begging by boys and also labour exploitation.

The evidence, however, is largely anecdotal, including those experiences that are documented in the secondary literature. Thi Tue Phuong Hoang, for example, refers to the trafficking of men for labour exploitation particularly from Lào Cai to China (2008). Trafficking of male Vietnamese labour migrants has also been documented by Duong and Khuat (2008: 119), who note that men involved in trafficking-like recruitment practices pay large fees in exchange for work in factories in Taiwan, South Korea, Japan and Malaysia, with the promised contract often not coming to fruition. Many leave these factories, abandoning their original paperwork and end up residing as irregular migrants in the destination country. Neither of these authors presents empirically-based evidence.

Andrew Bruce, former Chief of Mission at IOM Vietnam, conceded the general lack of knowledge about the traffic of men. Bruce stated that the most egregious known form of male trafficking involved the fishing industry, with 'misbehaving' men thrown overboard, although the scope of this form of exploitation is unknown. Another informant, of Vietnamese origin, shared his recently acquired knowledge of 41 male victims trafficked from the Central Highlands of Vietnam, identified through an 'assessment centre' in Lac Duong. The men, the informant stated, had been trafficked to work on a farm in China:

> … they were promised to get a job there and the contract was supposed to be for 3 months. But after 2 weeks, they reported to the police and they were returned. So we have recently come across male victims. I think the reason people did not talk about male victims of trafficking previously is because so few cases are reported … Now that people are being identified, I think people will be talking about it more. (Anon., Trafficking Project Coordinator, UN Agency, Vietnam, 16 October 2009)

Other reasons offered by another informant for the lack of identification of male victims included the absence of support mechanisms, shelters and reintegration services for Vietnamese men who are exploited under trafficking-like conditions:

> It is hard to know because there are no shelters for men. There are no groups working for men. We work closely with a Taiwanese partner and there are a lot of absolutely exploited men. There is just not much documented. (P. Changmanee, Regional Programme Director, Regional Anti-Human Trafficking Programme, Oxfam Quebec, 16 October 2009)

The informant's comment, although legitimate, fails to note the fact that shelters for returned Vietnamese female victims are often empty (Vijeyarasa, 2010b). There is little reason to suggest that shelters for men would be any more utilised than those currently designed only for female victims, raising doubts as to whether this would substantially influence the collection of data on male victims.

However, this same gender-bias in reintegration programmes and the impact on the identification of male victims was also noted in Ukraine. Lysenko referred to the tendency of NGOs providing services to victims to adopt names like 'Women's Consulting Centre', 'Women of Donbass', and 'Business Ladies'. She identified these non-gender neutral names as a direct barrier: 'So men could not go', with male victims feeling like 'loser[s]' in this group of primarily female victims (20 August 2009). According to Lysenko, NGOs with 'neutral' names like 'Road to Life' and 'Revival of the Nation' are at least able to 'check' if there are male victims.

Lysenko's argument is a logical one that was similarly upheld by my own data. Of the 14 male respondents to my questionnaire, eight sought reintegration support from the NGO 'Dovira Met' ('We achieve')[12] in Sumy in the northeast and four sought reintegration from the Kyiv Rehabilitation Centre. Two sought reintegration support from the 'Donetsk League of Business and Professional Women' in the southeast (both were single/unmarried and therefore not seeking reintegration support together with female partners). According to this breakdown of my data, the vast majority (12 out of 14 male respondents) found reintegration support in centres with gender-neutral names, although two male respondents accessed support from an organisation named as being for 'business women'.

In the case of Ghana, human trafficking across the border is considered to be synonymous with the traffic of women into the sex industry, whereas internal trafficking is largely understood as the traffic of children. This leaves the male trafficked population completely invisible, with 'women [...] even discussed a little more than men' (T. Amuzu, Executive Director, Legal Resource Centre, 13 August 2010). A dichotomy appears to divide discussions about irregular migration and trafficking in Ghana: discourse on irregular migrants focuses largely on men while discussions on adult trafficking appear to focus largely on women. In this case, the sex industry is the primary sector under analysis. In fact, no Ghanaian informants referred to trafficking of adult Ghanaian women outside of Ghana to any industry other than the sex industry, with trafficking into domestic work mentioned only in relation to the internal traffic of young girls.

This perception that 'trafficking' primarily concerns women and child victims was reiterated by the report of the Centre for Migration Studies at the University of Ghana discussed earlier in this book. Drawing on data from 60 informants and 60 households, the report does not state exactly how many women were involved in the research. As noted further below, one informant from the Centre indicated during our interview that they had managed to identify two women to participate. The report, which focuses on irregular migration and not trafficking, reinforces a gendered distinction drawn between irregular migration – as dominated by men – and trafficking abroad – primarily concerning women moved for sexual exploitation.

---

12   According to one informant, this name roughly translates to confidence or belief in something.

It is indisputable that trafficking affects both men and women, although the extent of the traffic of men is unclear. However, if trafficking is conceptually understood as predominantly, or almost exclusively, involving female victims of sexual exploitation rather than male victims, this might explain the increased likelihood that women have of being *identified* as victims of trafficking. What is clear is that being female is not per se a vulnerability factor and we cannot definitively conclude that being a woman increases the likelihood of being trafficked in the first place. Arguably, the manner in which gendered norms affect both male and female populations may be a more accurate descriptor of the relationship between gender and trafficking, including why people depart source countries in the first place, victims' experiences abroad as well as the industries into which they are trafficked, this being the topic of the next section.

The Gendered Nature of Exploitation

Gender-Segregated Work in Destination Countries

An often ignored area of exploration in trafficking discourse is the sectors into which people of different genders are trafficked. Gendered divisions of labour are evident across the globe (Hegewisch et al., 2010; Bettio and Verashchagina, 2009; ILO and Asian Development Bank, 2011). Data on trafficking similarly reveals that the nature of exploitation suffered among victims of trafficking is also gendered. This is unsurprising if we view trafficking within a migration spectrum and understand its relationship to the exploitation of migrant labour.

This gendered division of exploitation was evident from my own research in Vietnam, Ghana and Ukraine. As one Vietnamese informant noted:

> In the countryside, usually men earn a living for the family. In the vicinity of Hanoi or big cities, most of the temporary migrant people are women because men are supposed to do the hardest work in agriculture. They see that trading or being a porter is not their work. They do not accept to do those types of jobs so women in very difficult situations have to sacrifice themselves for jobs with low salaries and in some cases are more mobile than men. This depends on the tradition of each area. If you look at the Quảng Bình [on Vietnam's north central coast] area, most collectors are women but most cyclo drivers are men. They are coming from the same area but the division of labour is clear. (Anon., Counter-trafficking expert, international organisation, 12 October 2009)

Table 7.1   The 'gendered' nature of exploitation experienced in destination countries

Sector	Frequency	F	M	Percentage of questionnaire respondents
Agriculture	4	4	0	3.8
Begging	2	2	0	1.9
Construction	13	1	12	12.5
Cooking[13]	2	2	0	1.9
Domestic work	1	1	0	1.0
Furniture Manufacturer	1	0	1	1.0
Garment Industry	2	2	0	1.9
Factory work[14]	2	2	0	1.9
Restaurant (including waitressing)	2	0	2	1.9
Sexual exploitation	67	67	0	64.4
Exploitation in other sectors in conjunction with sexual exploitation[15]	4	4	0	3.8
Work in shop	3	3	0	2.9
Victim prevented from leaving Ukraine	1	0	1	1.0
No data	1	0	1	1.0

The gendered nature of exploitation was also evident in the data collected from my questionnaire respondents from Ukraine as indicated in Table 7.1. The majority of the male respondents (12) had been trafficked into the construction industry (see also USAID, 2010; Verité, n.d., and Surtees, 2008a which identify a similar dominance of trafficking of men into the construction industry, along with agriculture and in the case of Surtees, factory work and fishing). The other two suffered exploitation as a furniture manufacturer and a restaurant worker

---

13   One informant indicated that she worked as a cook as well as in the construction sector. This explains why the total number of figures in the frequency column accounts for 105 rather than 104 respondents.

14   Ice-cream and manufacturing.

15   Two of these informants indicated that they had been trafficked into the tea-packing industry and subsequently sexually exploited while one indicated that she had been a janitor. The fourth indicated that she had been a seller in England and Turkey before being trafficked into sexual exploitation.

respectively. No men were involved in domestic work, garment factory work, cooking or forced sexual services.

A significant number of respondents, 71 in total, accounting for 68.3 per cent of all female respondents, indicated that they had been trafficked for sexual exploitation, with four of these women exploited in other sectors in conjunction with sexual exploitation. The question concerning the industry into which victims were trafficked was worded as indicated below to avoid any impact of re-traumatisation, stigmatisation or stereotyping regarding the nature of trafficking. That is, I made a deliberate decision not to include "sexual exploitation" as a category, leaving informants to indicate "other" if they chose to share this information, as demonstrated in Figure 7.1.

---

28. When you were working overseas, what work did you do?

Garment industry/sewing   ☐

Waitress (Restaurant, bar, hotel)   ☐

Domestic work   ☐

Worked in hair or beauty salon   ☐

Worked in shop   ☐

Agriculture   ☐

Construction   ☐

Other (Specify) _____

Figure 7.1   Type of work engaged in overseas

Given the stigma often attached to such exploitation, it is perhaps surprising that there was nonetheless such a significant number of informants who marked the category of 'other' and specified some form of sexual exploitation (most commonly indicated by informants through the use of the Ukrainian phrase meaning 'sexual services', but also 'prostitution' and 'sexual entertainment'). Only one informant did not provide any information on the nature of the exploitation experienced in the destination country, while another indicated that 'border police prevented my "export" out of Ukraine' (trans.).[16] As with Ukraine, all five survey respondents

---

16 Проституция.

in Vietnam marked 'other' and indicated 'selling of prostitution services in a brothel' (trans.).[17]

Among the 71 Ukrainian women who indicate that they had be trafficked into sexual exploitation, two cases stand out for the fact that these victims indicated that they had worked as sex workers before leaving Ukraine. Both were from the Mykolaiv region, one aged 26 years and the other aged 19. Both had relatively low levels of school completion when compared to their peers. The older woman attended school up to the age of 15 years, while the younger had attended school only up to the age of 13 years. Prior to their departure from Ukraine, they had engaged in sex work for 9 years (since the age of 17) and 6 years (since the age of 13) respectively.

Importantly, both women were minors at the time they began selling sexual services – although both were adults when they were trafficked. The younger woman, who left school at the age of 13, began working as a child prostitute immediately after leaving school. Extensive literature exists that explores in depth the lack of capacity of a minor to make autonomous decisions with regard to sex work (Jeffreys, 2000; ECPAT, 1998; Montgomery in Kempadoo and Doezema, 1998). Even in jurisdictions where sex work is decriminalised, child prostitution is prohibited. While there is a limit to what we can extrapolate from the two cases, they raise the question of whether child prostitution is a vulnerability factor for trafficking. Unfortunately, many of the existing studies or reports that address both child prostitution and trafficking tend to draw on the stereotypes challenged in this book and offer limited reliable analysis for a more detailed exploration of this possible correlation (e.g. Hughes, 2002)

Returning to the gendered nature of exploitation, several informants in Ghana noted the traffic of girls into domestic servitude and some into the fishing industry. Former ILO manager Margaret Sackey explained that girls are not involved in diving or deep fishing, but are involved in fish preservation, with some being 'forced to work in commercial agriculture'. However, the majority of girls in urban areas are forced into 'domestic work' (22 July 2010). A similar view was shared by UNICEF's child protection specialist, Eric Okrah, who noted, 'in Ghana, you can have more boys than girls being sent to work in the fishing industry ... but the work that they do is also gender specific. The girls tend to do jobs that are more typical for girls, like processing the fish or selling the fish, while the boys go to do the catch'.

Breaking the Stereotypes: Sexual Exploitation of Men and the Traffic of Male Sex Workers

To give attention to the issue of sexual exploitation of male victims, I draw on two cases that I consider noteworthy as they contradict common assumptions of both victimhood and the nature of exploitation in regard to human trafficking. The first

---

17   Bán dâm trong một nhà nghỉ.

case concerned the alleged traffic of 17 Brazilian men for sexual exploitation in Spain in 2010; some of the men expected to work as models or dancers while a few expected to work as sex workers but were unaware they would be on-call 24 hours a day and moved from province to province (BBC News Europe, 2010).[18] The men were mostly in their 20s and were allegedly given stimulants to be able to provide sexual services 24 hours a day. The landlord was said to receive half of their earnings to cover food and lodgings, which according to the media coverage, was provided in mattress-cramped, neon-lit rooms. The story breaks many of the stereotypes of trafficking into sexual exploitation which may be the reason why it received media coverage in the first place.

The second case involved the sexual exploitation of two men identified in the Surtees study discussed earlier. Unlike the above example, I would argue that one of the two cases in the Surtees study stands out as a case of sexual slavery and rape. Surtees describes the experience of a Belarusian man as follows:

> The young man – aged 19 at assistance – was recruited with the offer of work in Russia. He was taken by his traffickers to a large city in northern Russia where he was kept in a private cottage on the outskirts of the city. He was informed that he had been sold to them and was to provide sexual services. He tried to resist but was chained and raped. He stayed in the cottage for two months after which time other victims were brought to the cottage and he was released. He was given a ticket home and threatened with death if he reported his experience. (IOM case file cited in Surtees, 2008a: 56)

This case is particularly noteworthy given how seldom men exploited in this way are identified and assisted. The other case in Surtees' study involved a Ukrainian man, who was recruited in a disco and promised work in Slovenia, where he worked as a dancer and was forced to provide sexual services to clients. He was obliged to drink alcohol – as a means of control and to ensure submission – and received no payment (Surtees, 2008a: 56).

The above cases present a stark contrast to the more frequently cited cases of trafficking of men into industries such as construction and agriculture. The two cases mentioned by Surtees account for only two out of around 685 cases and are evidently atypical. The experience of the man trafficked to Slovenia appears to parallel the example of the Brazilian men. The example of the 19-year-old man recruited to Russia, however, appears to be a one-off case from a methodological perspective. Although interesting, it is impossible to draw any sound conclusions from these examples which really may be outlier cases that are not representative

---

18   The 2010 US Trafficking in Persons Report notes that, '[t]here is evidence that some Brazilian transsexuals have been subjected to forced prostitution abroad'. The authors also contend that '25,000 Brazilian men are subjected to slave labor within the country, typically on cattle ranches, logging and mining camps, sugar-cane plantations, and large farms producing corn, cotton, soy, and charcoal' (US Department of State, 2010: 90).

of the norm. However, they are nonetheless important for highlighting that trafficking for sexual exploitation is not suffered only by women.

The Sex of Traffickers

Limited attention is given in the literature to the sex of recruiters.[19] This lack of attention to the role of the *female* perpetrator in recruitment has been noted elsewhere (Piper, 2005: 217). More has been written about female exploiters in destination countries, especially referring to migrant domestic workers and their relationship with female employers (Kindler, 2009 discussing Ukrainian migrant women in Poland; Dobner and Tappert, 2010 on Spain, and Anderson, 2001 on the EU generally). Erin Denton also identifies the failure of media reporting to identify the sex of traffickers. In her analysis of 191 incidents of human trafficking that were reported in international electronic media over a 6 month period, the gender of traffickers was not mentioned in 32 per cent of cases (2010: 18).

The available empirical evidence that exists reveals that recruiters tend to be female. For example, Duong and Khuat discuss the experiences of 213 female trafficked returnees, where 'the majority of traffickers were women, although occasionally there were men involved' (2006: 6). The IOM Ukraine database of its 2004 to 2006 caseload also reflects the finding that women are more often than men traffickers, with 57 per cent of recruiters having been female (A. Nguyễn, Counter-Trafficking Coordinator, IOM Mission in Ukraine, 13 August 2009). These examples recall the Australian case of Wei Tang, female Melbourne brothel owner, who was convicted of slavery offences under Australia's *Criminal Code* (see also Vijeyarasa, 2010a, and also Vijeyarasa and Bello-Villarino, 2013 for an analysis of both the Trafficking Protocol and Slavery Conventions and discussion of the legal reasoning in *Tang* and *Rantsev*).

However, these examples are not widely recognised and despite this evidence, misconceptions exist. When I asked my informant from the Government of Vietnam to describe the profile of a typical trafficker, he offered this:

> The human trafficker is a young carpenter who moves from the Red River Delta to Lào Cai province to work for small wood processing factory. He has the gift of the gab, so he is very persuasive ... During the time he is working in the factory, he meets and falls in love with a girl from Giầy ethnic minority. He tells her family that he will take her to his home village to introduce her to his

---

19   There is in fact limited research on the profiles of traffickers. Existing studies tend not to explore gender in depth. See for example a fairly general but recent study on the profile of traffickers in Tanzania (Kamazima, Kazaura, Ezekiel and Fimbo, 2011). Chenda Keo provides some demographic data in a study on Cambodia in which the author notes that among those incarcerated for human trafficking, convicted women tended to be poor and uneducated (Keo, 2013: 202).

family. In fact he has taken the girl to China and sold her to a prostitute house. (District level government official, Department of Social Evils Prevention, Lào Cai, 1 October 2009)

Similarly, writing on trafficking in Eastern Europe, Hughes draws on stereotypes in her assertions: 'The recruiters may be traffickers or work directly with traffickers. The woman may meet with a man who promises marriage at a later date. The man may use the woman himself for a short period of time, then coerce her into making pornography and later sell her to the sex industry, or he may directly deliver the woman to a brothel' (2006: 6).

Yet the figure of the female trafficker emerged particularly prominently in my research in Ukraine.[20] Lilia Koveshnikova, Director of the NGO Women of Donbass, noted, '[c]riminals who are involved in trafficking in persons are mostly women', for which she offered this explanation: 'In some cases they were former prostitutes or sometimes victims of trafficking in persons. Some of them were pressed into criminal activities by financial hardship' (Trans., Email comm., 29 July 2009). Olena Kustova from the US Embassy in Ukraine offered another reason from a legal perspective:

> I would say that according to Ukrainian legislation, for instance, a woman who has children can request the court to reduce her sentence or release her because no one can care for her small children. Sometimes traffickers take these into account and pick up recruiters who can later be released because of these circumstances ... Sometimes they are used as success stories. This woman says, 'I was there. I earned a lot of money. I purchased an apartment for my parents or myself. It is easy. Do not worry'. (2 September 2009)

Whatever the reason for what seems to be a higher number of traffickers being female (none of the suggested explanations has been verified by data or secondary research), there is a significant body of evidence that suggests that women are often involved as perpetrators of trafficking and that they may even outnumber men as recruiters. It would be particularly interesting to clarify if this finding regarding the greater incidence of female perpetrators is confirmed in instances of trafficking for both sexual as well as labour exploitation.

While this analysis of the female trafficker is brief, it is important to note the frequency with which perpetrators/traffickers are presumed to be male and how this reinforces a stereotypical gender dichotomy. This evidence against the female

---

20 In her findings on Ukraine, Rebecca Surtees also refers to mixed-sex (male/female) recruitment teams, Ukrainian nationals who had offered victims work in either Ukraine or in Russia, Japan, Poland, Turkey and Portugal (Surtees 2008, 45). The cooperation of male and female recruiters was noted in 26.7 per cent of cases assisted between 2004 and 2006. This trend was particularly pronounced in 2005 and 2006, with 26.5 per cent and 36.3 per cent of victims respectively recruited in this way.

victim/male perpetrator dichotomy directly challenges the mainstream trafficking framework as it attacks another element of the myths and misconceptions of trafficking that are not supported by existing empirical data.

The Gendered Nature of Stigma

In this final section, I look into trafficking-related stigma. Victims of trafficking are highly stigmatised, an experience which is exacerbated by the stigma associated with sex work. The concept of stigma is often associated with Gail Pheterson's (1993) earlier writings on 'whore stigma'[21] in which she discussed women's socialisation about sexual practices and concepts such as dishonour. Richard Parker and Peter Aggleton, two of the leading authors on stigma, add that stigma is about power relations, with stigma 'producing and reproducing relations of power and control' (2003: 16). Through the use of words, images and practices, certain groups and their behaviours are marginalised, with stigma used to establish a social hierarchy and social order, causing some groups to feel devalued and others superior (Parker and Aggleton, 2003: 16, 18). Stigma also plays a role in exacerbating pre-existing inequalities, whether in relation to race, gender, religion or ethnic status (Parker and Aggleton, 2003: 19; see also the much earlier writings on stigma by Canadian sociologist Erving Goffman, 1963). In the next pages, I analyse how this stigma affects men and women and I demonstrate in particular how the conflation of sex work and trafficking has had a stigmatising effect that has generated a further gender bias in the mainstream trafficking framework.

Stigma, Sex Work, Victimhood and Silence

The examples of Vietnam, Ghana and Ukraine reveal the importance of analysing the impact of stigma on victim identification, self-identification and what we know about trafficking. In the case of Vietnam, this stigma is aggravated by the government's labelling of trafficking as a social evil, whereas in Ukraine, it appears to derive from social perceptions. In Ghana, my informants tended to apply labels to both sex workers and victims and showed considerable discomfort in discussing sex work.

Of the three countries where I conducted my research, criminalisation of sex work and trafficking have arguably had the greatest impact on creating stigma in Ghana. According to the Assistant Director of Migration from the Ghana Immigration Services, Judith Dzokoto, upon return some victims are 'not treated

---

21   There is an increasing tendency of feminist activists and academics to reclaim the language of 'whore'. See for example the use of 'whore' by Luette Chavez, who drew attention to the intersections of race, class and transphobia towards sex workers at the *Berkeley Journal of Gender, Law & Justice* symposium entitled 'Uncovered: The Policing of Sex Work' (Alsgaard, 2011: 200).

like victims, they are treated like criminals. So it is difficult for them to come forward unless you provide reassurance when they return' (17 November 2010).

I discussed at length the issue of research on sex work and sex workers in Ghana with one informant. An academic with the Centre for Migration Studies at the University of Ghana, the informant referred to failed attempts of fellow researchers to obtain first-hand empirical data from women presumed to be working as sex workers in Koforidua in eastern Ghana. He referred to not only the unwillingness of the presumed madam to speak with the researchers but also to her denial that her workers were engaged in sex work in the first place as the main reasons.

The informant's story raises a range of issues that cannot be explored at length in this book. Perhaps these women were not sex workers, a situation that speaks to the widespread myths and rumours surrounding sex work in Ghana. Perhaps this experience reflects the unintended role of researchers in undermining the anonymity of sex workers who might choose not to be public about their work and where researchers might give priority to their own goals over the rights and best interests of informants including their safety (on this point, see Harrison, 2006 and Andrees and van der Linden, 2005, but on trafficking for sexual exploitation and not sex work). Finally it may simply reflect the illegality and therefore silencing of sex work in the country.

Similar comments regarding how stigma is a barrier for these sex workers to speak to researchers were made by other informants. This included victims' unwillingness to talk about actual experiences abroad beyond showing photos of Europe (E. Peasah, IOM Ghana, Counter-Trafficking Field Manager, technical Cooperation Department, 21 July 2010). The stifling of discourse on female victims in Ghana has the direct consequence of reinforcing the child victim archetype.

I also found evidence of labelling and categorisation in Ghana, which has already been documented in terms of HIV-related stigma in the country (see Mill, 2001; Mill, 2003). For example, one informant while talking about the 'high' numbers of Ghanaian migrant sex workers who in the past worked in Cote d'Ivoire explained that these girls are referred to as 'Monrovia girls', having travelled west through Liberia (Eric Peasah, IOM Ghana, Counter-Trafficking Field Manager, technical Cooperation Department, 21 July 2010). Another informant commented that – as an irregular migrant – if you have ever travelled that way through Libya, you are presumed to have engaged in sex work (Anon., Centre for Migration Studies, University of Ghana, 18 November 2010). The informant went on to note, '[t]hey will deny that they ever travelled to Libya because it is a problem. If the person wants to get married, it is difficult'. I would suggest a link between this discomfort with the existence of sex work and the migrant sex worker, and trafficking-related stigma. What results is a very limited and non-evidence based understanding of the demographics of victims in Ghana. This is exacerbated by the fact that little distinction is made between voluntary sex work and trafficking for sexual exploitation.

Victim blaming is also an issue in Ukraine, where the media was critiqued by one of my informants for making 'stigmatising statements'. The informant continued by noting that 'very often the blame is still on the victims which is a big problem because that then leads to victims not being able to come out and identify and victims suffering deeper trauma' (T. Ivanyuk, Counter-trafficking specialist, IOM Ukraine, 3 September 2009). Two other informants similarly referred to victim blaming, with one contending that this 'perception – that it is their own fault – probably feeds into prosecution' (Anon., Senior management, Inter-governmental organisation, 27 August 2009). Another argued that the perception that '"they were just prostitutes and that it was their own fault" […] has changed somewhat but it has not [changed] wholly' (J. Labovitz, former Chief of Mission, IOM Ukraine, 27 August 2009). By influencing criminal prosecutions and how victim's agency is discussed in these cases, I would contend that stigma in Ukraine plays a direct role in encouraging testimony focused on the 'coerced victim', with the voluntary victim otherwise blamed and punished for this voluntariness.

Trafficking and sex work-related stigma is similarly evident in Vietnam. Earlier in this book, I have discussed the impact of the designation of sex work as a 'social evil' and the related stigmatisation on victim identification. As one shelter staff noted:

> Returnees seem too often [to] be affected by stigma with all their surroundings. They generally walk the streets wondering who knows of where they've been and what they've done. One female told us about how she was refused nail service because the nail technician knew that she had been in Cambodia and that anyone who had come back from Cambodia must be HIV/AIDS infected. Families of the victims also have been known to be ashamed of their daughters and reject them upon return. (Shelter staff, Vietnam (cited in Vijeyarasa 2010b, 93)

However, saying that there is stigma does not mean that this stigma represents an insurmountable obstacle for reintegration or a deterrent to trafficking in the first place. In a study conducted in 2002 in Thailand, one social worker was quoted as saying: 'The parents here say, "The problem isn't that our daughter sells her body (khai tua), it's that we have no food to eat"' (Rende Taylor, 2005: 416). Rende Taylor, author of the study, concluded that '[f]rom this perspective, the filial piety of the daughter outweighs any stigma. Once a woman returns there is not much talk about her work experience unless she returns as a recruiter or agent and brings up the subject herself' (Rende Taylor, 2005: 416).

Rende Taylor cites authors who have drawn similar conclusions regarding sex work stigma in other areas of Thailand. Sara Peracca, John Knodel and Chanpen Saengtienchai (1998), for example, contend that the stigma is not sufficient to have an impact on a former sex worker's chances of marriage. In some cases, the men even appear attracted to the woman's earnings. Rende Taylor, nonetheless notes one study in which the authors argue that these workers have the reputation of being 'bad women' with diseases (Van-Landingham and Trujillo, 2002), highlighting that we cannot generalise as to the source, nature or impact of the stigma. Findings such as these suggest that stigma clearly varies – perhaps from country to country or regionally – but in this instance has a notable impact on female victims and shapes the sexually exploited female victim archetype.

Male Victim Stigma

There is significantly less research on male victim stigma particularly outside of the context of male homosexuality. There is an almost complete gap when it comes to the stigma experienced by male victims of trafficking. As noted above, the only study I have identified that addresses male trafficking victim stigma is that of Rebecca Surtees, discussed earlier in this chapter, on the trafficking of Belarusian and Ukrainian men. As noted by Surtees, '[s]ome men may not see themselves as trafficked; others may feel that their agreement to go abroad makes them complicit with their trafficker. Further, the terminology of "trafficking victim" and the social construction of "victimhood" may be problematic for some men to accept and apply to their situation' (2008, 9).

This is consistent with existing research that fear of stigma may also be a barrier to men seeking help (Chandra and Minkovitz, 2006; Deane and Chamberlain, 1994; Mahalik, Good and Englar-Carlson, 2003; Pederson and Vogel, 2007). As a result, men hold less favourable views of face-to-face counselling and arguably those men who are most in need are most at-risk of underutilising such services (Pederson and Vogel, 2007).

Findings from my own fieldwork in both Ghana and Ukraine support the notion of stigma being 'gendered'. This stigma has a direct impact on the extent to which male victims access reintegration services and, through that process, are identified and counted as victims of trafficking. In relation to reintegration or prevention programmes, one informant noted: 'A man going forward and saying, "I am unemployed and I need assistance", this is not likely. It is more often the women who go. In most of our empowerment activities, we have less than one per cent of men' (Dr M. Sackey, Former ILO-IPEC, Ghana 22 July 2010).

Similar comments were made by several informants in Ukraine. When it comes to male identification, '[m]en are less willing to recognise themselves as victims. Men are less visible. They tend to keep to themselves whereas women come out easier and bond with others' (T. Ivanyuk, Counter-trafficking specialist, IOM Ukraine, 3 September 2009).

The gender of the social worker was also noted as relevant. Referring to one victim from the Donetsk region, a psychologist at a reintegration centre shared the view that male victim bravado is a challenge when reintegration services are provided by women. She continued by noting:

> They say they were cheated or mention labour migration but nothing specifically to do with trafficking. To find out what actually happened [to them], about freedom of movement, whether they were beaten […] is difficult. They are scared because the traffickers or guards almost killed the person who tried to speak out. But for them to tell a woman or even a man that they were scared

because of what happened to other victims is really very difficult. (Dr I. Lysenko, Psychologist, IOM Rehabilitation Centre, Kyiv, 20 August 2009)

Similar views were shared by the Director of a local NGO who referred to 'shame' as the main barrier to identifying what otherwise appears to be a large number of Ukrainian men trafficked from the Lugansk Oblast (L. Koveshnikova, Director, Women of Donbass, Lugansk Oblast, Trans., Email comm., 29 July 2009).

These findings reveal a very important but often forgotten gendered aspect of trafficking: male victim stigma can be a fundamental challenge to male victim identification. If stigma for trafficked men is proven to be more powerful an inhibitor for self-identification than stigma for female victims – as suggested by several of my informants – this would likely result in an overrepresentation of women as victims in trafficking statistics. This may have widespread implications for data that, similar to my own, are collected from self-identified victims and this potential bias must be taken into account. This is also relevant when assessing the veracity of the mainstream trafficking framework which, on many occasions, relies on these cumulative statistics to support the possible misconception that trafficking overwhelmingly affects women.

Conclusion

This chapter aimed to critique the assumption that victims are women, exploited and taken advantage of by male perpetrators. Nevertheless, gendered patterns of migration are a reality and many stakeholders working on trafficking argue that gender inequality *directly* correlates to increased vulnerability to trafficking. This may be based on the need to escape inequality and violence in the home or pursue opportunities in response to obligations to provide for one's family. However, many of the correlations drawn between gender inequality and vulnerability to trafficking are often unfounded. Domestic violence is one example where empirical evidence is severely lacking. If we are to pursue an evidenced-based framework, such misconceptions must be questioned.

The 'non-gendering' of male victims is also a challenge in trafficking discourse: if male victims are discussed at all, their gender is rarely analysed. There is, however, increasing anecdotal evidence emerging and a growing body of empirical data, including in Ukraine, Vietnam, Belarus, the Philippines and the Middle East, that justify the demands for better analysis of male victims. Yet in Ghana a strong perception continues to exist that trafficking relates to children (and in some cases the sexual exploitation of adult women), whereas exploited irregular migrants are men. In this respect, there are stark global differences in terms of the extent to which different countries recognise male victims of trafficking.

Several elements of the gendering of trafficking discussed above are unsurprising. Men and women tend to be trafficked into gender-stereotypical industries. However, even here there are some exceptions, with female victims, for example, those from Ukraine, also trafficked into such sectors as agriculture and construction. However, the assumption that the majority of *identified* victims are trafficked into sexual exploitation was confirmed by my own fieldwork. Almost 66 per cent of all female Ukrainian respondents to my questionnaire, or 61.5 per cent of my total pool of respondents indicated that they had been trafficked into sexual exploitation. All five of my informants from Vietnam had been trafficked for sexual exploitation. While it is therefore not difficult to see why the sexually exploited victim archetype persists, we cannot ignore that we know very little about unidentified victims and that nearly 40 per cent of my surveyed population in Ukraine were trafficked for purposes other than sexual exploitation. In general, too little attention is paid to trafficking for non-sexual exploitation in the mainstream trafficking framework. In addition, more research should be done on the issue of stigma in the trafficking context, particularly because it plays a role in fostering such gender bias in the mainstream framework and reinforcing various myths and misconceptions about victims.

I believe that my analysis in this chapter is among the few in-depth studies of gender assumptions of trafficking. This chapter has attempted to give an overview of the multi-dimensional character of gender within trafficking, an issue otherwise understood as a linear relation – gender inequality increases vulnerability to trafficking. Among the several findings presented, the female trafficker is one that is particularly ignored. Although evident in the case law and databases of trafficking victims, this gender dimension of trafficking has received minimal attention and hardly any analysis.

Despite all these caveats, we can conclude that, in general terms, there is some truth to the female victim archetype and that gender inequality may correlate in certain circumstances with individual cases of trafficking. This may be the case, for example, when it comes to the expectations to provide for one's family. Nonetheless, such manifestations of the inequality suffered by women may also impact men, albeit in different ways. Further, we do not have any certainty as to the scope of trafficking in men globally. Nevertheless, the existing data on male victims, male victim stigma, the non-stereotypical industries into which both men and women are trafficked and the female perpetrator provide substantial evidence to discredit the mainstream female victim archetype.

PART III
An Alternative Approach
to Trafficking

Chapter 8
The Shortcomings of a Criminal Justice Focus

The chapters of this book demonstrate how the mainstream trafficking framework is unrepresentative of the various dimensions of human trafficking. What results is the promotion of scientifically unfounded causes of the practice. This is exacerbated by the fact that trafficking means different things to different people, including different actors directly involved in anti-trafficking interventions on the ground. For some, trafficking involves the kidnapping and selling of girls. For others, trafficking involves the deception of a woman who is convinced into accepting a fraudulent offer of work abroad, or lower pay or less freedom of movement than previously negotiated. Finally, others see trafficking as the exploitation of women and men who prove to be unlucky when undertaking a migratory adventure abroad in pursuit of money and social betterment.

The variations in these definitions reflect the different lenses or approaches adopted when it comes to the topic of trafficking, whether these are feminist, women's rights, gender and development, labour, migration-oriented or a combination of the above. However, an emphasis on the criminal underworld and the organised crime component of trafficking is evident throughout the existing literature. Given that criminal law is the frame of reference for many governments, as well as for the UN Office on Drugs and Crime (UNODC), it is fair to say that this viewpoint continues to dominate current discourse.

As noted throughout this book, significant shortcomings emerge from this criminal justice approach. In this chapter, I elaborate on the shortcomings that have resulted from a Trafficking Protocol driven primarily by the need to combat organised crime or 'trafficking syndicates'. Victim assistance and even prevention are de-prioritised when compared to the stronger obligations on states parties to fulfil the criminal law provisions of the Trafficking Protocol (Todres, 2011: 57). Jonathan Todres highlights, for example, how 'issues of poverty, development, and equality collectively merit only a single sentence in the Trafficking Protocol, with no detail on steps to be taken or specific requirements on states parties vis-à-vis these issues'. This can be compared to the extensive language on acts that must be criminalised, the need for law enforcement training, law enforcement information exchange and border control measures (Todres, 2011: 58).

It is also important to recall that the definition of trafficking in the Trafficking Protocol is applied in multi-disciplinary circles which are not only legal in nature. In light of its use beyond the law, at a representational level, the Trafficking Protocol acts to dilute the attention paid to the active drivers behind the victim's decision-making, undermining the dual identity of agent and victim (Vijeyarasa, 2010e: 218). An individual can voluntarily choose to migrate, initiate and undertake the process of migration, find themselves in trafficking-like conditions and yet still be deemed a victim, deserving redress for exploitation suffered following those decisions. What follows is an analysis of the criminal law approach, including its role in driving a non-victim-centred understanding of trafficking. In the next and final chapter of this book, I lay out steps towards a more inclusive, victim-centred approach for understanding human trafficking.

The Criminal Underworld of Sex and Exploitation

It is unsurprising that the Trafficking Protocol adopts a criminal law lens, particularly given its annexation to an Organised Crime Convention. For some practitioners, the criminal law focus is excusable, justified by the valid goal of securing successful prosecutions and facilitating clear steps for action by national-level actors. These include the identification and arrest of the accused and rescue of victims (Chambliss, 1964; Potter and Kappeler, 1998; and Rafter, 1990 cited in Farrell and Fahy, 2009: 618).

However, the sensationalism that accompanies this criminal focus is a direct contributor to the mainstream trafficking framework. Once described by Interpol as the fastest growing industry, even authors known for more nuanced writing describe trafficking's annual 'guestimated' turnover to be USD7–10 billion per year (Cwikel and Hoban, 2005: 306). These authors blame growth of the internet and more accessible telecommunications for 'generating a supply of women, generally from economically disadvantaged countries' (Cwikel and Hoban, 2005: 306).

It is clear too that this emphasis on the 'criminal underworld' directly contributes to the fascination with and over-emphasis on trafficking for sexual exploitation. Academics describe efforts to move sex workers between brothels to avoid police detection 'and to meet the demand for new and exotic women' (Cwikel and Hoban, 2005: 307). Sara Elizabeth Dill writes '[i]nternational crime syndicates benefit from trafficking, as it is a less risky yet more profitable form of organised crime ... [E]very day, investigations uncover brothels, strip clubs, and other venues where illegal trafficking in human beings has forced women and children into sexual slavery' (2006: 12).

From one of the most sensationalist pairs of academics comes this statement: 'Trafficking occurs because of a transnational political criminal nexus, which is comprised of individual criminals, organized crime groups, corrupt police and governmental officials, foreign governments, and NGOs' (Hughes and Denisova, 2001: 1). Migration, socio-economic contexts, cultural factors and women's and men's agency are all ignored. Rather, '[t]he networks are highly organized, have large-scale operations, and are connected to corrupt officials. The networks delegate specialized tasks related to trafficking in women, such as recruitment of women, preparation of documents, organization of travel, and delivery of the women' (Hughes and Denisova, 2001: 6).

From an evidentiary point of view, there is a divergence of opinions as to the extent to which large-scale criminal networks are involved in human trafficking. Nonetheless, academics such as Joyce Outshoorn argue that there are indeed widespread criminal networks to the extent that the 'framing of prostitution-related migration as a matter of women travelling and looking for a livelihood' is too simplistic (2005: 148).

There is nonetheless a growing and substantial body of literature that recognises the centrality of both migration and labour to trafficking. Moreover, the above analysis is not intended to suggest the criminal law has no role. Criminal law is fact essential in the prosecution of what may in some cases amount to heinous crimes. However, my main preoccupation is the use of this criminal justice lens to frame a broader, multi-dimensional discourse. Moreover, given the evident agendas of various stakeholders involved in human trafficking debates, this narrow focus opens the door for its use to sensationalise, stereotype and at its most extreme, criminalise both trafficking *and* its victims.

Elements of the Crime

As the following analysis shows, there are several ways in which the criminal justice approach fosters the myths and misconceptions that were questioned in Part II of this book. In particular, I find fault with several elements of the Trafficking Protocol's definition, including the overall approach to migration and movement among criminal law practitioners, as well as its provisions relating to 'abuse of a position of vulnerability' and 'for the purpose of exploitation'. Analysis of the shortcomings reveals why we need to move beyond a law-enforcement model in our understanding of what constitutes human trafficking.

A Focus on the Trafficker Over and Above the Victim

The primary goal of the Convention and its Trafficking Protocol is the successful prosecution of the alleged trafficker. The definition of trafficking therefore focuses on both the actions (*actus rea*) of the trafficker(s) and their 'mental element', or the purpose of the crime (*mens rea*). According to the Trafficking Protocol, an individual can be prosecuted for trafficking for their involvement in any one aspect of the actions that lead to trafficking: the recruitment, the transportation, the transfer, harbouring or receipt of persons.

It might be conjectured that the treatment of the trafficker as the active and most central individual is no different from how a criminal prosecution treats a murdered individual as passive by focusing on the acts and intentions (*mens rea* and *actus rea*) of the murderer. The criminal law approach also appears workable from a legal and justice perspective, allowing for perpetrators to be identified, arrested and tried and standards of *mens rea* and *actus rea* to be applied. However, a criminal justice lens deflects attention away from the decision-making process of the individual migrant that may have led them to engage in unsafe and risky migration – and even negotiate with the trafficker – when faced with barriers to legal migration abroad.

Namely, the criminal justice lens acts to radically skew the 'facts' of trafficking and our perception of victims. The victim is moved by the trafficker and they are framed as playing a limited, if any role, in their own movement. A victim's voluntariness, the expectations that were established before their departure, and a nuanced understanding of what amounts to a vulnerability or risk-factor for potential migrants and the drivers of their migratory decisions are lost when this criminal-justice oriented definition is the guiding framework for our understanding of trafficking. Indeed, this begs the question, why have we allowed a criminal law definition to provide the lens through which we view and understand human trafficking, an issue that can only properly be addressed from a multi-disciplinary approach? Outside of the criminal law, a trafficking framework must allow for greater attention to the active role of the individual and give scope to determining the autonomy and drivers of their decision-making.

The 'Movement' of the Victim is Inherent to Trafficking

Across the trafficking literature, we can see how many academics and policy makers use the term 'movement' – in my view correctly – to capture the terms 'recruitment, transportation, transfer, harbouring or receipt of persons'. For example, Moshoula Capous Desyllas notes that, '[t]rafficking in persons is considered to be the forced, illegal movement of people across national and international borders' (2007: 57). Thanh-Dam Truong also frames her discussion on trafficking around 'countering the illicit movement of, and trade in people' (2006: 21). Other authors make similar statements: 'Increasing human movements in the new globalized environment have both positive and negative consequences. Trafficking in human beings is one of these negative effects. An emerging transnational crime problem, human trafficking occurs in almost every part of the world' (Demir and Finckenauer, 2010: 58). This leads Aika van der Kleij to conclude: 'Trafficking occurs if there is a movement of a person, through deceptive, coercive or other means into a situation of sexual exploitation, i.e. prostitution' (2002: 14).[1]

---

1   The same can be said of the United Nations. UNESCAP note that, '[t]rafficking, migration and labour exploitation are interrelated concepts'. While noting that movement is not a necessary component of trafficking as per the criminal law approach described in this chapter, the report continues by stating that '[t]rafficking in persons often occurs in connection with the movement of people from rural areas to urban areas or across international boundaries' (2003: 26). Movement has been the chosen language in the definition of trafficker given by the UN Special Rapporteur on Trafficking, Joy Ngozi Ezeilo citing the United Nations Global Initiative to Fight Human Trafficking (UNGIFT):

When it comes to the terms 'transportation' or 'transfer', the use of the term movement is not disputed for obvious reasons. However, criminal justice practitioners in particular emphasise that, from a legal perspective, a person may be found guilty of trafficking without the element of movement being present. This becomes clear with the examples of harbouring or receipt. While a victim may have been trafficked from Thailand to Australia and, by their account, their experience has involved their movement from one country to another, for the purpose of a prosecution, a perpetrator can be prosecuted for trafficking even if they only played the role of harbouring the victim while they were in Australia, or if they received the victim at the destination point in Australia. That is, this person can be considered a trafficker even if they played no role in the actual movement of the victim from Thailand. This has resulted in authors, writing from that criminal law mind-set, that 'trafficking does not require movement' (Gallagher, 2010: 31–2).[2] This approach is understandable from a criminal law perspective. Seen through this lens, trafficking involves numerous actors, all of whom should be targeted for prosecution regardless of the particular role they played in the victim's experience of exploitation.

While this approach to movement has logic from a criminal law perspective, it is not helpful in ensuring a holistic approach to trafficking, nor a victim-centred one, particularly when the Trafficking Protocol's definition is applied outside of the

---

'Third parties involved in the process (recruiters, agents, transporters and others who participate knowingly in the movement of persons for the purposes of exploitation)' (Ngozi Ezeilo, 2009: ¶ 53). The Drugs and Crime Prevention Committee of Victoria in Australia, recognising the distinction between the legal requirements and reality, has also noted, '[c]ontrary to popular belief, trafficking does not necessarily require the movement of people across borders, although in most cases it does. Nor is it to be confused with people smuggling and more broadly illegal migration, although sometimes it may also involve this. The issue has been further confounded with stories surrounding refugees, entry of illegal migrants and "mail order brides"' (Drugs and Crime Prevention Committee, 2010: 4).

2 Gallagher writes, ' ... the references to harbouring and receipt operate to bring not just the process (recruitment, transportation, transfer) but also the end situation of trafficking within the definition. In other words, whereas buying or otherwise taking possession of an individual through any of the stipulated means for purposes of exploiting would fall within the definition of trafficking, maintaining an individual in a situation of exploitation through any stipulated means would, according to the plain meaning of the text, also amount to trafficking' (2010: 30). It is the use of a plain text reading in contexts outside of the criminal law that is problematic. Moreover, Gallagher continues by contending that, 'while the text [of the *travaux préparatoires*] does not support such a conclusion, it could be read such that you do not need any preceding process and you do not need cases where an individual is "trafficked *into* the exploitative situation" i.e. a workplace that has changed from acceptable to exploitative could count as "potential trafficking without any preceding process"' (2010: 31). This is an extremely broad interpretation and the author fails to note the challenge of distinguishing legally between trafficking and exploitative labour. As the author herself concedes, there is no evidence in the *travaux préparatoires* 'to support a contention that this is what the drafters had in mind' (2010: 31).

criminal law. Trafficking, from the victims' perspective, involves their movement from their place of origin to the destination point. It is an act that involves their recruitment in a particular location, transportation from, transfer to, harbouring along the way or receipt at the end of a journey to the destination point, regardless of how many actors are involved or what role they played.

The importance of understanding movement as central to trafficking is affirmed by the fact that the Trafficking Protocol was enacted pursuant to a convention on transnational crime. The transnational nature of trafficking highlights the reality that the victim's vulnerability to exploitation is exacerbated by the fact that they are not in their home or source country or locality. This 'foreigner' status, including the potential to be deported as an 'illegal migrant' and the ability of a trafficker to exploit this potential as well as possible language and cultural barriers, are key factors in their vulnerability. To understand trafficking as the 'movement' of victims by means of fraud or coercion for the purpose of exploitation reflects the holistic experience of the victim from point A to B. Movement, therefore, should be understood as an element as inherent to trafficking as it is to migration.

The Abuse of Power and Position of Vulnerability

The Trafficking Protocol identifies 'abuse of power or a position of vulnerability' as an additional means by which a person can be trafficked. A narrower formulation, 'abuse of authority', appeared in the International Convention for the Suppression of the 'White Slavery Traffic' of 1910. At the time, the drafters noted that the language of 'authority' should be understood to recognise that male family members may exercise power over female members as well as the power that parents exercise over children. The drafters therefore assumed that inequality within the home is a driver of human trafficking, despite the questionable evidentiary links discussed in Chapter 7. 'Abuse of power or a position of vulnerability' is, however, unique to the Trafficking Protocol, this language not appearing in earlier documents. Both phrases focus on the trafficker's state of mind and their intention to exploit or take advantage of the victim's vulnerabilities. They thereby perpetuate the notion of the weak victim who lacks agency.

Some assistance in understanding the intention of the drafters is provided in the *travaux préparatoires* to the Protocol. These explicitly state: 'The reference to abuse of a position of vulnerability is understood to refer to any situation in which the person involved has no real or acceptable alternative but to submit to the abuse involved' (UNODC, 2006: 347). However, as discussed earlier in this book, for many abolitionists who seek an end to prostitution, entry into the sex sector arises from socio-economic exclusion which leaves – in this case – women with little alternative other than to sell their bodies through a system of exploitation (e.g. Farley, 2004; Raymond, 2004; Jeffreys, 1997; Balos, 2004). For pro-sex work defenders of the 'agency' argument, however, sex work for the migrant sex worker is a choice that can offer more income and freedom than the alternatives at home (e.g. Busza, 2004: 240–41; Piscitelli, 2008). This leaves open the question of what is a 'real and acceptable alternative'. This, in turn, is related to the question of what amounts to consent in the context of sex work and migration and how much voluntariness can we believe is exercised by the undocumented migrant in her entry into sex work (Vijeyarasa, 2010a: 15). Interpretation is open to moral judgment.

However, a more fundamental challenge arises from presuming that victims lack power and suffer from particular vulnerabilities when compared to non-victims. As we have seen in Part II, this entails a misconception of the demographics of victims. This book suggests higher levels of education than otherwise presumed among victims. A relationship of inverse causality would suggest victims are more educated than their non-trafficked peers. The evidence contained in this book also reveals the existence of economic opportunities at home for many migrants who are later exploited by traffickers. Victims may not be driven by economic necessity but rather legitimate desires for social and economic betterment. These expectations give rise to deception. In summary, many of the stories of the victims described in the previous chapters fail to reflect a 'position of vulnerability'. What meaning should be given to the phrase 'abuse of power or of a position of vulnerability' when particular presumed vulnerabilities may not exist?

The UNODC Model Law on Human Trafficking (UNODC, 2009a) proposes a fairly detailed list of situations that could be considered an abuse of a position of vulnerability, whereby the trafficker(s) takes advantage of the vulnerable position of a person arising from:

   i. Having entered the country illegally or without proper documentation; or
  ii. Pregnancy or any physical or mental disease or disability of the person, including addiction to the use of any substance; or
 iii. Reduced capacity to form judgements by virtue of being a child, illness, infirmity or a physical or mental disability; or
 iv. Promises or giving sums of money or other advantages to those having authority over a person; or
  v. Being in a precarious situation from the standpoint of social survival; or
 vi. Other relevant factors.

The passage continues by recommending national-level definitions that focus on the intention of the offender and their awareness of the victim's vulnerability. The UNODC Model Law notes that this is 'easier to prove, as it will not require an inquiry into the state of mind of the victim but only that the offender was aware of the vulnerability of the victim and had the intention to take advantage of it' (UNODC Model Law, 2009: 9–10). Often seen as victim-friendly, it is also practical from a criminal justice perspective and the goal of prosecuting traffickers by interrogating their *actus* and *mens rea* as discussed earlier.

However, the above definition of vulnerability in the context of trafficking appears unsubstantiated. No study of trafficking that I have identified evidences the higher vulnerability of pregnant women, to offer one example. The findings in Part II with respect to absolute poverty also shed doubt on the suitability of including living in a "precarious situation" with respect to "social survival" in the definition. On a positive note, there is some attention paid in this UNODC Model Law provision to the possibility that a victim may enter the destination country voluntarily, with no need to show coercion or force; vulnerability can arise where a person illegally entered the country or lacked the proper documentation.

As a result of the need to fit cases of trafficking within the boundaries of the definition of trafficking offered in the Trafficking Protocol, we repeatedly see emphasis placed on demographic characteristics that may have no evidenced-based causal relationship to the situation of exploitation that later arises. The vulnerability of victims that is indisputably relevant to human trafficking is their migration status. Rather than, or in addition to, the criminal law framework, there is much value in focusing our attention on the migration status of victims, whether regular or irregular migrants, and the risks that this status poses for the protection of their human rights. To the contrary, assuming that victims suffer from family-related, social or economic vulnerabilities necessarily presumes that these are causes of trafficking without a sound evidence-base.

An Organised Intention to Exploit

The Trafficking Protocol's definition demands movement, transport, transfer or harbouring *for the purpose of exploitation*. Underlying this is a premise that trafficking necessarily involves a network of individuals, all driven towards this central purpose. While conceding that the scope of transnational crime and individual trafficking webs are unknown, authors still suggest that such movement necessarily involves multiple transit points and perhaps multiple countries and therefore some level of organisation (Putt, 2007:2).

However, exploitation in the destination country may have never been the intention of the 'trafficker' or any other individuals who assisted, supported or arranged the movement of a victim from their point of departure. The friend who provides a potential migrant with contacts in the destination country, the agent who secures the would-be migrant sex worker a visa or a mode of transport, or the parents who finance their child's journey, may have had no intention or certainly no desire for that journey to end in a situation of exploitation. In many instances, the roles these individual play may be entirely unrelated to the victim's experience in the destination country and they may themselves have a vested interest in the migrants' success. Such actors would not be prosecutable under most national laws addressing trafficking precisely because they were engaged to move the victim, possibly by the victim themselves, and had no notion of the possibility of, or intention for, the victim to be exploited in the destination country.

Yet the focus on the methods adopted by these actors, who are in fact migration agents and in some cases may meet the definition of smuggler, feeds the notion that trafficking is a form of organised crime – that separate individuals involved in the process are necessarily linked in a network. As a result, the literature describes trafficking's links to 'fraud, kidnapping, identity crime, bribery and corruption, and deprivation of liberty – all of which have to be successfully coordinated and managed clandestinely to ensure that the operation is run sufficiently effectively and often enough to generate profit' (Putt, 2007: 2; see also Bell, 2001). Such a conclusion brings to mind films like *Human Trafficking* (2005) and *Taken* (2008) critiqued earlier in this book for their incorrect and sensationalist portrayals of traffickers, their networks and the naive victim. Moreover, it deflects attention from the underlying socio-economic context that shapes the migratory decisions of potential migrants, shifting our focus away from the migration, labour and human rights issues that sit at the heart of human trafficking. Barriers to legal migration and inadequate protection by states of migrants working within their borders are the more central concerns.

Conclusion

To encompass the complex realities of human trafficking accurately, an alternative definition is required. This would involve a shift in focus away from the trafficker who takes criminal advantage of the so-called vulnerabilities of victims. Instead, greater attention needs to be placed on trafficking's intimate connection with the desire of potential migrants who seek adventure, economic and social opportunities and relatively improved circumstances when compared to what is offered at home. This shift allows us to better appreciate how it is that an individual's migrant status in particular – which is often irregular – gives rise to heightened vulnerability to exploitation.

This discussion raises legitimate concerns about the limitations of a criminal justice approach to trafficking and the need for a more migration and victim-centred one. However, this simultaneously begs the question of whether such a shift in orientation can actually be implemented from a legal perspective, whether criminal or civil. In the following chapter, I provide suggestions for an alternative legal lens to the current focus on the perpetrator taking 'criminal advantage' of the victim and discuss how this non-perpetrator, victim-centred definition of human trafficking can be used in legal and non-legal contexts. In particular, I recommend the use of a contract law approach to frame deception and redress and emphasise the need for an overarching human rights and particularly labour rights framework.

Chapter 9

The 'Voluntary' Victim, Unmet Expectations and Contractual and Labour Rights Redress

This book demonstrates the need for a more inclusive framework for understanding human trafficking. Victim voluntariness, their unmet expectations, a nuanced understanding of what amounts to a vulnerability or risk-factor and the drivers of migratory decisions are lost when a criminal-justice oriented definition is the guiding framework for our understanding of trafficking in all contexts.

My focus in this chapter, however, remains on the legal treatment of human trafficking. Here I explain why courts should take into account the 'unmet expectations' of victims that are formed on the basis of their negotiations[1] prior to departure or upon arrival in the destination country. While several authors have asserted the need to move away from a criminal justice framework, this simple assertion occludes the problem that arises in the migration framework. It is essential for such a migration-centred approach to retain a central concern for injustice and exploitation at its core. The notion of unmet expectations is a potential path for its implementation.

Recognising and analysing the expectations of the migrant that were in fact set by the would-be employer, recruiter, transporter etc., could help courts to establish the redress to which victims are entitled. This was seen in the Australian case of *R v Dobie* (2010) in which the Supreme Court of Queensland used evidence of the victims' negotiations with their trafficker – by email and text – about their conditions of work in Australia to determine the extent to which the intention of Mr Keith Dobie differed from the expectations that were created in the minds of his Thai victims.

An alternative definition of trafficking is provided in this chapter. In endeavouring to develop such a definition, one point needs reiterating. This concerns the variable levels of autonomy exercised by individuals when making decisions and how these variances reflect upon victim responsibility and redress. As I have argued throughout this book, evidence of a victim's voluntary role in making decisions that lead to exploitative labour should never render 'victimhood', or redress, impossible. A victim's negotiations with their trafficker(s) and their expectations concerning work and living conditions in destination countries are highly relevant in establishing their entitlement to, and scope of that redress. In this respect, strictly from a legal point of view, the Trafficking Protocol is correct –

---

1   One challenge that arises is the question of whether such negotiations are explicit. In some cases, victims may have simply accepted the conditions that were offered to them.

although its definition is not faultless – in preventing such consent from being used in a trafficker's defence where there is evidence of fraud or deception. However, from a social sciences perspective, this consent is central to our recognition of the 'victim-agent' whose autonomous decision-making discredits the naive and unknowing victim archetype.

Turning to Principles from Contract Law: Unmet Expectations, Deception and Redress

If we wish to retain the law as our lens for analysis, a contractual approach to trafficking may offer value. When one enters into a contract to buy a house, or – to better parallel the nature of human trafficking – a contract for employment to work as a waitress or a construction worker, the contract may be rendered void if the conditions of work are misrepresented or if the potential employee is deceived as to the nature of the object of the contract. While the agreement may have *initially* been entered into voluntarily by a migrant seeking social or economic betterment at the destination point, the individual may be recognised as a victim of fraud or deception and entitled to compensation in some circumstances. In my view, trafficking – when analysed from a legal perspective – should be considered from a similar lens. Indeed, I suggest that the Trafficking Protocol's inclusion of such concepts as 'fraud' and 'deception' permit the adoption of a contractual approach to trafficking.

This 'contractual' perspective to trafficking has multiple advantages. By adopting this approach, we move beyond the current emphasis on criminal law enforcement, which is often aimed at identification and prosecution of traffickers rather than support and redress for victims. We avoid other shortcomings in this criminal justice framework, which has also been misused to rescue, rehabilitate or criminalise non-trafficked, voluntary sex workers. Most importantly, the contractual approach provides us with the conceptual tools to recognise women's agency in a situation of trafficking. Some women do migrate irregularly for economic betterment based on some process of rational decision-making and their expectations about opportunities away from home. There tends to be little hesitation to recognise this in relation to men. I believe that evidence of such agency and voluntariness should not be a barrier to prosecuting traffickers. A more migration-centred definition may also be better suited to non-legal discourse as well.

A more appropriate definition of trafficking – particularly when compared to that offered in the Trafficking Protocol – would be:

A process by which a person, whose origin is Point A, has:

(a) been moved (recruited in their home country,[2] transported, transferred, harboured along the way or received in the destination country) to point B for the purpose of exploitation; or

(b) has consensually travelled from point A to B, but whose induced expectations created during the period of negotiation are unmet (i) upon arrival in point B or (ii) at some stage while residing in point B, in a way that his or her situation in point B rises to the level of exploitation.

Such movement may be within the country of origin or across borders. Unmet expectations of the victim may arise from deception or lack of information regarding living and working conditions in the destination country.

I propose the following definition of a victim of trafficking:

A migrant:

(a) who is coercively moved to the destination country; or

(b) whose induced expectations of work and life abroad are unmet, either (i) at the point of arrival in the destination country or (ii) at some stage while residing in the destination country, placing the victim in a situation of exploitation.

The fact that a potential migrant has engaged in some process of self-determined decision-making about their migration and expectations of work and life abroad, prior to departure, should not be seen as a reason to deny their victimhood.

The latter part of this definition highlights the fact that, although I emphasise evidence of voluntary or consensual movement throughout this book, at no point do I contend that the men and women identified during my research are not victims of trafficking. To express this idea, I have coined the phrase 'voluntary victim'. This concept reflects the increasing evidence of non-coerced recruitment and/or transportation of victims at the preliminary stage of the trafficking process and provides a vivid image to contrast the kidnapped victim archetype. This apparent oxymoron also addresses, in part, the concerns of many academics with how to recognise both agency and victimhood simultaneously.

Here also the 'spectrum of migration' offers much value. This lens of analysis recognises the divergence of experiences that fall within its parameters, including 'trafficking' i.e. failed migration and also recalls the importance of migrant expectations. If we accept the subjective view of the individual migrant of what

---

2   It is unclear whether the use of the term 'recruitment' in the Trafficking Protocol meant pre-departure recruitment. Further confusion arises from the lack of any interpretive materials on the 'action' element of trafficking (Gallagher, 2010: 29 footnote 74). However, if we read the term recruitment in its context, as we are expected to do under the basic principles of interpreting legal text, the language suggests pre-departure recruitment, after which would follow transport, transfer, harbouring and then receipt.

constitutes a satisfactory meeting of their expectations when embarking on the search for work abroad, we would be looking at 'success' from their point of view. Success might constitute economic betterment for themselves and/or for their families (remittances); it might be linked to new experiences for themselves (socially and economically); or as observed in countries like Ghana, it might involve something as intangible as social prestige (the 'burger mommy'), particularly upon returning home. Recognising such factors requires a victim and migration centred perspective more than a criminal justice one.

Legitimate and Non-Legitimate Expectations

The above critique and the introduction of principles from contract and labour law still requires us to define the perimeters of what will and will not constitute a case of human trafficking.

From a legal perspective, courts should take into account these 'unmet expectations' of victims that are formed on the basis of their negotiations prior to departure or upon arrival in the destination country. However, two challenging situations arise. The first is where potential migrants have excessively low expectations, that is, they accept conditions that by social standards involve unacceptable levels of servility. The second is where the potential migrant has unreasonable expectations.

As to the first, I would contend that we would need to clearly specify what society deems to be unacceptably exploitative situations. The rational of John Stuart Mill is helpful in establishing the boundaries of these standards:

> In this and most other civilized countries, for example, an engagement by which a person should sell himself, or allow himself to be sold, as a slave, would be null and void; neither enforced by law nor by opinion ... The reason for not interfering, unless for the sake of others, with a person's voluntary acts, is consideration for his liberty. His voluntary choice is evidence that what he chooses is desirable, or at the least endurable, to him, and his good is on the whole best provided for by allowing him to take his own means of pursuing it. But by selling himself for a slave, he abdicates his liberty; he foregoes any future use of it, beyond that single act ... The principle of freedom cannot require that he should be free not to be free. It is not freedom to be allowed to alienate his freedom. (Mill, 1859: 299–300)

Based on the meaning of liberty, we cannot accept that a decision to enslave oneself is a voluntary contractual transaction that needs to be upheld. Rather such a decision must be nullified. In terms of defining the criteria for unacceptable, servile conditions of work, the definitions offered in the Slavery and Supplementary Slavery Conventions are helpful. Cases may be instances of slavery or may be cases of both trafficking and slavery. Any offer of employment involving such conditions as enslavement, debt bondage, serfdom, servile marriage or child servitude – as defined in the Slavery Convention and Supplementary Slavery Convention – even where they are accepted and tolerated by the individual victim, should be treated as exploitative and contested. Based on the analysis in this book, the cases that fall in this category sit at the extreme end of the migration spectrum and are less representative of the majority of cases verified by the empirical data.

Nonetheless, research by Bélanger offers further considerations. In Vietnam, several returnees expressed the view that having to work for 6–18 months to reimburse expenses – i.e. to pay off a debt – was a reasonable cost of migration (Bélanger, 2014: 102). Not only does this highlight the transactional and calculated nature of movement but it also gives further additional guidance for defining the framework for 'reasonable' and 'unreasonable' expectations. Specifically on this question of debt bondage, further data collection is needed to establish the boundaries of reasonableness, taking into account Mill's guidance above that it is not freedom to be able to alienate one's freedom.

As to the second challenge of unreasonable expectations, this is easier to address in practice than to describe in abstract terms. A social and legal standard of reasonableness must be specified. This may include setting standards about what may be reasonable remuneration, hours and conditions of work. However, the notion of unmet expectations rests on the victim's expectations created through a process of negotiation. If a person is given reason to believe that their expectations will be met, even where such expectations are 'unreasonable' and a more rational person would not have believed them to be true, the individual may or may not be a victim. Such a situation would need further exploration. Courts may draw on principles such as the 'reasonable person'[3] as is commonly applied in law while analysing the particular circumstances of the victim who was led to believe that their unreasonable expectations would be met. This, for example, would allow judges to take into consideration factors such as lack of basic education, psychological vulnerability or extreme poverty, *if and when they prove to be relevant*, when looking at the individual case.

Labour Laws: Exploitation and Regulating Conditions of Work

It is important to reiterate the overarching principles of human rights law that must govern any analysis of trafficking. Trafficking of men and women, by its

---

3   The principle of the reasonable person, often referred to as the 'reasonable man', is a common law concept that applies an objective standard against which the reasonableness of a person's behaviour, perspective or interpretation is assessed. A particular challenge of applying the reasonable person test in the context of trafficking is whether to apply a standard of what is reasonable in the source country – most likely – or at the destination point. In the case of *R v Dobie*, discussed earlier, the courts considered the victim's experiences as sex workers in their home country, Thailand, to establish their expectations for work and life in Australia.

very nature, entails violations of the human rights of individuals. A human rights-based approach emphasises the human dignity of the individual, including the right to freedom from exploitation. Yet this overarching human rights framework is frequently missing in trafficking discourse.

Moreover, labour protections for workers are sometimes given very little attention, despite employment being at the heart of the issue. The Convention on the Protection of the Rights of All Migrant Workers and Members of Their Families is rarely cited in trafficking discussions. This is despite the fact that it requires the human rights, treatment, and welfare of all migrant workers to be protected, regardless of the workers' legal status. Wherever an individual is placed on the migration spectrum, common experiences include arduous journeys, low wages, hazardous working environments and unsanitary living. Regardless of the choices made by those who find themselves facing exploitation, the law should reconcile the individual's voluntary movement with their status as a victim deserving redress. To be simultaneously a victim and an agent of one's destiny should not be impossible under the law. This could be perfectly addressed through the protection of migrant workers' rights.

Such an approach is already provided for in many national labour laws. Many progressive legal regimes address issues that are common to many victims' experiences, including restrictions on freedom of movement, withholding wages and unsafe working conditions (Richards, 2004: 160). ILO Convention 97 on Migration for Employment (1949),[4] as well as ILO Convention 143[5] specifically on migrant workers must be brought into the legal framework that addresses trafficking. Other international legal standards are also central to a holistic approach to addressing trafficking, including well-accepted – although not necessarily implemented – principles related to social protection, decent work and pay, prohibiting discrimination and harassment in the workplace and ensuring rights to unionise. Many of the problems faced pre-departure, in transit and in destination countries are also set out by the CEDAW Committee in its General Recommendation No. 26 on women migrant workers.[6]

---

4   It should be noted that this Convention makes no reference to trafficking.

5   Only minimal reference is made to trafficking in this document. This includes in relation to prosecution (Article 5) and in its preamble, which calls for further standards to address trafficking for labour exploitation.

6   It is unfortunate that, in its General Recommendation, the CEDAW Committee did not use the opportunity to call for trafficking to be viewed within a migration framework and highlight more explicitly that its General Recommendation should be used as guidance on the protections of both regular and irregular migrants. In footnote 4, it waivers and attempts to avoid making a clear and explicit statement on the issue: 'This general recommendation deals only with the work-related situation of women migrants. While it is a reality that in some instances women migrant workers may become victims of trafficking due to various degrees of vulnerability they face, this general recommendation will not address the circumstances relating to trafficking. The phenomenon of trafficking is complex and needs more focused attention. The Committee is of the opinion that this phenomenon

Conclusion

This discussion sets out steps towards a more inclusive and victim-centred framework, both when operating within the law and beyond it. From a legal point of view, some of the stronger elements of the Trafficking Protocol, like references to deception, highlight the value of contract law principles to our understanding of victim's experiences and redress. Above all else, borrowing from contract law reflects the agency and autonomy of victims, the negotiations and expectations of migrants involved in human trafficking and the fact that labour relations are at the heart of the issue. Including and beyond the law, this reflects the importance of applying an overarching human rights framework. Labour and migration rights in particular, both of which are well-articulated in international law, can offer a victim-centred and rights-based approach.

---

can be more comprehensively addressed through article 6 of the Convention which places an obligation on States parties "to take all appropriate measures, including legislation, to suppress all forms of traffic in women and exploitation of prostitution of women". The Committee emphasises however, that many elements of General Recommendation No. 26 are also relevant in situations where women migrants have been victims of trafficking'.

Conclusion: Towards a More Inclusive, Victim-Centred Framework

It is always a problem to generalise and get a profile ... I was trying to get an average statistic for victims: female, male, sexual exploitation, labour exploitation. If it is 50 per cent of the case load, is it good enough to say it is a profile? If it is 40 per cent and you fall into this average category, are you a typical victim? In that way, you need to be careful what you call a profile. People of various ages and backgrounds and education fall victims of trafficking.

(T. Ivanyuk, Counter-Trafficking Programme Specialist, IOM Ukraine, 3 September 2009)

This book aimed to examine some of the most commonly held assumptions about the demographics of victims of trafficking. The goal was to challenge the mainstream trafficking framework and its related myths and misconceptions concerning the naive, uneducated, poor, female victim. Building on the work of a growing body of academics who seek to challenge the image of the coerced victim, this analysis sought to provide empirical evidence to confront head-on the mainstream framework and present an alternative approach to understanding trafficking.

Part I of this book was focused on examining the main stakeholders and their agendas – from academic literature and the reports of NGOs to pieces in the popular press. This was set alongside an analysis of the international, regional and national laws that have a significant and identifiable impact on how trafficking is understood. This analysis revealed how the mainstream trafficking framework is constructed upon often unfounded assumptions about victims and the so-called 'push' factors of trafficking. Constant reiteration within trafficking discourse acts to amplify these myths and misconceptions.

The challenge to the mainstream framework presented in this book consisted of two main aspects. First, I began with the image of the coerced victim of trafficking which was shown to be an atypical and misleading representation of human trafficking. Some degree of voluntariness on the part of potential migrants is present in situations that end in trafficking. While developing this critique of the coerced victim archetype, it became evident that there is a split in the treatment of 'victim voluntariness'. On the one side are analysts – both academics and non-academics – who see little or no voluntariness in the initial movement of victims. These authors tend to view trafficking as typically involving the kidnapping, abduction or selling of women and girls. On the other side are those analysts who recognise some degree of voluntariness in the initial movement and yet, even in this case, often identify structural factors as responsible for shaping migratory decisions. Poverty, gender inequality and other vulnerability factors, such as ethnic minority status and conflict, are said to push victims abroad and shape trafficking patterns.

Part II of this book challenged, to different degrees, the assumptions presented by both groups of analysts. First, movement as a result of physical or psychological force – that is, by 'coercion' as legally defined – was shown not to be typical of human trafficking. As a counterpoint, I proposed an alternative representation, termed the 'voluntary victim', a phrase used to refer to those victims who exercise some degree of autonomous decision-making. It became evident that a victim's entry into exploitative conditions of work abroad is frequently initiated by a voluntary decision. The image of the voluntary victim acts to directly challenge that of the kidnapped or abducted slave.

Second, this book turned to the factors that are assumed to shape, influence or structure the decisions made by potential migrants. Such factors are often deemed causes of human trafficking by those stakeholders who argue that they limit opportunities or exacerbate vulnerability to exploitation. Three demographic factors that are most commonly labelled as 'causes' within mainstream trafficking discourse were examined in detail: low levels of education; poverty and labour market barriers; and gender inequality. My analysis revealed how sound evidence demonstrating a correlation with human trafficking is frequently lacking in academic and other studies.

This book also examined the actors who create and/or reiterate such assumptions and their particular agendas. For example, I have explored the role of both abolitionist and pro-sex work feminist theorists in reinforcing a voluntary/involuntary dichotomy and hence the coerced victim archetype. I have challenged the lack of attention given to trafficking as a form of migratory movement. Driven by expectations for a better life through the pursuit of opportunities abroad, the 'migrant' and the 'victim of trafficking' in the pre-departure stage are one and the same; when exploitation arises, trafficking is the end result of this migration gone wrong.

The arguments presented bolster the evidence emerging from the new school of thought on trafficking and the work of a growing body of scholars who call for recognition of the rarity of the kidnapped coerced victim. Further, it validates the argument that in many instances the mainstream perspective is one-sided and limited in its understanding of the multiple dimensions of human trafficking.

The Voluntary Victim of Trafficking

There is limited appreciation of the extent to which coerced movement is not actually present in situations of trafficking. Rather, the image of the abducted woman or sold daughter has filtered through even to academic discourse. Yet, this book reveals how kidnapping is rare, with stories of coercive movement largely anecdotal and unverified. While coerced movement is a reality in some instances, trafficking more typically results from non-coerced migratory movement. Some informants from the field even argue that many victims are fully aware of the possible risk of exploitation when they set out on their 'adventures'. With such coerced movement proving exceptional, the image of the 'voluntary victim' appears to be a more accurate reflection of human trafficking. Recognising this voluntariness is central for an accurate understanding of the dual status of 'victim-agent'.

Luck, adventure or the craze to travel are also all relevant but oft ignored themes. While some victims are lucky and successful in their migration pursuits – with success often defined in financial terms – others are less fortunate and may have entered into an exploitative situation through the advice of a 'false friend'. Yet even this 'false friend' imagery may be a myth, an additional story that conforms to the 'ideal' victim.

The widespread presence of pre-planning among victims also discredits the typicality of coercion. Such evidence points to the error of situating trafficking outside of a migration framework. Imagery concerning the 'burger' and the 'burger mommy' in Ghana or Brazilian soap operas and Cinderella stories in Ukraine explain potentially unrealistic expectations of success abroad as well as the setting of individual and perhaps family goals – particularly concerning monetary success and personal wealth – that influence victims' decision-making processes at the pre-departure stage. On this point, I argue that we may question whether these are completely autonomous decisions, given that they are often driven by false or exaggerated information, including through the popular press and returned migrants 'parading' their successes. Regardless, this evidence calls into question the representative nature of the picture of coercive movement.

Yet there are some clear exceptions and coercion certainly does exist. Anecdotal stories, for example, describe the selling of young Vietnamese girls, although these are often based on the limited existing body of literature from the 1990s and early 2000s. More importantly, however, these stories identify a complex mix of factors, including parental decision-making, expectations and the desires of children to contribute to household expenses. They also remind us of the challenge we face in recognising the evolving capacities of a child to make decisions about their own labour. All of these factors must be considered if we are to achieve a more accurate and nuanced understanding of trafficking and victims' own legitimate roles in decisions regarding potential migration.

A New Victim Profile

The Educated Victim

The mainstream trafficking framework assumes a strong correlation between education levels and vulnerability to human trafficking, with education deemed an 'obvious' protection factor against trafficking. To the contrary, the empirical evidence shows that a significant number of victims may have education levels higher than their non-trafficked peers. This is most stark in Ukraine, where the evidence suggests the possibility of a *direct correlation* between levels of education and risk of trafficking. That is, given barriers to legal migration, higher levels of education may in fact correlate with – or even lead to – higher levels of irregular and unsafe migration.

The evidence presented in Chapter 5, however, also revealed other influences that education may have on trafficking. This includes how levels of education may guide the distances travelled by potential migrants. In Ghana, for example, the limited evidence that exists suggests that the least educated (primary or no schooling) are perhaps more likely to migrate than those with middle, secondary and vocational schooling, although largely to other countries in West Africa. Irregular migrants are, however, reaching North America and Europe and appear to leave Ghana after achieving a higher level of schooling than their peers. The quality of education and its relevance to the domestic job market also prove relevant.

Finally, there is a persistent assumption that naivety and ignorance are at play in trafficking. This is a particularly non-evidenced-based portrait. Perhaps the picture of the uneducated and naive victim makes it easier to forgive the erroneous choices of these migrants that led to their exploitation abroad, whereas the brave and adventurous victim is considered too culpable.

The Job Seeker

Poverty and human trafficking are almost universally linked in the literature and in trafficking discourse, with 'high poverty rates and unemployment for women' assumed to 'leave them vulnerable to the enticements of traffickers' (Kligman and Limoncelli, 2005: 128). Poverty is a concept with a precise meaning in development discourse. The analysis in Chapter 6 appears to be the first within existing trafficking debates to analyse the relationship between trafficking and poverty by taking into account the distinctions between absolute and relative poverty. Given the extent to which poverty is assumed to be at play, particularly in driving movement from low-income to middle-income and upper-income countries, adopting a more nuanced analysis of how poverty affects patterns of trafficking is essential.

Despite poverty being labelled by various informants from the field as '[t]he root of the problem', in order to have a substantial basis to deem 'poverty' a driver, more systematic analysis of income levels and livelihoods of a large pool of returned victims is needed. This is particularly the case if we want to determine whether and to what extent household needs, pre-departure employment opportunities, the conditions of work at home or those presumed to exist abroad shape the decision to leave.

When discussing the assumed correlation between trafficking and poverty, I took my analysis one step further and looked into one of the possible key causes of poverty for women: the incapacity of women to gain a sufficient income from labour in their own countries. Based on my analysis of the labour market experiences of individuals before departure, a correlation between barriers to access well-paid jobs – whether real or perceived – and human trafficking proved to be one of the clearest correlations. This was particularly the case in Ukraine and, to a degree, in Vietnam. Further research is needed that explores how women migrants and their decisions are impacted by lack of satisfaction with conditions of work at home and perceptions of work abroad. Vulnerability to economic shocks and a potential link to human trafficking also need further analysis, alongside the particular vulnerabilities facing youth.

Male and Female Victims and Traffickers

An overarching theme across all of the assumptions explored in this book is the assumed sex of victims, with women presumed to face a heightened level of vulnerability to trafficking based on high drop-out rates of girls from school, the feminisation of poverty, gender discrimination in the labour market and other manifestations of gender inequality. The extent to which 'gender inequality' is simply assumed to be a cause of trafficking is in fact stark. Although there is increasing recognition of the traffic of men, there is simultaneously a distinct failure to note the incoherence between this evidence of male trafficking and gender inequality being an assumed cause of trafficking. Moreover, while many stakeholders in the field continue to argue that gender inequality correlates in some way to trafficking, few can substantiate this claim with evidence of specific manifestations that have a relationship with trafficking. There is little solid evidence, for example, of domestic violence as a driver, despite this being an assumed 'cause'.

This does not mean that trafficking is not *gendered*. If anything, the most gendered aspects of trafficking are those most frequently ignored. Men are unquestionably victims, exploited in such sectors as construction, agriculture, fishing and factory work. Where data on male victims is lacking at the national-level, we must question whether victims are predominantly women or whether we are simply failing to identify male victims. This may be because of lack of reintegration services for men or because men are viewed as exploited irregular migrants rather than as victims of trafficking. What results is an erroneous understanding of adult trafficking whereby exploitation (of women) in the sex sector is equated with trafficking and non-sexual exploitation is simply seen as a by-product of migration.

The data also challenge our understanding of gender-segregated labour and exploitation. Female victims are trafficked into such sectors as agriculture and construction, while trafficking for sexual exploitation of men does exist. In some respects, this may reflect a shift in patterns of labour segregation. At the same time, it highlights that there will always be cases that fall outside of those experiences considered most typical. Overall, most people do indeed appear to be trafficked into gender stereotypical industries – women and girls into sex work and men into construction.

There has been very limited systematic analysis of the gender of the trafficker – frequently, perhaps surprisingly, female – or the gendered nature of stigma. In my analysis, I claim that both male and female victims suffer from the male trafficker/ female victim dichotomy often presented in the trafficking discourse. Women are framed as vulnerable, passive, naive and weak. This misconception also results in a failure to recognise the agency and often reasoned decision-making of women, who are instead seen as falling prey to male perpetrators. Furthermore, the male victim is rendered invisible in this picture, with the dichotomy instead conjuring up imagery of the trapped and fallen female sex slave. This undermines identification of male victims. Finally, this archetype also downplays the role of women as perpetrators of trafficking.

Of the myths and misconceptions analysed in this book, the gender stereotypes that pertain to trafficking proved to be the most dominant. The analysis contained here reveals the sheer complexity of the role of gender in trafficking. Moreover, it exposes how this complexity is overshadowed by the debates preoccupying governments, theorists, activists and the media, the current discourse only capturing the surface of this complexity.

Other Potential Drivers Beyond the Scope of this Book

This book has focused on those myths and misconceptions which are believed to most commonly skew trafficking imagery. Inevitably, this book is limited in scope and several other potential drivers of trafficking are worth further investigation. For example, with constantly increasing barriers for regular international migration, marriage migration is one option left for (predominantly women but also male) residents of developing or transitional economies. In 2006, more women from developing countries gained residency in Norway through marriage to non-immigrant Norwegians than they did through asylum as refugees or through marriage with an immigrant Norwegian (Tyldum and Tveit, 2008; 19) (Tyldum, 2013: 104). Dependence and vulnerability may be heightened in such transnational marriages, reflecting – as discussed in Chapter 4 – possible reduced voluntariness or autonomy at both the departure and destination point.

In addition, a strong connection is often drawn, including by NGO activists and government authorities, between ethnic minority status and trafficking. It is presumed that the mountainous ethnic minority communities of Vietnam, for example, are particularly prone to trafficking. However, my own research suggests that this assumption, unjustifiably, assumes that Vietnam's ethnic minorities experience patterns of trafficking similar to that of Thailand's ethnic minority population and in fact conflates migration among ethnic minorities with trafficking. Certainly, ethnic minorities are among those who have been identified as trafficked. What is problematic is the non-empirically based assumption that ethnic minority status heightens vulnerability to trafficking.

A surprising number of inter-governmental documents refer to conflict as a driver of trafficking, including the Ouagadougou Action Plan (Ouagadougou Action Plan, 2006: General principles; see also European Commission, 2012: §1). Writing on Bosnia and Herzegovina, international NGO Human Rights Watch reported that due to local corruption, as well as complicity of international officials, trafficking networks were allowed to 'flourish', with women tricked, threatened, physically assaulted and sold as chattel (Human Rights Watch, 2002: 4). Most of these women were reported as having been trafficked from Moldova, Romania and Ukraine. While beyond the scope of this book, such variables as these require further investigation through the lens of analysis applied in this book.

Rising Above Individual Agendas

This book has highlighted the importance of not ignoring the actors who are behind these myths and misconceptions. It is evident that these stereotypical assumptions are often defined and promoted by various stakeholders who have a vested interest in promoting these assumptions. This includes governments whose moral panic over prostitution and concerns over crime and insecurity result in the pursuit of an end to migrant sex work. Abolitionists, meanwhile, pursue the criminalisation of prostitution and trafficking alike for their alleged role in furthering the subjection and objectification of women and their bodies. Rescue and rehabilitation of sex workers is deemed justified by a world view that both prostitution and trafficking exploit the secondary and unequal status of women. The profit-driven media sell papers full of sensationalist narratives of crack-downs and raids to save innocent women victims.

It is unlikely that any of these stakeholders can set aside these agendas when making their contributions to trafficking debates and policy developments. After all, these agendas are the reason for their interest in human trafficking in the first place. At the same time, there is some indisputable common ground, even among those stakeholders who have seemingly distinct interests. Viewing trafficking through the lens of voluntary victimhood and unmet expectations may help all stakeholders to rise above these individual agendas.

Consensus may, for example, be reached in terms of addressing the unmet expectations of migrant sex workers with regard to longer hours of work or having to service more clients than agreed, lack of protections from brothel owners when faced with violence at the hands of clients or forced or unprotected sex. An end to such unmet expectations would help to address the majority – although certainly not all – of the major (practical, although not necessarily the theoretical) preoccupations of abolitionists with prostitution while simultaneously aligning with years of labour rights advocacy of pro-sex work feminists. Similarly, anti-immigration campaigning that alerts potential migrants to the possibilities of fraud and deception, thereby heightening their awareness when negotiating with potential employers, may simultaneously address some of the concerns of those governments who perceive a relationship between immigration and crime. Nonetheless, reorienting not only our definition of, but also practical approaches to, trafficking requires a demonstration of will among stakeholders to pursue this common ground.

Final Remarks: Trafficking as Failed Migration

This book articulates evidence-based arguments to dispute the coerced and naive female victim archetype. The exploitation of men and women in trafficking often arises in the course of their voluntary pursuit of economic and social goals, rather than being shaped or causally correlated with low education, poverty or gender equality. My findings act to challenge the victim archetype reinforced in trafficking discourse and imagery across the globe.

While an evolution in trafficking literature has occurred in recent years, the extent to which the mainstream trafficking framework persists is surprising. The voices of authors such as Siddharth Kara, Benjamin Skinner, Nicholas Kristof and Donna Hughes dominate debates; other more nuanced discourse is silenced or stifled. Adopted and amplified by other powerful voices, including the United States Government and international organisations, the mainstream framework exercises a decisive influence on the meaning attributed to trafficking globally. Particularly outside of academic circles, this discourse is largely unquestioned. Families are seen as unable to afford to send girls to schools; women are desperate to escape violent homes; and family values demand that women sacrifice themselves to guarantee that food is placed on the table. Women and children are therefore in danger of exploitation.

As we have seen, one of the most fundamental flaws in the conflation of trafficking with enslavement is the inability to see trafficking as a phenomenon that falls *within* the field of migration. Like the image of the slave trader, 'trafficking' is associated primarily with the criminal acts of the trafficker and not the legitimate social and economic goals of the potential migrant. This book has disputed the coerced and naive female victim archetype and has demonstrated that the exploitation of men and women in trafficking often arises in the course of their voluntary pursuit of (legitimate) economic and social goals, rather than being shaped or causally correlated with the demographics victims are assumed to share.

Trafficking should be understood as failed migration, arising when a migrant faces a situation of exploitation that substantially departs or diverges from their expectations. Women and men do often migrate irregularly for economic betterment based on some process of voluntary and often carefully reasoned decision-making and their expectations of opportunities away from home. The girl whose boyfriend assisted her in planning her departure from Vietnam, with the knowledge of her siblings, the Ghanaian woman who expected to be a nanny in Russia and was forced into sex work, and the Ukrainian couple whose search for business capital led to their exploitation, all had unmet expectations, even if to differing degrees.

Such expectations are often based on deception, fraud and lack of transparency during the negotiations of a migrant prior to leaving their home country, or on the exaggerated stories of success shared by returned migrants. Deception and fraud prove to be far more central to the concept of trafficking than coerced movement. In this respect, academics and policy makers in this field need to concede the error of allowing a criminal law definition to provide the lens through which we view and understand the multi-dimensional arena of human trafficking.

As I close my analysis, I find it important to reiterate the grave consequences of leaving such myths and misconceptions unchecked. The existing framework for trafficking determines what is meant by the phenomenon and who fits within its boundaries. Hence, the trafficking framework creates the phenomenon under discussion. Sensationalist voices have given meaning to what is a complicated and inadequate definition of trafficking in the UN Protocol. Data are collected that reaffirm trafficking's stereotypes, with other cases conveniently ignored or given limited attention. The regular repetition of the story of the archetypal victim – whether because it attracts donor resources, generates sympathy or reflects the focus of an NGO, a government policy or serves another agenda – affirms the stereotypical and unrepresentative understanding of trafficking that was generated many years ago when human trafficking began to draw so much attention. To the contrary, I have outlined the contours of a migration framework that both expands, and at times narrows, the boundaries of how trafficking is understood so as to ensure that we capture, more accurately, the demographics of victims and the causes of their movement. Failure to do so will leave us in a vicious cycle of asserting the same victim archetype, one that fails to reflect accurately human trafficking and its realities.

Annex 1:
Questionnaire

I am conducting research on the age, education, employment and family history of women and girls who are returnees to [Vietnam/Ukraine]. This questionnaire is anonymous. No names are required. This questionnaire is for research purposes only. Your answers will have no impact on your legal status or the services that are available to you. The questionnaire is optional. You do not need to complete this questionnaire if you do not want to. If you start completing the questionnaire and change your mind, you are free to stop at any stage. If there are any questions you do not want to answer, please leave them blank. The questionnaire should take around 15 minutes of your time.

We will start with a few questions about you:

1. What is your sex?

Male   ☐
Female   ☐

2. What is your age?

3. What is your current marital status? Tick all relevant answers

Single   ☐
Married   ☐
Divorced   ☐
Widow   ☐
Living with partner   ☐

4. [Ukraine] Do you practise or follow any of these religions?

Jewish ☐	Ukrainian Orthodox – Kyiv Patriarchate	☐
Protestant ☐	Ukrainian Orthodox – Moscow Patriarchate	☐
Roman Catholic ☐	None	☐
Ukrainian Autocephalous Orthodox ☐	Other	☐
Ukrainian Greek Catholic ☐		

4. [Vietnam] Do you practise or follow any of these religions

None	☐	Hoahao	☐
Buddhism	☐	Muslim	☐
Caodai	☐	Protestant	☐
Catholicism	☐	Other	☐

5. [Ukraine] Do you consider yourself a member of any of these groups?

Belarusian	☐	Polish	☐
Bulgarian	☐	Romanian	☐
Crimean Tatar	☐	Russian	☐
Hungarian	☐	Ukrainian	☐
Jewish	☐	Other	☐
Moldovan	☐		

5. [Vietnam] Do you consider yourself a member of any of these groups

None	☐	Hoahao	☐
Buddhism	☐	Muslim	☐
Caodai	☐	Protestant	☐
Catholicism	☐	Other	☐

Now let's talk about your life before leaving [Ukraine/Vietnam]

6. Have you ever attended school?

Yes   ☐
No   ☐ (If no, skip to Question 12)

7. If you have attended school, up to what age did you attend?

Up to Age 5	☐	Up to Age 10	☐	Up to Age 15	☐
Up to Age 6	☐	Up to Age 11	☐	Up to Age 16	☐
Up to Age 7	☐	Up to Age 12	☐	Up to Age 17	☐
Up to Age 8	☐	Up to Age 13	☐	Up to Age 18	☐
Up to Age 9	☐	Up to Age 14	☐		

8. In total, how many years of school have you attended? _____ (Years).

9. Did any of following people pay for your school fees or other costs related to your schooling? Tick yes or no where relevant.

	Yes	No
Mother		
Father		
Grandparents		
Siblings		
Aunt		
Uncle		
Cousins		

I don't know ☐

10. Before leaving [Ukraine/Vietnam], did you attend College/University?

Yes ☐
No ☐ (If no, skip to Question 12)

11. Did you complete and receive the College/University degree?

Yes ☐
No ☐

12. Before leaving [Ukraine/Vietnam], did you receive any vocational training?

Yes ☐ If yes, for what type of job? _____
No ☐

13. [Ukraine] Where was your home before you left Ukraine (oblasti, autonomous republic, or municipality)?

_____

13. [Vietnam] Where was your home before you left Vietnam?
District _____
Province _____

14. How long did you live there prior to leaving [Ukraine/Vietnam]?
Number of months/years? _____
I don't remember ☐

15. What age were you when you left [Ukraine/Vietnam? _____ (age in years)
I don't remember ☐

16. Did you live with any of the following people before you left [Ukraine/Vietnam]? Tick yes or no where relevant

	Yes	No
Mother		
Father		
Grandparents		
Husband/Wife/		
Boyfriend/Girlfriend/		
Partner		
Siblings		
Aunt		
Uncle		
Cousins		
Other (Specify)		

I don't remember ☐

17. In total, immediately prior to leaving [Ukraine/Vietnam], how many people were living with you in your household ?
Number of people (not including yourself)? _____

18. Prior to leaving [Ukraine/Vietnam], were you earning an income outside of your home?

Yes ☐
No ☐   (Skip to Question 23)

19. If you were earning an income, what was your occupation? _____

20. How long did you work in this occupation before leaving?
Number of years? _____

21. Had you ever received training for your position in this occupation?
Yes ☐
No ☐

22. Was the money you earned enough to cover your own expenses and any contribution you made to family expenses?

Yes ☐
No ☐

Just a couple more minutes, thank you for your patience. If you do not mind, I will now ask you 2 questions on your decision to leave Ukraine.

23. Were any of the people listed below aware that you were leaving [Ukraine/ Vietnam]? Tick yes or no where relevant

	Yes	**No**
Mother		
Father		
Grandparents		
Husband/Wife/		
Boyfriend/Girlfriend/		
Partner		
Siblings		
Aunt		
Uncle		
Cousins		
Other (Specify)		

24. Did any of the people below participate in arranging your departure from [Ukraine/Vietnam]? Tick yes or no where relevant

	Yes	**No**
Mother		
Father		
Grandparents		
Husband/Wife/		
Boyfriend/Girlfriend/		
Partner		
Siblings		
Aunt		
Uncle		
Cousins		
Other (Specify)		

And now just 6 more questions about your experience living outside of [Ukraine/ Vietnam] and the survey is finished.

25. How long did you spend living outside of [Ukraine/Vietnam]?

| Less than 6 months ☐ | From 1–2 years ☐ | From 3–5 years ☐ |
| Less than 1 year ☐ | From 2–3 years ☐ | More than 5 years ☐ |

26. Did you leave [Ukraine/Vietnam] because you planned to marry to a [non-Ukrainian/non-Vietnamese]?

Yes ☐
No ☐ (Skip to Question 28)

27. Did you finally marry a [non-Ukrainian/non-Vietnamese]?

Yes ☐
No ☐

28. When you were working overseas, what work did you do?

Garment industry/sewing   ☐
Waitress (Restaurant, bar, hotel)   ☐
Domestic work   ☐
Worked in hair or beauty salon   ☐
Worked in shop   ☐
Agriculture   ☐
Construction   ☐
Other (Specify) _____

29. When you were working overseas, did you send any of your income back to your family in [Ukraine/Vietnam]?

Yes ☐
No ☐ (Skip to Question 32)

30. How often did you send money home?

Rarely   ☐   Every few months   ☐
Approximately once a month ☐   Approximately every year   ☐

31. During your time working outside of [Ukraine/Vietnam], approximately what portion of your total income did you send home?

Less than ¼ of income   ☐   Approximately ¾ of income   ☐
Approximately ¼ of income   ☐   Almost all of income   ☐
Approximately ½ of income   ☐

And finally

32. Is there anything you would like to add about leaving [Ukraine/Vietnam] or your experiences outside of [Ukraine/Vietnam]?

_____

_____

_____

_____

_____

_____

33. Do you have any questions of comments about this questionnaire?

_____

_____

_____

_____

_____

_____

Thank you for your time and cooperation.

Annex 2:
Overview of data collected from Ukraine, Vietnam and Ghana

Table A2.1 **Number of questionnaires completed and key informant interviews conducted across Ghana, Vietnam and Ukraine**

Country	No. of questionnaires completed by trafficked returnees		No. of key informant interviews	
	Male	Female	Male	Female
Ukraine	14	90	3	15
Vietnam	0	5	8	7
Ghana	0	0	9	8
Total	14	95	20	30

TableA2.2 **Overview of questionnaire data collected from victims of trafficking returned to Ukraine**

NGO	Region	No. of questionnaires completed	Sex of respondents	
			Female	Male
Revival of a Nation	Ternopil	15	15	0
Donetsk League of Business and Professional Women	Donetsk	14	12	2
Dovira Met	Sumy	15	7	8
Lubystok	Mykolaiv	9	9	0
Women's Information and Consulting Centre	Zhytomyr	33	33	0
IOM Rehabilitation Centre	Kyiv	18	14	4
Total	-	104	90	14

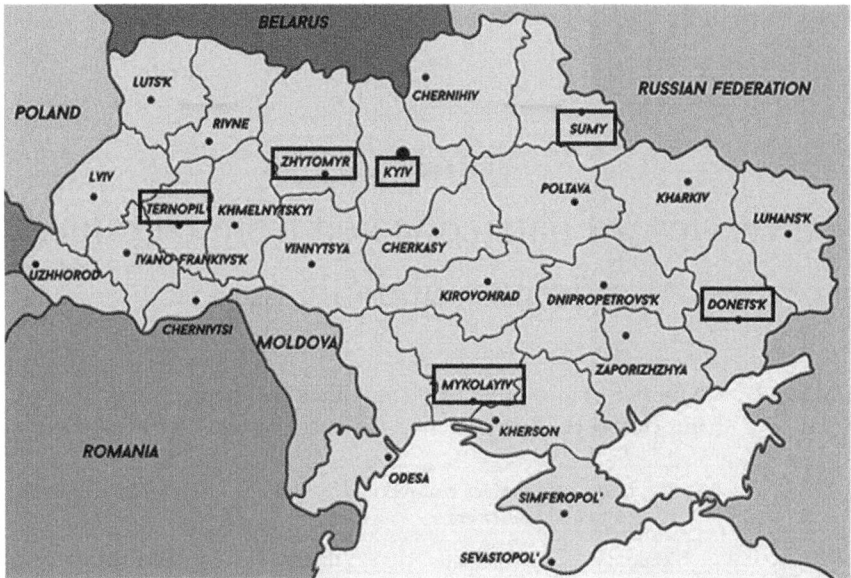

Map A2.1   Map of Ukraine highlighting the location of the IOM Rehabilitation Centre Kyiv and NGOs participating in quantitative data collection

Source: Carnegie Council (via Shutterstock), 2014. Modified by author.

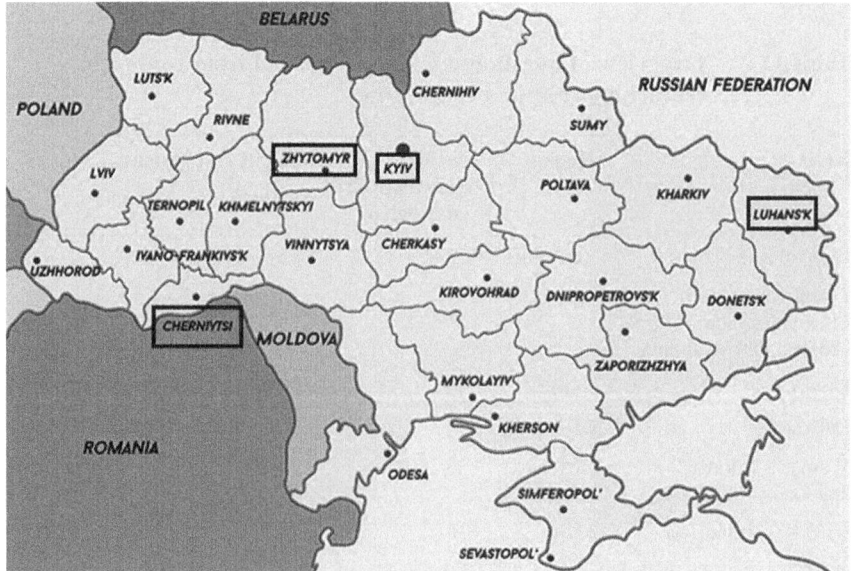

Map A2.2   Map of Ukraine marking locations of face-to-face and email key informant interviews

Source: Carnegie Council (via Shutterstock), 2014. Modified by author.

Table A2.3   Overview of questionnaire data collected from victims of trafficking returned to Vietnam

NGO	Locality	No. of questionnaires completed	Sex of respondents	
			Female	Male
Centre for Women and Development	Hanoi	5	5	0
Total	-	5	5	0

Map A2.3   Location of the Centre for Women and Development (CWD), Hanoi

Source: Centers for Disease Control and Prevention, 2013. Modified by author.

Map A2.4   Map of Vietnam marking locations of key informant interviews

Source: Centers for Disease Control and Prevention, 2013. Modified by author.

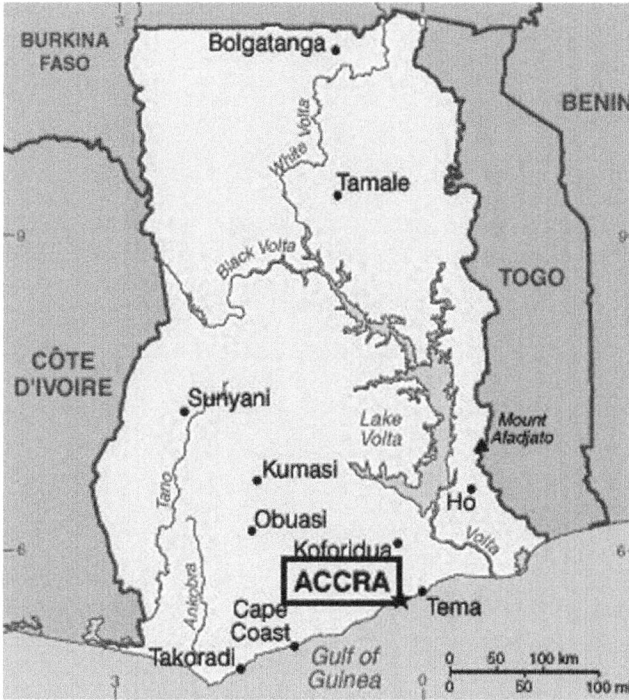

Map A2.5 Map of Ghana, marking the capital Accra, location of key informant interviews, as well as Lake Volta, the most commonly documented site of internal trafficking of children into the fishing industry

Source: Central Intelligence Agency, The World Factbook, 2007. Modified by author.

Bibliography

Legislation, Case Law, Resolutions and Policy Documents

International Legal Instruments and Related Documents

Convention to Suppress the Slave Trade and Slavery (adopted 25 September 1926, entered into force 7 March 1927), 60 LNTS 253 {Slavery Convention].

Convention Concerning Forced and Compulsory Labour (adopted 28 June 1930, entered into force 1 May 1932), 39 UNTS 55 [ILO Convention No. 29].

Convention for the Suppression of the Traffic in Persons and of the Exploitation of the Prostitution of Others (adopted 2 December 1949, entered into force 25 July 1951), 96 UNTS 271 [Trafficking Convention].

Supplementary Convention on the Abolition of Slavery, the Slave Trade and Institutions and Practices Similar to Slavery (adopted 7 September 1956, entered into force 30 April 1957), 226 UNTS 3 [Supplementary Slavery Convention].

Convention Concerning the Abolition of Forced Labour (adopted 25 June 1957, entered into force 17 January 1959), 320 UNTS 291[ILO Convention No. 105].

Convention on the Elimination of All Forms of Discrimination against Women (adopted 18 December 1979, entered into force 3 September 1981), 1249 UNTS 13, [CEDAW].

Convention on the Rights of the Child (adopted 20 November 1989, entered into force 2 September 1990), 1577 UNTS 3.

International Convention on the Protection of the Rights of all Migrant Workers and Members of their Families 2003 (adopted 18 December 1990, entered into force 1 July 2003), UNGA Res. 45/158.

Convention Concerning the Prohibition and Immediate Action for the Elimination of the Worst Forms of Child Labour (adopted 17 June 1999, entered into force 19 November 2000) [ILO Convention No. 182].

CEDAW Committee. 2008. General Recommendation No. 26, Women Migrant Workers, UN Doc. CEDAW/C/2009/WP.1/R.

CEDAW Committee. 1999. General Recommendation No. 24, Article 12: Women and health, 20th Sess.

CEDAW Committee. 1992. General Recommendation No. 19, Violence against women, 11th Sess.

United Nations Protocol to Prevent, Suppress and Punish Trafficking in Persons especially Women and Children, supplementing the United Nations Convention against Transnational Organised crime (adopted 12 December 2000, entered into force 25 December 2003), UNGA Res. 55/25 [Trafficking Protocol].

United Nations Protocol against the Smuggling of Migrants by Land, Air and Sea, supplementing the United Nations Convention against Transnational Organised Crime (adopted 12 December 2000, entered into force 28 January 2004), UNGA Res. 55/25 [Smuggling Protocol].

United Nations Convention against Transnational Organised Crime (adopted 15 November 2000, entered into force 29 September 2003), 2225 UNTS 209.

United Nations Office on Drugs and Crime. 2006. Trauvaux Préparatoires of the negotiations for the elaboration of the United Nations Convention against Transnational Organized Crime and the Protocols thereto.

United Nations Office on Drugs and Crime (UNODC). 2009a. Model Law on Trafficking in Persons, UN Sales No. E.09.V.11 [UNODC Model Law].

Regional Legal Instruments and Related Documents

Europe

European Union. 2002. Brussels Declaration on Preventing and Combating Trafficking in Human Beings, Doc. No. 14981/02. < http://www.refworld.org/docid/4693ac222.html > [Accessed 2 April 2014].

IOM. 2003. Budapest Declaration on Public Health and Trafficking in Human Beings. <http://www.aidsactioneurope.org/system/files/publications/files/1585-0.pdf> [Accessed 2 April 2014].

Council of Europe Convention on Action against Trafficking in Human Beings and its Explanatory Report. 2005, ETS 197, Warsaw, Poland [European Convention on Trafficking].

Organisation for Security and Co-operation in Europe (OSCE). 2005. OSCE Action Plan to Combat Trafficking in Human Beings. 562nd Plenary Meeting, PC.DEC/557/Rev. 1. <http://www.osce.org/pc/15944> [Accessed 2 April 2014].

European Parliament Resolution on Preventing Trafficking in Human Beings. 2010 (adopted by the European Commission on 10 February 2010), B7-0029/2010 [European Parliament Resolution].

European Commission. 2012. An EU Strategy towards the eradication of trafficking in human beings. MEMO/12/455, 19 June 2012. <http://europa.eu/rapid/pressReleasesAction.do?reference=MEMO/12/455&format=HTML&aged=0&language=EN&guiLanguage=en> [Last modified 19 November 2013].

Asia

Asian Regional Initiative against Trafficking (ARIAT) Plan of Action (adopted 1 March 2000, Manila, Philippines).

South Asian Association for Regional Cooperation (SAARC) Convention on Preventing and Combating Trafficking in Women and Children for Prostitution (adopted 5 January 2002, Kathmandu, Nepal) [SAARC Convention].

ASEAN Declaration against Trafficking in Persons Particularly Women and Children. 2004 (adopted on 29 November 2004, Vientiane, Lao People's Democratic Republic).

Africa

African Charter on Human and Peoples' Rights (adopted on 27 June 1981, entered into force on 21 October 1986), 1520 UNTS 217; OAU Doc. CAB/LEG/67/3/ Rev. 5.

African Charter on the Rights and Welfare of the Child (adopted 11 July 1990, entered into force 29 November 1999), OAU Doc. CAB/LEG/24.9/49.

Economic Community of West African States (ECOWAS) Initial Plan of Action against Trafficking Persons 2002–2003 (adopted December 2001, Dakar, Senegal).

Protocol to the African Charter on Human Rights and People's Rights on the Rights of Women (adopted on 11 July 2003, Maputo, Mozambique, entered into force 25 January 2004), OAU Doc. CAB/LEG/66.6.

Domestic Law and Related Documents

Australia

Criminal Code Amendment (Trafficking in Persons and Debt Bondage) Act 2005 (Cth) at s 271.2(1).

Criminal Code Amendment (Slavery and Sexual Servitude) Act 1999 (Cth)

Prostitution Control Act 1994 (Vic).

Ukraine

Constitution of Ukraine, 1996 (adopted 28 June 1996).

Civil Code of Ukraine (enacted 16 January 2003), Law No. 435-IV.

Criminal Procedure Code Ukraine (enacted 18 May 2004), Law No. 1723-IV.

Decree on Amending Criminal Code of Ukraine with regard to Enhancement of Liability of Human Trafficking and the Engaging into Prostitution (enacted 12 January 2006), No. 3316-IV.

Criminal Code of Ukraine, (enacted 10 February 2006), Law No. 2341-III.

Decree on Approving the State Program of Combating Trafficking in Human Beings for the period until 2010 (enacted 7 March 2007), No. 4010.

Law of Ukraine on Combating Trafficking in Human Beings (enacted 22 September 2011, entered into force 15 October 2011), No. 8469.

Vietnam

Constitution of Vietnam, 1992 (adopted 15 April 1992).

Penal Code of the Socialist Republic of Vietnam (entered into force 1 July 2000), No. 15/1999/QH10 (1999) [Penal Code of Vietnam].

Ordinance on Prostitution Prevention and Combat (entered into force 31March 2003), No. 10/2003/L-CTN.

National Plan of Action against Crime of Trafficking in Children and Women during 2004–2010 (entered into force 14 July 2004), No. 120/2004/QD-TTg, 14 July 2004 [National Plan of Action 2004–2010].

Law on Vietnamese Guest Workers (entered into force 29 November 2006), No. 72/2006/QH11 [Guest Workers Act].

Law on Gender Equality (entered into force 1 July 2007), No. 73/2006/QH11 [Law on Gender Equality]

Regulation on Receipt and Support to Community Reintegration of the Trafficked Women and Children Returned Home from Overseas (entered into force 29 January 2007), No. 17/2007/QD-TT [Decision 17].

Guidance on the Organization and Operation of Victim Support Unit pursuant to the Prime Minister's Decision No. 17/2007/QD-TTG (entered into force 17 February 2009), Circular No. 05/2009/TT-BLĐTBXH [Circular No. 5].

Law on Human Trafficking Prevention and Combat (entered into force 1 January 2012), No. 66/2011/QH12.

Ghana

Consolidation of Criminal Code, 1960 (enacted 12 January 1961), Act No. 29.

Constitution of the Republic of Ghana, 1992 (approved 28 April 1992).

Immigration Act, 2000 (enacted 2 February 2000), Act No. 573.

Human Trafficking Act, 2005 (enacted 5 December 2005), Act No. 694.

Economic and Organised Crime Act, 2010 (enacted 6 September 2010), Act No. 804.

Cases

Rantsev v Cyprus and Russia (2010) Eur Court HR, App. 25965/04, 7 January 2010.

R v Tang [2007] 16 VR 454 [12] (Eames JA, Maxwell P and Buchanan JA agreeing), reversed.

R v Tang (2008) 237 CLR 1 (Gleeson CJ, Gummow, Kirby, Hayne, Heydon, Crennan and Kiefel JJ, 28 August 2008).

R v Dobie [2009] QCA 394 [4] (Fraser JA).

Government Reports and Policy Statements

Centers for Disease Control and Prevention (CDC). 2013. Atlanta, United States <http://wwwnc.cdc.gov/travel/destinations/traveler/none/vietnam> [Accessed 7 May 2014].

Central Intelligence Agency. 2007. Ghana. <https://www.cia.gov/library/publications/cia-maps-publications/Ghana.html> [Accessed 7 May 2014].

Cholewinski, R. 2005. *Irregular migrants access to social rights*. Council of Europe: Council of Europe Publishing (Migration Collection).

Danish Immigration Service. 2008. *Protection of victims of trafficking in Ghana: Report from Danish Immigration Service's fact-finding mission to Accra, Ghana.* Copenhagen, Denmark: Danish Immigration Service. <http://www.nyidanmark.dk/NR/rdonlyres/EB5BAEDA-0D96-46C2-B2D2-E48BA8911B2C/0/Ghanaffrapport2008.pdf>. [Last accessed 2 April 2014].

Drugs and Crime Prevention Committee, Parliament of Victoria (Australia). 2010. *Inquiry into people trafficking for sex work,* No. 312 Session 2006–2010, Melbourne, Australia: Parliament of Victoria.

Gallagher, A. and Pearson, E. 2008. *Detention of trafficked persons in shelters: A legal and policy analysis.* Canberra, Australia: Australian Agency for International Development (AusAID).

Ghana Statistical Service (GSS) and Ghana Health Service (GHS). 2008. *Ghana Demographic and Health Survey,* Accra, Ghana and Maryland, US: GSS, GHS and ICF Macro. <http://dhsprogram.com/pubs/pdf/FR221/FR221%5B13Aug2012%5D.pdf> [Last accessed 8 April 2014].

Government of Sweden. 1997. *The Rights of the Poor – Our Common Responsibility,* Government Report 1996/1997: 169.

Government of Ukraine. 2008. *National report submitted in accordance with paragraph 15(a) of the annex to the Human Rights Council Resolution 5/1.* UN Doc. No. A/HRC/WG.6/2/UKR/1, [Government of Ukraine UPR Report].

Hugo, G. 2009. *Migration between Africa and Australia: A demographic perspective.* African Australians: A review of human rights and social inclusion issues. Sydney, Australia: Australian Human Rights Commission.

Iredale, R. and Piper, N. 2003. Identification of the Obstacles to the Signing and Ratification of the UN Convention on the Protection of the Rights of All Migrant Workers: The Asia-Pacific Perspective, International Migration and Multicultural Policies Section, UNESCO.

Ministry of Culture, Sport and Tourism (MOCST), General Statistics Office (GSO) and Institute for Family and Gender Studies and UNICEF, 2008. Results of the Nationwide Survey on the Family in Vietnam 2006: Key Findings, Hanoi: MOCST, GSO, Institute for Family and Gender Studies and UNICEF.

Ministry of Economy of Ukraine. 2005. *Ukraine: Millennium Development Goals 2000+5.* <http://www.un.org.ua/files/MDG_Ukraine_2000_plus_5_ENG.pdf>. [Last accessed 8 April 2014].

Ministry of Foreign Affairs of Vietnam, 2012. Review of Vietnamese migration abroad. Hanoi, Vietnam. <http://eeas.europa.eu/delegations/vietnam/documents/eu_vietnam/vn_migration_abroad_en.pdf>.

Tengey, W. and Oguaah, E. 2002. *The little Ghanaian slaves: A cry for help: Child trafficking in Ghana.* Accra, Ghana: Danish International Development Agency – Ghana Office (DANIDA).

US Department of State. 2012. *Trafficking in persons report.* Washington, D.C.: US Department of State.

US Department of State. 2011a. *Remarks on the release of the 2011 Trafficking in persons report.* <http://www.state.gov/secretary/20092013clinton/rm/2011/06/167156.htm>. [Last accessed 8 April 2014].

US Department of State. 2011b. *Trafficking in persons report.* Washington, D.C.: US Department of State.

US Department of State. 2010. *Trafficking in persons report.* Washington, D.C.: US Department of State.

US Department of State. 2009. *Trafficking in persons report.* Washington, D.C.: US Department of State.

US Department of State. 2005. *Trafficking in persons report.* Washington, D.C.: US Department of State.

US Department of State. 2004. *The link between prostitution and trafficking.* Human trafficking: Data and documents. <http://digitalcommons.unl.edu/cgi/viewcontent.cgi?article=1037&context=humtraffdata&sei-redir=1#search=%22link%20between%20prostitution%20trafficking%22> [Last accessed 8 April 2014].

USAID. 2010. *Trafficking of adult men in the Europe and Euroasia region.* Social Transition Series, Washington D.C., US: USAID Development Experience Clearinghouse,

USAID. 2008. *Combatting trafficking in persons in the 21st Century.* Washington D.C., US: USAID Office of Women in Development.

Sources from the United Nations System

Bustamante, J. 2011. *Report of the Special Rapporteur on the Human Rights of Migrants*, UN. Doc. No. A/HRC/17/33, 21 March 2011, New York.

CEDAW Committee. 2007. *Concluding Observations: Vietnam*, UN. Doc. No. CEDAW/C/VNM/CO/6, 37th Sess. 2 February 2007.

Coomaraswamy, R. 2000. *Integration of the human rights of women and the gender perspective.* Report of the Special Rapporteur on Violence against Women, its Causes and Consequences, on trafficking in women, women's migration and violence against women, UN Doc. E/CN.4/2000/68, 29 February 2000.

Crépeau, F. 2014. *Report of the Special Rapporteur on the Human Rights of Migrants: Labour exploitation of migrants*, UN. Doc. No. A/HRC/26/35, 3 April 2014, New York.

D'Cunha, J. 2002. *Trafficking in persons: A gender and rights perspective.* United Nations Expert Group Meeting on Trafficking in women and girls, Doc. No. EGM/TRAF/2002/EP.8, 8 November 2002, Glen Cove, New York.

De Lind van Wijngaarden, J.W. 2007. *Assessment of HIV/AIDS vulnerability, responses and STI/HIV prevention, care and support needs of institutionalized children aged 14 to 19 in selected labour and social education institutions and reform schools in Vietnam.* Hanoi, Vietnam: UNICEF.

ILO. 2012. *ILO global estimate of forced labour: Results and methodology.* Special Action Programme to Combat Forced Labour, Geneva, Switzerland: ILO.

ILO. 2009. The cost of coercion: Global report under the follow-up to the ILO Declaration on Fundamental Principles and Rights at Work. In: *98th Session of International Labour Conference*, Geneva, Switzerland 3–19 June 2009. <http://www.stopht.ca/files/cost_of_coercion_forced_labour.pdf>. [Last accessed 8 April 2014].

ILO. 2005. A global alliance against forced labour: Global report under the follow-up to the ILO Declaration on Fundamental Principles and Rights at Work. In: *93rd Session of International Labour Conference*, Geneva, Switzerland 31 May-16 June 2005. <http://www.ilo.org/public/english/standards/relm/ilc/ilc93/pdf/rep-i-b.pdf>. [Last accessed 8 April 2014].

ILO-IPEC. 2001. *Combating Trafficking in Child Labour Exploitation in West and Central Africa: Synthesis Report based on studies in Benin, Burkina Faso, Cameroon, Côte d'Ivoire, Gabon, Ghana, Nigeria and Togo.* Geneva, Switzerland: ILO-IPEC.

ILO and Asian Development Bank (ADB). 2011. *Women and labour markets in Asia: Rebalancing towards gender equality in labour markets in Asia.* Bangkok, Thailand: ILO Regional Office for Asia and the Pacific and Asian Development Bank.

Lyttleton, C. 2002. *Prevention of HIV/AIDS among ethnic minorities of the Upper Mekong Region through community-based non-formal and formal education: Final report of phase 1 – Needs assessment.* Bangkok, Thailand and Sydney, Australia: UNESCO Asia Pacific Regional Bureau for Education. <http://portal.unesco.org/pv_obj_cache/pv_obj_id_D8A9AC30F393ED9F884E59A9A2F53889BB0F1300/filename/167+EX+Prevention+of+HIV-AIDS+among+Ethnic+Minorities+Mekong.pdf>.

Ngozi Ezeilo, J. 2012a. *Report of the Special Rapporteur on Trafficking in Persons, especially Women and Children.* UN Doc No. A/HRC/20/18, 6 June 2012, New York.

Ngozi, Ezeilo. J. 2012b. *Report of the Special Rapporteur on Trafficking in Persons, especially Women and Children: Mission to Australia.* UN Doc. No. A/HRC/20/18/Add.1, 18 May 2012, New York.

Ngozi Ezeilo, J. 2009. *Report submitted by the Special Rapporteur on trafficking in persons, especially women and children,* UN doc. A/HRC/10/16, 20 February 2009.

Office of the High Commissioner for Human Rights (OHCHR). 2010. *UN OHCHR Commentary on Recommended Principles and Guidelines on Human Rights and Human Trafficking.* UN.Doc. HR/PUB/10/2. <http://www.ohchr.org/Documents/Publications/Commentary_Human_Trafficking_en.pdf> [Accessed 4 January 2013].

OHCHR. 2002. *Recommended Principles and Guidelines on Human Rights and Human Trafficking.* UN. Doc. E/2002/68/Add.1. <http://www.unhcr.org/refworld/docid/3f1fc60f4.html> [Last accessed 8 April 2014].

Truong, T. 2006. *Poverty, gender and human trafficking in Sub-Saharan Africa: Rethinking best practices in migration management.* Paris, France: UNESCO. <http://unesdoc.unesco.org/images/0014/001432/143227e.pdf> [Last accessed 8 April 2014].

Truong, T. and Belen-Angeles, M. 2005. *Searching for best practices to counter human trafficking in Africa: A focus on women and children.* Paris, France: UNESCO

UNAIDS and WHO. 2004. *Epidemiological factsheets on HIV/AIDS and sexually transmitted infections: Ghana.* <http://data.unaids.org/publications/ Fact-Sheets01/ghana_en.pdf> [Last accessed 8 April 2014].

United Nations Center for International Crime Prevention. 2003. *Assessing transnational organized crime: Results of a pilot survey of 40 selected transnational organised criminal groups in 16 Countries.* Report from the UN Center for International Crime Prevention, Vienna, Austria. <http:// www.unodc.org/pdf/crime/publications/Pilot_survey.pdf>. [Last accessed 8 April 2014].

UNICEF. n.d. *Country profile: Education in Ukraine.* <http://www.unicef.org/ ceecis/Ukraine.pdf> [Accessed 10 July 2012].

UNICEF. 2001. *Profiting from abuse: An investigation into the sexual exploitation of our children.* UNICEF New York. <http://www.unicef.org/publications/ files/pub_profiting_en.pdf> [Last accessed 8 April 2014].

UNDP. 2013. *Human development report – The rise of the south: Human progress in a diverse world.* NY, US: UNDP. <http://hdr.undp.org/sites/default/files/ reports/14/hdr2013_en_complete.pdf> [Last accessed 18 April 2014].

UNDP. 2009. *Equal opportunities and women's rights in Ukraine Programme: Report for 2008.* <http://www.undp.org.ua/files/en_11592EOWR_prodoc_ eng.pdf> [Last accessed 8 April 2014].

UNDP. 2008. *Human Development Report Ukraine: Human development and Ukraine's European choice.* UNDP Ukraine. <http://hdr.undp.org/en/ reports/national/europethecis/ukraine/Ukraine_NHDR_2008_EN.pdf>. [Last accessed 8 April 2014].

UNDP. 2007. *Human Development Report 2007 (West Gonja District): Vulnerability and attainment of the MDGs at the local level.* <http://hdr.undp. org/en/reports/national/africa/ghana/UNDPWestGonjareport2007.pdf> [Last accessed 8 April 2014].

UNDP. 2006. *Globalisation, Gender and Work in the Context of Economic Transition: The Case of Viet Nam*, report prepared by Naila Kabeer and Van Anh Tran Thi, Hanoi, Vietnam: UNDP.

UNDP. 2003. *Gender issues in Ukraine: Challenges and opportunities.* <http:// socialtransitions.kdid.org/sites/socialtransitions/files/resource/files/ST1022_ en_64099super.pdf>. [Last accessed 8 April 2014].

UNIFEM East and Southeast Asia Office and UNIAP. n.d. *Trafficking in persons: A gender and rights perspective (Briefing kit).* <http://www.unrol.org/files/ traffkit_eng.pdf>. [Last accessed 8 April 2014].

United Nations Educational, Scientific and Cultural Organisation (UNESCO). 2012. *World Atlas of Gender Equality in Education*. Paris, France: UNESCO Publishing.

UNESCO Institute for Statistics (UIS). 2008. *Global education digest*. Montreal, Canada: UIS.

UNESCO. 2007. *Human Trafficking in South Africa: Root causes and recommendations*. Policy Paper Poverty Series No. 14.5(E), Paris, France: UNESCO. <http://unesdoc.unesco.org/images/0015/001528/152823E.pdf>. [Last accessed 8 April 2014].

UNESCO. 2006a. *Human trafficking in Mozambique: Root causes and recommendations*. Policy Paper No. 14.1(E), Paris, France: UNESCO. <http:// unesdoc.unesco.org/images/0014/001478/147846e.pdf> [Last accessed 8 April 2014].

UNESCO. 2006b. *Human trafficking in Nigeria: Root causes and recommendations*. Policy Paper No. 14.2(E), Paris, France: UNESCO. <http://unesdoc.unesco. org/images/0014/001478/147844e.pdf>.[Last accessed 8 April 2014].

UNESCO. 1997. *International Standard Classification of Development (ISCED) 1997*. <http://www.unesco.org/education/information/nfsunesco/doc/isced_1997. htm>. [Last accessed 8 April 2014].

UNESCO. n.d. Trafficking and HIV Project: Trafficking statistics project. <http:// www.unescobkk.org/culture/cultural-diversity/trafficking-and-hivaids- project/projects/trafficking-statistics-project/>. [Last accessed 8 April 2014].

UNFPA. 2006. *A passage to hope: Women and international migration*. State of the World Population 2006. < http://www.unfpa.org/swp/2006/pdf/en_sowp06. pdf> [Last accessed 8 April 2014].

UNIAP. 2010. *Human Trafficking Laws: Legal provisions for victims; Comparing legal definitions and frameworks against the United Nations Protocol on Human Trafficking: Cambodia, People's Republic of China, Lao PDR, Malaysia, Myanmar, Thailand and Vietnam*. <http://www.no-trafficking.org/ reports_docs/legal_prov_vics.pdf>. [Last accessed 8 April 2014].

UNIAP. 2008. *Guide to ethics and human rights in counter-trafficking: Ethical standards for counter-trafficking research and programming*. Bangkok, Thailand: UNIAP. <http://www.no-trafficking.org/reports_docs/uniap_ethics_ guidelines.pdf>. [Last accessed 8 April 2014].

UNDOC. 2013a, Blue Heart Campaign against Human Trafficking. <http://www. unodc.org/blueheart/en/about.html>. [Last accessed 8 April 2014].

UNODC. 2013b. UNODC on human trafficking and migrant smuggling. <https:// www.unodc.org/unodc/en/human-trafficking/index.html>.

UNODC. 2009b. *A global report on trafficking in persons*. UN. GIFT. <http:// www.unodc.org/unodc/en/frontpage/unodc-report-on-human-trafficking- exposes-modern-form-of-slavery-.html>. [Last accessed 8 April 2014].

UNODC. 2009c. *International framework for action to implement the trafficking in persons protocol*. Vienna, Austria: UNODC. <http://www.unodc.org/ documents/human-trafficking/Framework_for_Action_TIP.pdf> [Last accessed 8 April 2014].

UNODC. 2008. *Human trafficking: An overview*. United Nations, New York: UN.GIFT.

UNODC. 2004. Compilation of United Nations Convention against Transnational Organised Crime and the Protocols thereto. Vienna, Austria: UNODC.

UNODC. n.d. *Trafficking in persons to Europe for sexual exploitation*. <http:// www.unodc.org/documents/publications/TiP_Europe_EN_LORES.pdf>. [Last accessed 8 April 2014].

UN Statistics Division. 2011. *Millennium Development Goals indicators*. <http:// mdgs.un.org/unsd/mdg/SeriesDetail.aspx?srid=634&crid>. [Last accessed 8 April 2014].

United Nations Office on Drugs and Crime (UNODC). 2008. *Human trafficking: An overview*. United Nations, New York: UN.GIFT.

International Organisation and Non-Governmental Organisation (NGO) Sources

Anarfi, J.K. et al. 2000. *Push and pull factors of international migration. Country report: Ghana*. Brussels: Eurostat Working Papers 2000/E(10).

ActionAid International Vietnam. 2005. *Synthesis report: The trafficking of Vietnamese women and children*.

Amnesty International. 2006. *Ukraine: Domestic violence – Blaming the victim*. AI Index EUR 50/005/2006.

Anarfi, J. and Kwankye, S. 2003. *Migration from and to Ghana: Background paper*. Brighton, UK: Development Research Centre on Migration, Globalisation and Poverty.

Anderson, B. and Davidson, J. O. 2003. *Is trafficking in human beings demand driven? A multi-country pilot study*. Geneva, Switzerland: IOM Research Series.

Anti-Slavery Think Tank. 2014. *From Experience: How to combat slavery in our generation – A discussion paper*. Hong Kong, China: Liberty Asia.

Asia Watch (Women's Rights Project). 1993. *A modern form of slavery: Trafficking of Burmese women and girls into brothels in Thailand*. New York, US: Human Rights Watch.

Beegle, Kathleen, De Weerdt, Joachim and Dercon, Stefan. 2010, *Migration and Economic Mobility in Tanzania: Evidence from a Tracking Survey*. Policy Research Working Paper No. 4798, Washington D.C., US: World Bank.

Bettio, F. and Verashchagina, A. 2009. *Gender segregation in the labour market: Root causes, implications and policy responses in the EU*. Brussels, Belgium: European Commission's Expert Group on Gender and Employment (EGGE), Directorate-General for Employment, Social Affairs and Equal Opportunities.

Bøas, M. and Hatløy, A. 2006. *After the 'storm': Economic activities among children and youth in return areas in post war Liberia: The case of Voinjama*, Oslo, Norway: Fafo.

Boateng, K. and Ofori-Sarpong, E. 2002. *An analytical study of the labour market for tertiary graduates in Ghana: A World Bank/National Council for Tertiary Education and National Accreditation Board Project*, Accra, Ghana. <http://www.usp.ac.fj/worldbank2009/frame/Documents/Publications_regional/Ghana_Labor_Market_tertiary_En02.pdf>.

Bourke-Martignoni, J. 2001. *Violence against women in Vietnam: Report prepared for the Committee on the Elimination of Discrimination Against Women*, Geneva, Switzerland: World Organisation Against Torture.

Brunovskis, A. and Surtees, R. 2007. *Leaving the past behind? When victims of trafficking decline assistance*. Oslo, Norway and Fafo and NEXUS Institute.

Brunovskis, A. and Tyldum, G. 2004. *Crossing borders: An empirical study of transnational prostitution and trafficking in human beings*. Oslo, Norway: Fafo.

Burke, A. and Ducci, S. 2005. *Desk Review: Trafficking in minors for commercial sexual exploitation: Thailand*. United Nations Interregional Crime and Justice Research Institute, Action Programme Against Trafficking in Minors for Sexual Purposes. <http://www.unicri.it/emerging_crimes/human_trafficking/minors/docs/dr_thailand.pdf>. [Last accessed 8 April 2014].

Carling, J. 2006. *Migration, human smuggling and trafficking from Nigeria to Europe*. IOM.

Carnegie Council. 2014. *Ukraine: A federalist future?* <http://www.carnegie council.org/publications/articles_papers_reports/0208.html> [Last accessed 7 May 2014].

Center of Social Expertise of the Institute of Sociology. 2004. *Rapid assessment of trafficking in children for labour and sexual exploitation in Ukraine*. Kyiv, Ukraine: International Programme on the Elimination of Child Labour [ILO-IPEC] and National Academy of Sciences.

Chenda, K. 2006. *Life after reintegration: The situation of child trafficking survivors*. Geneva, Switzerland: IOM.

Chiongson, R.A. 2009. *CEDAW and the law: A gendered and rights-based review of Vietnamese legal documents through the lens of CEDAW*. United Nations Development Fund for Women [UNIFEM].

Corsini, V. 2010. *Population and social conditions: Highly educated men and women likely to live longer*. Brussels, Belgium: Eurostat (Statistics in focus). <http://epp.eurostat.ec.europa.eu/cache/ITY_OFFPUB/KS-SF-10-024/EN/KS-SF-10-024-EN.PDF>. [Last accessed 8 April 2014].

De Haas, H. 2008. *Migration and development: A theoretical perspective*. International Migration Institute (IMI) Working Papers, Paper 9. Oxford, UK: IMI.

De Haas, H. et al. 2008. *Mobility and human development*. IMI Working Papers, Paper 14, Oxford, UK: IMI.

Department of Peacekeeping Operations. 2004. *Human trafficking and United Nations peacekeeping.* DPKO Policy Paper.

Derks, A, Henke, R. and Ly, V. 2006. *Review of a Decade of Research on Trafficking in Persons,* Cambodia. San Francisco, US: The Asia Foundation.

ECPAT Australia. 1998. *Youth for Sale. ECPAT Australia's National Inquiry into the Commercial Sexual Exploitation of Children and Young People in Australia.* Melbourne, Victoria: ECPAT Australia.

Fahey, S. 2002. *Women in Vietnam.* Asian Development Bank (ADB). Manila, The Philippines: ADB. <http://www.adb.org/sites/default/files/pub/2002/women_vie.pdf>.

Hegewisch, A.H.L., Hayes, J. and Hartmann, H. 2010. *Separate and Not Equal? Gender segregation in the labor market and the gender wage gap.* Washington: Institute for Women's Policy Research.

Higazi, A. 2005. *Ghana country study: A part of the report on informal remittance systems in Africa, Caribbean and Pacific (ACP) countries.* ESRC Centre on Migration, Policy and Society (COMPAS), London, UK: Emerging Markets Group. <http://www.dfid.gov.uk/r4d/PDF/Outputs/EC-PREP/InformalRemittanceSummary.pdf>. [Last accessed 8 April 2014].

Horwood, C. 2009. *In pursuit of the Southern Dream: Victims of necessity – Assessment of irregular movement of men from East Africa and the Horn to South Africa.* Geneva, Switzerland: IOM.

Huguet, J. and Ramangkura, V. 2007. *A long road home: Analysis of regional and national processes for the return and reintegration of victims of trafficking in the Greater Mekong Sub-region.* IOM.

Human Rights Watch (HRW). 2002. *Hopes betrayed: Trafficking of women and girls to post-conflict Bosnia and Herzegovina for forced prostitution.* 14(9), pp. 1–76.

IN Network Ghana. n.d. *Report on child labour in fishing in the Gomoa and Awutu Efutu-Senya Districts,* Ghana. <http://www.innetwork.org.gh/docs/materials/ChildLabourwebsite.pdf> [Last accessed 8 April 2014].

IOM. 2012a. HIV and Bangladeshi women migrant workers: An assessment of vulnerabilities and gaps in services. Geneva, Switzerland: IOM.

IOM. 2012b. Behavioural study of female sex workers along Ghana's Tema-Paga transport corridor, Accra, Ghana: IOM.

IOM. 2011. *Unaccompanied children on the move: The work of the International Organisation for Migration.* Geneva, Switzerland: IOM.

IOM. 2007. *The IOM Handbook on Direct Assistance for Victims of Trafficking.* Geneva, Switzerland: IOM. <http://publications.iom.int/bookstore/free/IOM_Handbook_Assistance.pdf> [Last accessed 8 April 2014].

IOM. n.d. *Trafficking from Caucasus: IOM case studies.* <http://www.iom.int/armenia/case_studies_caucasus_eng.pdf> [Accessed 16 May 2012].

IOM. 2006. *Human trafficking survey: Belarus, Bulgaria, Moldova, Romania, and Ukraine.* Kyiv, Ukraine: IOM ((Prepared by GfK).

IOM and Nexus Institute. 2012. *Trafficked at Sea: The exploitation of Ukrainian seafarers and fishers*. Geneva, Switzerland: IOM and Washington. D.C., US: Nexus Institute

Kelly, E. 2002. *Journeys of jeopardy: A review of research on trafficking in women and children in Europe*. IOM Migration Research Series.

Khuat, T.H.O. 2007. *HIV/AIDS policy in Vietnam: A civil society perspective*. Hanoi, Vietnam: Institute for Social Development Studies (ISDS) and Open Society Institute. <http://www.soros.org/publications/hivaids-policy-vietnam-civil-society-perspective>.[Last accessed 8 April 2014].

Kufogbe, S.K. 2005. *Child labour in fishing in the Gomoa and Awutu-Efutu-Senya districts*. Accra, Ghana: IN Network (formerly International Needs) Ghana.

Kunfaa, E.Y. 1999. *Consultations with the poor: Ghana*. Kumasi, Ghana: World Bank.

La Strada. 2008. *Violation of women's rights: A cause and consequence of trafficking in women*. Amsterdam, Netherlands: La Strada International.

Lainez, N. 2011. *Prostitution mobility and representations: The case of Vietnamese prostitutes going to Cambodia, Hô Chi Minh City and Bangkok*. Ho Chi Minh City, Vietnam: Alliance Anti-Trafic Vietnam & IRASEC/Observatory on illicit trafficking.

Lăzăroiu, S. and Alexandru, M. 2003. *Who is the Next Victim? Vulnerability of young Romanian women to trafficking in human beings*. Bucharest, Romania: IOM.

Lee, S. 2008. *How do women fare in education, employment and health? Gender analysis of the 2006 Vietnam household living standard survey*. World Bank, Report No. 47433-VN.

Lemistre, Philippe and Magrini, Marie-Benoît. 2009. *Education level and the distance income migration trade-off*. Marseille, France.

Levchenko, K. 1999. *Legal study on the combat of trafficking in women in forced prostitution in Ukraine*. Vienna, Austria: Ludwig Bolzmann Institute of Human Rights.

Lim, L.L. ed. 1998. *The sex sector: The economic and social bases of prostitution in Southeast Asia*. Geneva, Switzerland: International Labour Office.

Luda di Cortemiglia, V. n.d. *Desk review trafficking in minors for commercial sexual exploitation Ukraine*. United Nations Interregional Crime and Justice Research Institute.

Malynovska, O. 2006. Caught between East and West, Ukraine struggles with its migration policy. *Migration Policy Institute*. http://www.migrationpolicy.org/article/caught-between-east-and-west-ukraine-struggles-its-migration-policy. [Last accessed 9 April 2014].

Martens, J., Pieczkowski, M. and van Vuuren-Smyth, B. 2003. *Seduction, sale and slavery: Trafficking in women and children for sexual exploitation in South Africa*, IOM.

McKibbon, S. 1992. Slavery of Mozambican refugees in South Africa. London, UK: Anti-Slavery International.

Sex, Slavery and the Trafficked Woman

Mediterranean Institute of Gender Studies. 2007. Mapping the realities of trafficking in women or the purpose of sexual exploitation in Cyprus. Cyprus, Mediterranean Institute of Gender Studies

Mendelsen, S. 2005. *Barracks and brothels: Peacekeepers and human trafficking in the Balkans*, Washington, D.C., US: Center for Strategic and International Studies (CSIS).

Odera, T.M. and Malinowski, R.L. 2011. *Guidelines for assisting victims of trafficking in the East Africa region.* Geneva, Switzerland: IOM.

Organisation for Security and Cooperation in Europe Office for Democratic Institutions and Human Rights (OSCE-ODIHR). 2008. *Compensation for trafficked and exploited persons in the OSCE region.* Warsaw, Poland: OSCE Office for Democratic Institutions and Human Rights.

Parson, C.R., Skeldon, R., Walmsley, T.L., and Winters, L.A. 2007b. Quantifying international migration: A database of bilateral migrant stock, World Bank Policy Research Working Paper no. 4165, Washington D.C., US: World Bank.

Pearson, E. 2002. *Human traffic, human rights: Redefining witness protection.* London, UK: Anti-Slavery International.

Poulain, M. and Herm, A. 2011. *Guide to enhancing migration data: West and Central Africa.* Geneva, Switzerland: IOM.

Pyshchulina, O. 2006. *Human trafficking and legal practice: A new challenge for Ukraine*, Budapest, Hungary: Center for Policy Studies European University and Open Society Institute.

Putt, J. 2007. *Human trafficking to Australia: A research challenge, trends and issues in crime and criminal justice.* Australian Institute of Criminology, 338, pp. 1–6.

Radu, P.C. 2003. *Freedom at midnight: Human trafficking in Romania.* Bucharest, Romania: Institute for War and Peace Reporting.

Raymond, J., D'Cunha, J., Ruhaini Dzuhayatin, S., Hynes, H.P., Ramirez Rodriguez, Z., and Santos, A. 2002. A comparative study of women trafficked in the migration process: Patterns, profiles and health consequences of sexual exploitation in five countries (Indonesia, the Philippines, Thailand, Venezuela, and the United States). North Amherst, MA: Coalition Against Trafficking in Women. <http://www.catwinternational.org/Home/Article/203-a-comparative-study-of-women-trafficked-in-the-migration-process>. [Last accessed 8 April 2014].

Raymond, J and Hughes, D. 2001. *Sex trafficking of women in the United States: International and domestic trends.* Coalition against Trafficking in Women.

Riisøen, K.H., Hatløy, A. and Bjerkan, L. 2004. *Travel to uncertainty: A study of relocation in Burkina Faso, Ghana and Mali.* Oslo, Norway: Faso.

Siddiqi, F. and Patrinos, H.A. 1995. *Child labor: Issues, causes and interventions.* Washington D.C., US: World Bank.

Siren (Strategic Information Response Network). 2008a. *Human Trafficking Data Sheet.* Hanoi, Vietnam: United Nations Inter-Agency Project on Human Trafficking (UNDIAP).

Siren (Strategic Information Response Network). 2008b. *Human Trafficking Data Sheet*. Bangkok, Thailand: United Nations Inter-Agency Project on Human Trafficking (UNDIAP).

Social Monitoring Center and Ukrainian Institute of Social Studies. 2001. *Trafficking in women as a social problem in Ukrainian society*. Kyiv, Ukraine: Winrock International. <http://pdf.usaid.gov/pdf_docs/Pnacy387.pdf> [Last access 8 April 2014].

Sölkner, A. 2008. *Needs assessment of the national referral mechanism for victims of trafficking in human beings in Ukraine: Assessment report*. Organization for Security and Co-operation in Europe (OSCE).

Surtees, R. 2008a. *Trafficking in men – A trend less considered: The case of Belarus and the Ukraine*. Kyiv, Ukraine: IOM.

Surtees, R. 2005. *Second annual report on victims of trafficking in South-Eastern Europe*. IOM.

Surtees, R. and Craggs, S. 2010. *Beneath the surface: Methodological issues in research and data collection with assisted trafficked victims*. Geneva, Switzerland: IOM and Washington, D.C., US: NEXUS Institute.

TAMPEP (European Network for HIV/STI Prevention and Health Promotion among Migrant Sex Workers). 2007. *National report on HIV and sex work: Ukraine*. Amsterdam, Netherlands: TAMPEP. <http://tampep.eu/documents/Ukraine%20National%20Report.pdf> [Last accessed 8 April 2014].

Taylor, E. 2002. *Trafficking in women and girls*. Accra, Ghana: IOM.

The Advocates for Human Rights. 2005. *Distinguishing trafficking from illegal migration*. <http://www.stopvaw.org/distinguishing_trafficking_from_illegal_migration.html> [Last accessed 8 April 2014].

Ukrainian Center for Social Reforms (UCSR), State Statistical Committee of Ukraine and Macro International. 2008. *2007 Ukraine Demographic and Health Survey: Key Findings*. Maryland, USA: UCSR and Macro International.

Van Klaveren, M., Hughie-Williams, M., and Ramos Martin, N. 2010. An overview of women's work and employment in Ukraine, Decisions for Life MDG3 Project, Country Report No. 8. <http://www.uva-aias.net/uploaded_files/publications/WP94-Klaveren,Tijdens,Hughie-Williams,Ramos-Ukraine.pdf>. [Last accessed 8 April 2014].

Verité, n.d. *Hidden Costs in the Global Economy: Human Trafficking of Philippine Males in Maritime, Construction and Agriculture*. Amherst, MA: USA.

Walker, A. 2013. Strange trafficking: Sex, slavery and the freedom principle. *Legal Studies Research Paper Series*, No. 2013-2, 1–37.

Walker, C., Aliber, M. and Nkosi, B. 2007. *Women's property rights, HIV/AIDS and domestic violence: South Africa country report*. Washington D.C., US: International Center for Research on Women (ICRW).

Warnath, S. 2007. *Examining the intersection between trafficking in persons and domestic violence*. Washington D.C., US: Social Transition Team, Office of Democracy, Governance and Social Transition of the United States Agency for International Development.

Watson, C. 2005. *Addressing the MDGs and targets for education and gender: Comments on Selected Aspects Linked to the ICPD Programme of Action.* UNICEF. <http://www.un.org/esa/population/publications/PopAspectsMDG/17_UNICEF2.pdf>. [Last accessed 8 April 2014].

Wells, M. 2005. *Vietnam: Gender situation analysis.* Manila, The Philippines: Asian Development Bank.

Wijers, M. and Haveman, R. 2006. *Guidelines on trafficking in human beings for the criminal justice chain in Ukraine.* Kyiv, Ukraine: IOM.

Wijers, M. and Lap-Chew, L. 1997. *Trafficking in women: Forced labour and slavery-like practices in marriage, domestic labour and prostitution.* Utrecht, The Netherlands: Foundation against Trafficking in Women.

World Bank. 2011. *Implementation completion and results report: Equal access to quality education in Ukraine.* Report No. ICR00001701, Human Development Second Unit. Europe and Central Asia Region: World Bank.

World Bank. 2009. *Country social analysis: Ethnicity and development in Vietnam.* Washington D.C., US: World Bank

World Bank. 2008. *Ukraine improving intergovernmental fiscal relations and public health and education expenditure policy: Selected issues.* Report No. 42450-UA, Washington D.C., US: World Bank.

World Bank. 2007a. *Poverty update.* Report No. 39887-UA, Washington D.C., US: World Bank.

World Bank. 2006. *Vietnam Aiming High: Vietnam development report 2007, Poverty reduction and economic management unit.* East Asia and the Pacific Region, Report No. 38064-VN, Washington D.C., U.S.: World Bank.

World Bank. 2005. *Ukraine: Poverty assessment: Poverty and inequality in a growing economy.* Report No. 34631-UA, Washington D.C., US: World Bank.

Women's Consortium of Ukraine et. al. 2008. *Alternative report on the implementation of the UN Convention on the Elimination of All Forms of Discrimination against Women in Ukraine,* Kyiv, Ukraine: Women's Consortium of Ukraine.

Zakharov, Y. and Yavorsky, V. 2009. *Human rights in Ukraine-2008.* Kharkiv, Ukraine: Prava Ludyny (Human Rights Monthly Bullletin).

Zimmerman, C. and Watts, C. 2003. *WHO ethical and safety recommendations for interviewing trafficked women.* Geneva, Switzerland: World Health Organisation.

Journals, Books and Other Sources

Adams, N. 2003. Anti-trafficking legislation: Protection or deportation? *Feminist Review,* 73, pp. 135–9.

Aghatise, E. 2004. Trafficking for prostitution in Italy: Possible effects of government proposals for legalization of brothels. *Violence against Women,* 10(10), pp. 1126–55.

Agustín, L. 2012. Kristof and the rescue industry: The soft side of imperialism. *Counter punch.* <http://www.counterpunch.org/2012/01/25/the-soft-side-of-imperialism/> [Last accessed 8 April 2014].

Agustín, L. 2009. Trafficking in persons, the no-methodology report. *The Naked Anthropologist.* <http://www.lauraagustin.com/tip-trafficking-in-persons-the-no-methodology-report> [Last accessed 8 April 2014].

Agustín, L. 2007. *Sex at the margins: Migration, labour markets and the rescue industry.* London, UK: Zed Books.

Agustín, L. 2006. The disappearing of a migration category: Migrants who sell sex. *Journal of Ethnic and Migration Studies*, 32, pp. 29–47.

Agustín, L. 2005. Migrants in the mistress's house: Other voices in the 'trafficking' debate. *Social Politics*, 12(1), pp. 96–117.

Agustín, L. 2004. Alternative ethics, or: Telling lies to researchers. *Research for sex work*, 7, pp. 6–7.

Agustín, L. 2003a. Forget victimization: Granting agency to migrants. *Development*, 46(3), pp. 30–36.

Agustín, L. 2003b. A migrant world of services. Social politics: *International Studies in Gender, State and Society*, 10(3), pp. 377–96.

Ahmed, A. and Seshu, M. 2012. 'We have the right not to be "rescued" ... ' When anti-trafficking programmes undermine the health and well-being of sex workers. *Anti-Trafficking Review*, 1, pp. 149–68.

Aidis, R., Friederike, W., Smallbone, D. and Isakova, N. 2007. Female entrepreneurship in transition economies: The case of Lithuania and Ukraine. *Feminist Economics*, 13(2), pp. 157–83.

Aikins, A.D. and Ofori-Atta, A.L. 2007. Homelessness and mental health in Ghana: Everyday experiences of Accra's migrant squatters. *Journal of Health Psychology*, 12(5), pp. 761–78.

Ali, H.M. 2010. Data collection on victims of human trafficking: An analysis of various sources. *Journal of Human Security*, 6(1), pp. 55–69.

Allain, J. 2012. *The legal understanding of slavery: From the historical to the contemporary.* Oxford University Press, Oxford: United Kingdom.

Allain, J. 2009. On the curious disappearance of human servitude from general international law, *Journal of the History of International Law*, 11, pp. 303–32.

Alsgaard, H. 2011. Uncovered: the policing of sex work. *Berkeley Journal of Gender, Law and Justice,* 26, pp. 198–202.

Altink, S. 1995. *Stolen lives: Trading women into sex and slavery.* London, UK: Scarlet Press.

Amar, P. 2009. Operation Princess in Rio de Janeiro: Policing 'sex trafficking', strengthening worker citizenship, and the urban geopolitics of security in Brazil. *Security Dialogue*, 40(4–5), pp. 513–41.

Andrees, B. and Belser, P. 2009. *Forced labour: Coercion and exploitation in the private economy.* London, UK: Lynne Rienner Publishers.

Andrees, B. and Van der Linden, M.N. 2005. Designing trafficking research from a labour market perspective: The ILO experience. *International Migration*, 43(1/2), pp. 55–73.

Andrijasevic, R. and Anderson, B. 2009. Anti-trafficking campaigns: Decent? Honest? Truthful? *Feminist Review*, 92, pp. 151–5.

Andrijasevic, R. 2007. Beautiful dead bodies: Gender, migration and representation in anti-trafficking campaigns. *Feminist Review*, 86, pp. 24–44.

Andrijasevic, R. 2004. Trafficking in women and the politics of mobility in Europe. PhD thesis, University of Utrecht, Utrecht, The Netherlands.

Androff, D.K. 2011. The problem of contemporary slavery: An international human rights challenge for social work. *International Social Work*, 54(2), pp. 209–22.

Anderson, B. 2013. *Us and Them? The Dangerous Politics of Immigration Control*. Oxford, UK: Oxford University Press.

Anderson, B. 2010. Mobilizing migrants, making citizens: Migrant domestic workers as political agents. *Ethnic and Racial Studies*, 33(1), pp. 69–74.

Anderson, B. 2002. Why madam has so many bathrobes? Demand for migrant workers in the EU. *Journal of Economic and Social Geography*, 92(1), pp. 18–26.

Anderson, S.A. 2002. Prostitution and sexual autonomy: Making sense of the prohibition of prostitution. *Ethics*, 1, pp. 748–80.

Anguita Olmedo, C. 2007. El tráfico ilegal de seres humanos para la explotación sexual y laboral: La esclavitud del siglo XXI. *Nomades: Revista Crítica de Ciencias Sociales y Jurídicas*, 15(1), pp. 3–16.

Ansah, N. 2006. Structural relations to the sex trade and its links to trafficking: The case of Ghana. *Agenda: Empowering Women for Gender Equity*, 20(70), pp. 100–106.

Ariffin, J. 2004. Gender critiques of the Millennium Development Goals: An overview and an assessment. In: International Council on Social Welfare (ICSW), *31st International Conference on Social Progress and Social Justice*. 16–20 August 2004, Kuala Lumpur, Malaysia.

Arneson, R. 1994. Autonomy and preference-formation. In: J.L. Coleman and A. Buchanan, eds. *In Harm's Way: Essays in Honor of Joel Feinberg*. Cambridge, US: Cambridge University Press, pp. 42–75.

Aronowitz, A.A. 2001. Smuggling and trafficking in human beings: The phenomenon, the markets that drive it and the organizations that promote it. *European Journal on Criminal Policy and Research*, 9(2), pp. 163–95.

Asiedu, A. 2003. Some benefits of migrants' return visits to Ghana. In: University of Sussex, *International workshop on migration and poverty in West Africa*. 13–14 March 2003, Brighton, UK.

Askola, H. 2007. *Legal responses to trafficking in women for sexual exploitation in the European Union*. Portland, Oregon: Hart Publishing.

Associação Brasileira de Defesa da Mulher, da Infância e da Juventude (ASBRAD). 2008. Direitos humanos e gênero no cenário da migração e do tráfico internacional de pessoas. *Cadernos Pagu*, 31, pp. 251–73.

Ausserer, C. 2008. 'Control in the name of protection': A critical analysis of the discourse of international human trafficking as a form of forced migration. *St Anthony's International Review,* 4(1), pp. 96–114.

Bales, K. 1999. *Disposable People: New slavery in the global economy*, Berkeley and Los Angeles, US: University of California Press.

Balos, B. 2004. The Wrong Way to Equality: Privileging consent and the trafficking of women. *Harvard Women's Law Journal*, 27, pp. 137–75.

Balos, B. 2001. Teaching prostitution seriously. *Buffalo Criminal Law Review*, 4, pp. 709–53.

Balos, B. 1999. A matter of prostitution: Becoming respectable. *New York University Law Review*, 74, pp. 1220–303.

Banerjee, U.D. 2006. Migration and trafficking of women and girls: A brief review of some effective models in India and Thailand. In: K. Beeks and D. Amir, eds. *Trafficking and the global sex industry*. Lanham, MD: Lexington Books, pp. 189–200.

Bankole A. 1995. Desired fertility and fertility behaviour among the Yoruba of Nigeria: A study of couple preferences and subsequent fertility. *Population Studies*, 49(2), pp. 317–28.

Barry, K. 1995. *The prostitution of sexuality*. New York, US and London, UK: New York University Press.

Barry, K. 1979. *Female sexual slavery*. New York, US and London, UK: New York University Press.

Bauman, Z. 1998. On postmodern uses of sex. *Theory, Culture and Society*, 15, pp. 19–33.

Becker, H. 1963. *Outsiders: Studies in the sociology of deviance*. New York, US: Free Press.

Bélanger, D. 2014. Labor migration and trafficking among Vietnamese migrants in Asia. *The Annals of the American Academy of Political and Social Science*, 653(1), pp. 87–106.

Bell, R.E. 2001. Sex trafficking: A financial crime perspective. *Journal of Financial Crime*, 9(2), pp. 165–78.

Bell, S. 1994. *Reading, writing and rewriting the prostitute body*. Bloomington, US: Indiana University Press.

Berman, J. 2010. Biopolitical management, economic calculation and 'trafficked women'. *International Migration*, 48(4), pp. 84–113.

Bernat, F.P and Zhilina, T. 2010. Human trafficking: The local becomes global. *Women and Criminal Justice*, 20, pp. 2–9.

Bernish, P. 2011. Upsetting the human trafficking apple cart. <http://www.freedomcenter.org/freedom-forum/index.php/?p=4135> [Accessed 16 May 2012].

Bernstein, E. 2008. O significado da compra: Desejo, demanda e o comércio do sexo. *Cadernos Pagu*, 31, pp. 315–62.

Bernstein, E. 2007. Sex work for the middle classes. *Sexualities*, 10(4), pp. 473–88.

Bettio, F. and Nandi, T.K. 2010. Evidence on women trafficked for sexual exploitation: A rights based analysis. *European Journal of Law and Economics*, 29, pp. 15–42.

Beyrer, C. 2004. Is trafficking a health issue? *The Lancet*, 363(9408), pp. 564–5.

Beyrer, C. and Stachowlak, J. 2003. Health consequences of trafficking in women and girls in Southeast Asia. *The Brown Journal of World Affairs*, 10(1), pp. 105–17.

Bilankiuk, L. 2003. Gender, language attitudes, and language status in Ukraine. *Language in Society*, 32, pp. 47–78.

Bindman, J. 1998. An international perspective on slavery in the sex industry. In: K. Kempadoo and J. Doezema, eds. *Global Sex Workers: Rights, Resistance and Redefinition*. New York, US: Routledge, pp. 65–8.

Birkenthall, S. 2012. Human trafficking: A human rights abuse with global dimensions. *Interdisciplinary Journal of Human Rights Law*, 6(27), pp. 27–40.

Bogusz, B., Cholewinski, R., Cygan, A. and Szyszczak, E. 2004. *Irregular migrants and human rights: Theoretical, European and International Perspectives*, The Hague: Martinus Nijhoff Publishers.

Bowles, L.R. 2009. Imagining migrant women and the embodied market: Accra, Ghana. In: C. Baker, ed. *Expressions of the body: Representation in African text and image*. Oxford: Peter Lang, pp. 313–36.

Brennan, D. 2005. Methodological challenges in research with trafficked persons: Tales from the field. *International Migration*, 43(1/2), pp. 35–54.

Brettell, C.B. and Hollifield, J.F. 2007. *Migration theory: Talking across the disciplines*. 2nd ed. New York, US: Routledge.

Brown, L. 2000. *Sex Slaves: The trafficking of women in Asia*. London, UK: Virago Press.

Brown, W. 2005. Freedom's silences. In: W. Brown, ed. *Edgework: critical essays on knowledge and politics*. Princeton, US: Princeton University Press, pp. 83–97.

Brownmiller, S. 1994. *Seeing Vietnam: Encounters of the road and heart*. Harpercollins, New York, US.

Bruch, E.M. 2004. Models wanted: The search for an effective response to human trafficking. *Stanford Journal of International Law*, 40(1), pp. 1–45.

Brunovskis, A. and Surtees, R. 2010. Untold stories: Biases and selection effects in research with victims of trafficking for sexual exploitation. *International Migration*, 48(4): 1–37.

Buckingham, A.D. and Saunders, P. 2004. *The survey methods workbook: From design to analysis*. Cambridge, UK: Polity Press.

Burkhalter, H. 2012. Sex trafficking, law enforcement and perpetrator accountability, *Anti-Trafficking Review*, 1, pp. 122–33.

Burn, J. and Simmons, F. 2006. Trafficking and slavery in Australia: An evaluation of victim support strategies. *Asian and Pacific Migration Journal*, 15(4), pp. 553–70.

Burn, J. and Simmons, F. 2005. Rewarding witnesses, ignoring victims: An evaluation of the new trafficking visa framework. *Immigration Review*, 24, pp. 6–13.

Burn, J., Blay, S. and Simmons, F. 2005. Combating human trafficking: Australia's responses to modern day slavery. *Australian Law Journal*, 79(9), pp. 543–52.

Busza, J. 2004. Sex work and migration: The dangers of oversimplification-A case study of Vietnamese women in Cambodia. *Health and Human Rights*, 7(2), pp. 231–49.

Busza, J., Castle, S. and Diarra, A. 2004. Trafficking and health. *British Medical Journal*, 328, pp. 1369–71.

Butcher, K. 2003. Confusion between prostitution and sex trafficking. *The Lancet*, 361, p. 1983.

Byrnes, B. 2013. Beyond Wei Tang: Do Australia's Human Trafficking Laws Fully Reflect Australia's International Human Rights Obligations? (Workshop on Legal and Criminal Justice Response to Trafficking in Persons in Australia: Obstacles, Opportunities and Best Practice delivered at the Australian Human Rights Commission, 2009), Sydney, Australia. Available at http://www.humanrights.gov.au/news/speeches/beyond-wei-tang-do-australia-s-human-trafficking-laws-fully-reflect-australia-s [Accessed 20 September 2013]

Cameron, M. and Schloenhardt, A. 2013. Punishing trafficking in persons: International standards and Australian experiences. *Bond Law Review*, 24(1), pp. 1–29.

Caraway, N. 2006. Human trafficking and existing contradictions in Asia-Pacific human politics and discourse. *Tulane Journal of International and Comparative Law*, 14(2), pp. 295–316.

Carline, A. and Pearson, Z. 2007. Complexity and queer theory approaches to international law and feminist politics: Perspectives on trafficking. *Canadian Journal of Women and Law*, 19(1), pp. 73–118.

Carrington, K. 2006. Does feminism spoil girls? Explanations for official rises in female delinquency. *The Australian and New Zealand Journal of Criminology*, 39(1), pp. 34–53.

Carrington, K. and Hearn, J. 2003. Trafficking and the sex industry: From impunity to protection. *Current Issues Brief*, 28, pp. 1–16.

Chambers, C. 2008. *Sex, justice and culture: The limits of choice*. University Park, US: Pennsylvania State University Press.

Chandra, A. and Minkovitz, C.S. 2006. Stigma starts early: Gender differences in teen willingness to use mental health services. *Journal of Adolescent Health*, 38(754), pp. e1-e8.

Chang, G. 2000. *Disposable domestics: Immigrant women workers in the global economy*. Cambridge, US: South End Press.

Chang, G. and Kim, K. 2007. Reconceptualising approaches to human trafficking: New directions and perspectives from the field(s). *Stanford Journal of Civil Rights and Civil Liberties,* 3(2), pp. 318–44.

Chapkis, W. 2003. Trafficking, migration and the law: Protecting innocents, punishing immigrants. *Gender and Society*, 17(6), pp. 923–37.

Chaudary, S. 2012. Trafficking in Europe: An analysis of the effectiveness of European Law, *Michigan Journal of International Law*, 33: 77–99.

Cheng, S. 2010. Review of Sex trafficking: Inside the business of modern slavery by S. Kara. *Journal of World History,* 21(2), pp. 363–8.

Chuang, J.A. 2013. Exploitation creep and the unmaking of human trafficking law, *American University Washington College of Law Research Paper*, 108(1).

Chuang, J.A. 2012. Article 6. In: M.A. Freeman, C. Chinkin and B. Rudolf, eds. The UN Convention on the Elimination of All Forms of Discrimination against Women: A Commentary. Oxford: Oxford University Press, pp. 169–96.

Chuang, J.A. 2010. Rescuing trafficking from ideological capture: Prostitution reform and anti-trafficking law and policy. *University of Pennsylvania Law Review*, 158, pp. 1655–728.

Chuang, J.A. 2006. Beyond a snapshot: Preventing human trafficking in a global economy. *Indiana Journal of Global Legal Studies*, 13, pp. 137–63.

Christman, J. and Anderson, J. eds. 2005. *Autonomy and the challenges to liberalism: New essays*. Cambridge, UK: Cambridge University Press.

Clark, M.A. 2003. Trafficking in persons: An issue of human security. *Journal of Human Development and Capabilities*, 4(2), pp. 247–63.

Cleveland, D.A. 1991. Migration in West Africa: A Savanna Village perspective. *Africa*, 61(2), pp. 222–46.

Cole, J. 2006. Reducing the damage: Dilemmas of anti-trafficking efforts among Nigeria prostitutes in Palermo. *Anthropologica*, 48(2), pp. 217–28.

Coontz, P. and Griebel, C. 2004. International approaches to human trafficking: The call for a gender-sensitive perspective in international law. *Women's Health Journal*, 4, pp. 47–58.

Corrin, C. 2005. Transitional road for traffic: Analysing trafficking in women from and through Central and Eastern Europe. *Europe-Asia Studies*, 57(4), pp. 543–60.

Cullen, M. and McSherry, B. 2009. Without sex: Slavery, trafficking in persons and exploitation of labour in Australia. *Alternative Journal*, 34(1), pp. 4–10.

Curtol, F., Decarli, S., Di Nicola, A. and Savona, E.U. 2004. Victims of human trafficking in Italy: A judicial perspective. *International Review of Victimology*, 11(1), pp. 111–41.

Cranford, C. 2012. Wage differentials between native and immigrant women in Spain: Accounting for differences in support. *Gender, Work and Organisation*, 33(1), pp. 118–64.

Crawford, M. 2010. *Sex trafficking in South Asia: Telling Maya's story*. New York, USA: Routledge.

Crawford, M. and Kaufman, M.R. 2008. Sex trafficking in Nepal: Survivor characteristics and long-term outcomes. *Violence against Women*, 14, pp. 905–16.

Cresswell, J. 1994. *Research design: Qualitative and quantitative approaches*. 3rd ed. California, US: Sage.

Cwikel, J. and Hoban, E. 2005a. Contentious issues in research on trafficked women working in the sex industry: Study design, ethics, and methodology. *Journal of Sex Research*, 42(4), pp. 306–16.

D'Anieri, P. 2007. *Understanding Ukrainian politics: Power, politics and institutional design*. New York, US: M.E. Sharpe.

Dandona, R. et al. 2006. Demography and sex work characteristics of female sex workers in India. *BMC International Health and Human Rights*. 6(5), pp. 1–10.

Day, S. 2009. Renewing the war on prostitution. *Anthropology Today*, 25(3), pp. 1–3.

Day, S. and Ward, H. Approaching health through the prism of stigma: Research in seven European countries. In: S. Day and H. Ward, eds. *Sex work, mobility and health in Europe*. London, UK: Keagan Paul.

DeStefano, A. 2007. The war on human trafficking: US policy assessed. NJ, US: Rutgers University Press.

Deane, F.P. and Chamberlain, K. 1994. Treatment fearfulness and distress as predictors of professional psychological help-seeking. *British Journal of Guidance & Counselling*, 22, pp. 207–17.

Decker, M.R., Miller, E., Raj, A., Saggurti, N., Donta, B. and Silverman, J.G. 2010. Indian men's use of commercial sex workers: Prevalence, condom use, and related gender attitudes. *Journal of Acquired Immune Deficiency Syndrome*, 53(2), pp. 240–46.

Defeis, E.F. 2000. Draft convention against sexual exploitation. In: K.D. Askin and D.M. Koenig, eds. *Women and International human rights law*. New York, US: Transnational Press, Vol. 2, pp. 319–49.

Demir, O.O. and Finckenauer, J.O. 2010. Victims of sex trafficking in Turkey: Characteristics, motivations, and dynamics. *Women and Criminal Justice*, 20(1–2), pp. 57–88.

Denton, E. 2010. International news coverage of human trafficking arrests and prosecutions: A content analysis. *Women and Criminal Justice*, 20(1–2), pp. 10–26.

Denzin, N. and Lincoln, Y. eds. 1998. *Collecting and interpreting qualitative materials*. Thousand Oaks: Sage.

Desyllas, M.C. 2007. Sex trafficking: The global market in women and children. *Journal of International Women's Studies*, 8, pp. 167–72.

Deveaux, M. 2006. *Gender and justice in multicultural liberal states*. Oxford: Oxford University Press.

Dill, S.E. 2006. Old crimes in new times: Human trafficking and the modern justice system. *Criminal Justice*, 21(1), pp. 12–18.

Ditmore, M.H. 2009. A Failure of understanding: Review of Sex trafficking: Inside the business of modern slavery by S. Kara. *Women's Review of Books*, 5, pp. 23–4.

Ditmore, M.H. 2005. Trafficking in lives: How ideology shapes policy. In: K. Kempadoo, J. Sanghera and B. Pattanaik, eds. *Trafficking and prostitution reconsidered: New perspectives on migration, sex work, and human rights*. Boulder, US: Paradigm Publishers, pp. 107–26.

Ditmore, M.H and Thukral, J. 2012. Accountability and the use of raids to fight trafficking. *Anti-Trafficking Review*, 1, pp. 134–48.

Dinan, K.A. 2002. Migrant Thai women subjected to slavery-like abuses in Japan. *Violence Against Women*, 8, pp. 1113–39.

Djajić, S. 1987. Illegal aliens, unemployment and immigration policy. *Journal of Development Economics*, 25, pp. 235–49.

Djajić, S. 1986. International migration, remittances and welfare in a dependent economy. *Journal of Development Economics*, 21, pp. 229–34.

Dobner, M. and Tappert, S. 2010. Female migrant domestic workers and their Spanish employers in times of crisis. A comparative analysis of consequences for women on both sides of the coin. In: SGIR, *7th Pan-European International Relations Conference*. 9–11 September 2010, Stockholm, Sweden. Available at: <http://stockholm.sgir.eu/uploads/Female%20migrant%20 domestic%20workers%20and%20their%20Spanish%20employers%20 in%20times%20of%20crisis.pdf> [Accessed 26 January 2011].

Doezema, J. 2005. Now you see her, now you don't: Sex workers at the UN Trafficking Protocol negotiations. *Social and Legal Studies*, 14(1), pp. 61–89.

Doezema, J. 2002. The ideology of trafficking. In: Center for Ethics and Value Inquiry, *Work conference on human trafficking*. 15 November 2002, Ghent, Belgium. <http://www.nswp.org/sites/nswp.org/files/DOEZEMA-IDEOLOGY.pdf> [Accessed 15 May 2012].

Doezema, J. 2001. Western feminists 'wounded attachment' to the 'third world prostitute'. *Feminist Review*, 67, pp. 16–38.

Doezema, J. 1998. Forced to choose: Beyond the voluntary v. forced prostitution dichotomy. In: K. Kempadoo and J. Doezema, eds. *Global sex workers: Rights, resistance, and redefinition*. New York and London: Routledge, pp. 34–50.

Domingo, A., Gil-Alonso, F. and Robertson, G. 2007. Immigration and changing labour force structure in the Southern European Union. *Population*, 62(4), pp. 709–27.

Dorevitch, A. and Foster, M. 2008. Obstacles on the road to protection: Assessing the treatment of sex-trafficking victims under Australia's migration and refugee law. *Melbourne Journal of International Law*, 9, pp. 1–46.

Dottridge, M. 2002. Trafficking in children in west and central Africa. *Gender and Development*, 10(1), pp. 28–42.

Dottridge, M. and Jordan, A. 2012. Children, adolescents and human trafficking: Making sense of a complex problem, Issue Paper 5. Center for Human Rights and Humanitarian Law, *American University Washington College of Law*. <http://www.childtrafficking.com/Docs/dottridge_making_problem_0812. pdf> [Accessed 13 June 2012].

Doussantousse, S. and Tooke, L. 2002. A cultural approach to HIV and AIDS prevention and care for sustainable development in Ha Long City, Quảng Ninh province, Vietnam. In: *14th International AIDS Conference*. 7–12 July, Barcelona, Spain.

Duong, L.B. and Khuat, T.H., eds. 2008. *Market transformation, migration and social protection in a transitioning Vietnam*. Hanoi: The Gioi Publisher.

Ebbe, O.N.I. and Das, D.K. 2007. *Global trafficking in women and children*. Boca Raton: CRC Press.

Edwards, A. 2010. Transitioning gender: Feminist engagement with international refugee law and policy 1950–2010. *Refugee Survey Quarterly*, 29(2), pp. 21–45.

Ekberg, G. 2004. The Swedish law that prohibits the purchase of sexual services: Best practices for prevention of prostitution and trafficking in human beings. *Violence Against Women*, 10, pp. 1187–218.

Elabor-Idemudia, P. 2003. Race and gender analyses of trafficking: A case study of Nigeria. *Canadian Woman Studies*, 22(3/4), pp. 116–23.

Emerton, R., Laidler, K.J. and Petersen, C.J. 2007. Trafficking of mainland Chinese women to Hong Kong's sex industry: Problems of identification and response. *Asia-Pacific Journal of Human Rights and the Law*, 2, pp. 35–84.

Engerman, S. 2007. Slavery, freedom and zen. In: A.K. Appiah and M. Bunzl, eds. *Buying freedom: The ethics and economics of slave redemption*, Princeton, US.: Princeton University Press, pp. 77–107.

Engstrom, D.W., Minas, S.A., Espinoza, M. and Jones, L. 2004. Halting the trafficking of women and children in Thailand for the sex trade: Progress and challenges. *Journal of Social Work Research and Evaluation*, 5(2), pp. 193–206.

Erickson, B.H. 1979. Some problems of inference from chain data. *Sociological Methodology*, 10, pp. 276–302.

Fallon, K.M. 2003. Transforming women's citizenship rights within an emerging democratic state: The case of Ghana. *Gender & Society*, 17(4), pp. 525–43.

Faria, C. 2008. Privileging prevention, gendering responsibility: An analysis of the Ghanaian campaign against HIV/AIDS. *Social & Cultural Geography*, 9(1), pp. 41–73.

Farley, M. 2004. 'Bad for the body, bad for the heart': Prostitution harms women even if legalized or decriminalized. *Violence Against Women*, 10(10), pp. 1087–125.

Farr, K. 2006. Sex trafficking: The global market in women and children. *British Journal of Criminology*, 46, pp. 373–4.

Farrell, A. and Pfeffer, R. 2014. Policing human trafficking: Cultural blinders and organisational barriers. *The Annals of the American Academy of Political and Social Science*, 653(1), pp. 46–64.

Farrell, A. and Fahy, S. 2009. The problem of human trafficking in the US: Public frames and policy responses. *Journal of Criminal Justice*, 37, pp. 617–26.

Fergus, L. 2005. Trafficking in women for sexual exploitation. *Human Rights Defender*, 14(3), pp. 11–13.

Fisher, H. 2002. The sex slave trade: Biological imperatives, cultural trends, and the coming empowerment of women. *Hastings Women's Law Journal Symposium*, 13, pp. 21–9.

Frances, R. 1996. Australian prostitution in international context. *Australian Historical Studies*, 106, pp. 127–41.

Frank, O. and Snijders, T.A.B. 1994. Estimating the size of hidden populations using snowball sampling. *Journal of Official Statistics*, 10, pp. 53–67.

Freedman, L. 2003. Strategic advocacy and maternal mortality: Moving targets and the millennium development goals. *Gender and Development*, 11(1), pp. 97–108.

Freeman, J. 1989/1990. The feminist debate over prostitution reform: Prostitutes' rights groups, radical feminists, and the (im)possibility of consent. *Berkeley Women's Law Journal*, 5, pp. 75–109.

Friedman, M. 2003. *Autonomy, gender, politics*. Oxford: Oxford University Press.

Foerster, A. 2009. Contest bodies. *International Feminist Journal of Politics*, 11(2), pp. 151–74.

Fowler, J., Che, N. and Fowler, L. 2010. Innocence lost: The rights of human trafficking victims. *Procedia Social and Behavioural Science*, 2, pp. 1345–49.

Gal, S. and Kligman, G. 2000. *Reproducing gender: Politics, publics and everyday life after socialism*. Princeton, US: Princeton University Press.

Gallagher, A.T. 2011. Improving the effectiveness of the international law on human trafficking: A vision for the future of the US Trafficking in Persons Report. *Human Rights Review*, 12(3), pp. 381–400

Gallagher, A.T. 2010. *The international law of human trafficking*. Cambridge, US: Cambridge University Press.

Gallagher, A.T. 2009. Human rights and human trafficking: Quagmire or firm ground? A response to James Hathaway. *Virginia Journal of International Law*, 49, pp. 789–848.

Gallagher, A.T. 2008. Using international human rights law to better protect victims of human trafficking: The prohibitions on slavery, servitude forced labour and debt bondage. In: L.N. Sadat and M.P. Scharf, eds. *The theory and practice of international criminal law: Essays in honour of M. Cherif Bassiouni*. The Hague: Martinus Nijhoff, pp. 397–430.

Gallagher, A.T. 2001. Human rights and the new UN protocols on trafficking and migrant smuggling: A preliminary analysis. *Human Rights Quarterly*, 23, pp. 975–1004.

Gallagher, A.T. and Holmes, P. 2008. Developing an effective criminal justice response to human trafficking: Lessons from the front line. *International Criminal Justice Review*, 18, pp. 318–43.

Gallagher, A.T. and Surtees, R. 2012. Measuring the success of counter-trafficking interventions in the criminal justice sector: Who decides – and how? *Anti-trafficking Review*, 1, pp. 10–30.

Ganson, H. and Laux, R. 2004. Improving labour market statistics in Ukraine. *Labour Market Trends*, pp. 37–43.

Getu, M. 2006. Human trafficking and development: The role of microfinance. *Transformation*, 23(3), pp. 143–56.

Gleeson, K. 2004. 'Having sunk as low as possible for a man to sink'- the pimp in law. *Australian Feminist Law Journal*, 21, pp. 101–20.

Giang, L.M. and Huong, N.T.M. 2008. From family planning to HIV/AIDS in Vietnam: Shifting priorities, remaining gaps. In: R. Parker, R. Petchesky and R. Sember, eds. *Reports from the Front Lines. Rio de Janeiro, Brazil: Sexuality Policy Watch*, pp. 277–309

Gilligan, C. 1982. *In a different voice: Psychological theory and women's development*. Cambridge, US: Harvard University Press.

Goldberg, M. 2009. *Means of reproduction: Sex, power and the future of the world*. New York, US: Penguin.

Goffman, E. 1963. *Stigma: Notes on the management of spoiled identity*. London, UK: Penguin.

Goodey, J. 2004. Sex trafficking in women from Central and East European countries: Promoting a 'victim-centred' and 'woman-centred' approach to criminal justice intervention. *Feminist Review*, 76, pp. 26–45.

Goodey, J. 2003. Migration, crime and victimhood: Responses to sex trafficking in the EU. *Punishment & Society*, 5(4), pp. 415–31.

Goschin, G.D.C. and Roman, M. 2009. The partnership between the state and the church against trafficking in persons. *Journal for the Study of Religions and Ideologies*, 8(24), pp. 231–56.

Gozdziak, E.M. and Collett, E.A. 2005. Research on human trafficking in North America: A review of the literature. *International Migration*, 43 (1/2), pp. 99–128.

Grabbe, H. 2002. The sharp edges of Europe: Extending Schengen eastward. *International Affairs*, 76(3), pp. 497–514.

Guinn, D.E. 2008. Defining the problem of trafficking: The interplay of US law, donor, and NGO engagement and the local context in Latin America. *Human Rights Quarterly*, 30, pp. 119–45.

Gulati, G. 2011. New frames and story triggers in the media's coverage of human trafficking. *Human Rights Review*, 12(3): 363–79.

Gushulak, B.D. and MacPherson, D.W. 2000. Health issues associated with the smuggling and trafficking of migrants. *Journal of Immigrant Health*, 2(2), pp. 67–78.

Halley, J., Kotiswaran, P., Shamir, H. and Thomas, C. 2006. From the international to the local in feminist legal responses to rape, prostitution/sex work, and sex trafficking: Four studies in contemporary governance feminism. *Harvard Journal of Law & Gender*, 29, pp. 335–423

Hallgrímsdóttir, H.K., Phillips, R., Benoit, C. and Walby, K. 2008. Sporting girls, streetwalkers, and inmates of houses of ill repute: Media narratives and the historical mutability of prostitution stigmas. *Sociological Perspectives*, 51(1), pp. 119–38.

Haque, M.S. 2006. Ambiguities and confusion in migration-trafficking nexus: A development challenge. In: K. Beeks and D. Amir, eds. *Trafficking and the global sex industry*, Lanham, US: Lexington Books, pp. 3–20.

Harrison, D. 2006. Victims of human trafficking or victims of research? Ethical considerations in research with females trafficked for the purposes of sexual exploitation. M.A. dissertation, University of East Anglia, Norwich, United Kingdom.

Hanna, C. 2002. Somebody's daughter: The domestic trafficking of girls for the commercial sex industry and the power of love. *William and Mary Journal of Women and the Law,* 9(1), pp. 1–29.

Haub, C. and Phuong, T.T.H. 2003. An overview of population and development in Vietnam. Hanoi, Vietnam: Population Reference Bureau. Unpublished. <http://www.prb.org/Articles/2003/AnOverviewofPopulationandDevelopmentinVietnam.aspx> (partially available), [Accessed 15 May 2012]

Hawkesworth, M.E. 2006. *Globalisation and feminist activism.* Lanham, US: Rowman & Littlefield.

Haynes, D. 2014. The celebritization of human trafficking. *The Annals of the American Academy of Political and Social Science*, 653(1), pp. 25–45.

Haynes, D.F. 2009. Exploitation nation: The thin and grey legal lines between the protection of victims of human trafficking and the lack of protection of exploited migrant workers. *Notre Dame Journal of Legal Ethics and Public Policy*, 23(1): pp. 1–58.

Haynes, D.F. 2004. Used, abused, arrested and deported: extending immigration benefits to protect victims of trafficking and to secure the prosecution of traffickers. *Human Rights Quarterly*, 26(2), pp. 221–72.

Hearn, J. and McKie, L. 2008. Gendered policy and policy on gender: The case of 'domestic violence'. *Policy and Politics: An International Journal*, 36(1), pp. 75–91.

Heckathorn, D.D. 2002. Respondent-driven sampling II: Deriving valid population estimates from chain-referral samples of hidden populations. *Social Problems*, 49(1), pp. 11–34.

Heckathorn, D.D. 1997. Respondent-driven sampling: A new approach to the study of human populations. *Social Problems*, 44(2), pp. 174–99.

Heijnders, M. and Van der Meij, S. 2006. The fight against stigma: An overview of stigma-reduction strategies and interventions. *Psychology, Health and Medicine*, 11(3), pp. 353–63.

Henshaw, S.K., Singh, S. and Haas, T. 1999. Incidence of abortion worldwide, *Family Planning Perspective*, 25: 30–38.

Hesli, V.L. and Miller, A.H. 1993. The gender base of institutional support in Lithuania, Ukraine and Russia. *Europe-Asia Studies*, 45(3), pp. 505–32.

Heyzer, N. 2002. Combating trafficking in women and children: A gender and human rights framework. In: *The Human Rights Challenge of Globalization: Asia-Pacific-US: The Trafficking in Persons, Especially Women and Children.* 13–15 November 2002, Honolulu, Hawaii.

Hoang, T.T.P. Legislating to combat trafficking in Vietnam, 17th Biennial Conference of the Asian Studies Association of Australia. 1–3 July 2008, Melbourne, Australia.

Holmes, L. 2010. Trafficking and human rights: European and Asia-Pacific Perspectives. Cheltenham, UK: Edward Elgar.

Hormel, L. and Southworth, C. 2006. Eastward bound: A case study of post-Soviet labour migration from a rural Ukrainian town. *Europe-Asia Studies*, 58(4), pp. 603–23.

Horowitz, M. 1974. The historical foundations of modern contract law. *Harvard Law Review*, 87, pp. 917–56.

Hoang, T.T.P. 2008. Legislation to combat trafficking in Vietnam. In: 17th Biennial Conference of the Asian Studies Association of Australia. 1–3 July 2008, Melbourne, Australia.

Hodge, D.R. and Lietz, C.A. 2007. The international sex trafficking of women and children: A review of the literature. *Affilia*, 22(2), pp. 163–74.

Hodžić, S. 2009. Unsettling power: Domestic violence, gender politics, and struggles over sovereignty in Ghana. *Ethnos*, 74(3), pp. 331–60.

Horsfield, S. 2002. Questioning inevitability: Globalisation and prostitution. *Australian Feminist Law Journal*, 17: 33–47.

Hotaling, N. and Levitas-Martin, L. 2002. Increased demand resulting in the flourishing recruitment and trafficking of women and girls: Related child sexual abuse and violence against women. *Hastings Women's Law Journal*, 13, pp. 117–26.

Howard, N. 2014. Teenage labor migration and antitrafficking policy in West Africa. *The Annals of the American Academy of Political and Social Science*, 653(1), pp. 124–40.

Huda, S. 2006. Sex trafficking in South Asia. *International Journal of Gynaecology & Obstetrics*, 94(3), pp. 374–81.

Hughes, D. 2004. The role of 'marriage agencies' in the sexual exploitation and trafficking of women from the former Soviet Union. *International Review of Victimology*, 11, pp. 49–71.

Hughes, D. 2002. Trafficking of children for prostitution. In: *Protecting our children: Working together to end child prostitution*, US Department of Justice, Office of Juvenile Justice and Delinquency Prevention, 13–14 December 2002, Washington, D.C, US

Hughes, D. and Denisova, T. 2001.The transnational political criminal nexus of trafficking in women from Ukraine. *Trends in Organized Crime*, 6(3/4), pp. 1–22.

Hughes, D. 2001. The 'Natasha' trade: Transnational sex trafficking. *National Institute of Justice Journal*, 246, pp. 9–14.

Hughes, D. 2000. The 'Natasha' Trade -The Transnational Shadow Market of Trafficking in Women. *Journal of International Affairs*, 53(2), pp. 625–51.

Hyland, K.E. 2001. Protecting human victims of trafficking: An American framework. *Berkeley Women's Law Journal*, 16, pp. 29–71.

Hyrcak, A. 2007a. Seeing orange: Women's activism and Ukraine's Orange Revolution. *Women's Studies Quarterly*, 35(3/4), pp. 208–25.

Hyrcak, A. 2007b. From global to local feminisms: Transnationalisms, foreign aid and women's movement in Ukraine. *Sustainable Feminisms*, 11, pp. 75–93.

Hyrcak, A. 2005. Coping with chaos: Gender and politics in a fragmented state. *Problems of Post-Communism*, 52(5), pp. 69–81.

Illes, P., Soares, T.G.L., Fiorucci, E da S. 2008. Tráfico de Pessoas para fins de exploração do trabalho na cidade de São Paulo. *Cadernos Pagu*, 31, pp. 199–217.

Imai, K., Gaiha, R.and Kang, W. 2011. Vulnerability and poverty dynamics in Vietnam. *Applied Economics*, 43(25), pp. 3603–618.

Jahic, G. and Finckenauer, J.O. 2005. Representations and misrepresentations of human trafficking. *Trends in Organised Crime*, 8(3), pp. 24–40.

Jearn, J. and McKie, L. 2008. Gendered and social hierarchies in problem representation and policy processes: 'domestic violence' in Finland and Scotland. *Violence against women*, 16(2), pp. 136–58.

Jeffreys, E. 2003.Transnational prostitution – A global feminist response? *Australian Feminist Studies*, 18, pp. 211–16.

Jeffreys, S. 2008. *The industrial vagina: The political economy of the global sex trade*. London: Routledge.

Jeffreys, S. 2002. Women trafficking and the Australian connection. *Arena Magazine* 58, pp. 44–7.

Jeffreys, S. 2000. Challenging the child/adult distinction in theory and practice on prostitution. *International Feminist Journal of Politics*, 2(3), pp. 359–79.

Jeffreys, S. 1997. *The Idea of Prostitution*. Melbourne: Spinifex.

Jones, A. 2009. *Gender inclusive: Essays on violence, men and feminist international relations*. London, UK: Routledge.

Jones, A. 2006. *Men of the Global South: A Reader*. London: Zed Books.

Jones, S.V. 2010. The invisible man: The conscious neglect of men and boys in the war on human trafficking. *Utah Law Review*, pp. 1143–88.

Jones, L., Engstrom, D.W., Hilliard, T. and Diaz, M. 2007. Globalisation and human trafficking. *Journal of Sociology and Social Work*, 34, pp. 107–22.

Jordan, A.D. 2002. Human rights or wrongs? The struggle for a rights-based response to trafficking in human beings. *Gender & Development*, 10(1), pp. 28–37.

Jordan, A.D. 2000. Commercial sex workers in Asia: A blind spot in human rights law. In: K.D. Askin and D.M. Koenig, eds. *Women and international human rights law*. Ardsley, NY: Transnational Press, Vol. 2, pp. 525–85.

Joudo Larson, J. 2011. The trafficking of children in the Asia-Pacific. *Trends and Issues in Crime and Criminal Justice*, 415, pp. 1–6.

Jupp, V. 2006. *The SAGE dictionary of social research methods*. Thousand Oaks, US: Sage.

Kabeer, N. and Tran Thi, V.A. 2006. *Globalisation, Gender and Work in the Context of Economic Transition: The Case of Viet Nam*. Hanoi, Vietnam: UNDP.

Kapur, R. 2005. *Erotic Justice: Law and the new politics of postcolonialism.* London, UK: Glasshouse Press.

Kamazima, S.R., Kazaura, M.R., Ezekiel, M.J. and Fimbo, B. 2011. Reported human traffickers' profiles: A key step in the prevention of trafficking in persons through HIV and AIDS interventions in Tanzania. *East Africa Journal of Public Health*, 8(2): 77–81.

Kara, S. 2009. *Sex trafficking: Inside the business of modern slavery.* New York, USA: Columbia University Press.

Karatnycky, A. 2005. Ukraine's Orange Revolution. *Foreign Affairs*, 84(2), pp. 35–52.

Kaur, A. 2010. Labour migration in Southeast Asia: Migration policies, labour exploitation and regulation. *Journal of Asia Pacific Economy*, 15(1): pp. 6–19.

Keo, C. 2013. *Human trafficking in Cambodia.* New York, USA: Routledge Southeast Asia Series.

Keo, C., Bouhours, T., Broadhurst, R. and Bouhours, B. 2014. Human trafficking and moral panic in Cambodia, *The Annals of the American Academy of Political and Social Science*, 653(1), pp. 202–24.

Kelly, E. 2005. 'You can find anything you want': A critical reflection on research on trafficking in persons within and into Europe. *International Migration*, 43(1–2), pp. 235–65.

Kempadoo, K. and Doezema, J. eds., 1998. *Global sex workers: Rights, resistance, and redefinition.* New York, US: Routledge.

Kempadoo, K. 2007. The war on human trafficking in the Caribbean. *Race and Class*, 49, pp. 79–85.

Khuat, H.T. 1998. *Study on Sexuality in Vietnam: The Known and Unknown Issues.* Hanoi, Vietnam: Population Council.

Kindler, M. 2009. The relationship to the employer in migrant's eyes: The domestic work Ukrainian migrant women in Warsaw, *Cahiers de l'Urmis*, 12. <http://urmis.revues.org/index853.html> [Accessed 15 May 2012].

King, R., Skeldon, R., and Vullnetari, J. 2008. Internal and international migration: Bridging the theoretical divide. In: *International Migration, Integration and social Cohesion (IMISCOE) Theories of Migration and Social Change Conference.* 1–3 July 2008, Oxford, United Kingdom.

Kis, O. 2005a. Choosing without choice: Predominant models of femininity in contemporary Ukraine. In: I.A. Morell, H. Carlback, M. Hurd and S. Rastback, eds. *Gender Transitions in Russia and Eastern Europe.* Stockholm, Sweden: Gondolin Publishers, pp. 105–36.

Kis, O. 2005b. Beauty will save the world!: Feminine strategies in Ukraine Politics and the case of Yulia Tymoshenko. <http://www.yorku.ca/soi/_Vol_7_2/_HTML/Kis.html> [Accessed 15 May 2012].

Kis, O. n.d. Ukraine's acute lack of feminism (trans.). *Politykantro.* <http://gender.at.ua/publ/1-1-0-23> [Accessed 15 May 2012].

Kleemans, E.R. 2011. Expanding the domain of human trafficking research: Introduction to the special issue on human trafficking. *Trends in Organised Crime*, 14(2/3), pp. 95–9.

Kligman, G. and Limoncelli, S., 2005, Trafficking women after socialism: To, through, and from Eastern Europe. *Social Policy*, 12, pp. 118–40.

Klomegah, R. 2000. Child fostering and fertility: Some evidence from Ghana. *Journal of Comparative Family Studies*, 31(1), pp. 107–15.

Kojima, Y.T. 2007. What ails effective implementation of measures to counter trafficking in women and girls? A structural analysis based on examples from Thailand and Sri Lanka. In: *Women in the Trafficking-Migration Continuum from the Perspective of Human Rights and Social Justice*, Maastricht, The Netherlands: Shaker, pp. 141–80.

Koser, K. 2010. Dimensions and dynamics of irregular migration. *Population, Place and Space*, 16, pp. 181–93.

Krieg, S. 2009. Trafficking in human beings: The EU approach between border control, law enforcement and human rights. *European Law Journal*, 15(6), pp. 775–90.

Kyle, D. and Koslowski, R. 2011. Introduction. In: D. Kyle and R. Koslowski, ed. *Global human smuggling: Comparative perspectives*. 2nd ed. Baltimore, US: Johns Hopkins University Press, pp. 1–25.

Laczko, F. 2005. Data and research on human trafficking. *International Migration*, 43(1/2), pp. 5–16.

Lainez, N. 2012. Commodified sexuality and mother-daughter power dynamics in the Mekong Delta. *Journal of Vietnamese Studies*, 7(1), pp. 149–80.

Lawrance, B.N. From child labour 'problem' to human trafficking 'crisis': Child advocacy and anti-trafficking legislation in Ghana. *International Labor and Working-Class History*, 78, pp. 63–88.

Le Bach, D. and Khuat, T.H. 2008. *Market transformation, migration and social protection in a transitioning Vietnam*. Hanoi, Vietnam: The Gioi Publisher.

Lee, J.J.H. 2005. Human trafficking in East Asia: Current trends, data collection, and knowledge gaps. *International Migration*, 43(1–2), pp. 165–201.

Leishman, M. 2007. Human trafficking and sexual slavery: Australia's response. *Australian Feminist Law Journal*, 27, pp.193–218.

Leggett, T. 2004. Hidden agendas? The risks of human trafficking legislation, *Crime Quarterly*, 9, pp. 1–5.

Lehmann, H., Pignatti, N. and Wadsworth, J. The incidence and cost of job loss in the Ukrainian labour market. *Journal of Comparative Economics*, 34, pp. 248–71.

Leichtentritt, R.D. 2005. Young male street workers: Life histories and current experiences. *The British Journal of Social Work*, 35(4), pp. 483–509.

Lépinard, E. 2011. Autonomy and the crisis of the feminist subject: Revisiting Okin's Dilemma. *Constellations*, 18(2), pp. 205–21

Leuchtag, A. 2003. Human rights, sex trafficking and prostitution. *The Humanist*, 63(1), pp. 10–13.

Leung, A. 2003. Feminism in transition: Chinese culture, ideology and the development of the women's movement in China. *Asia Pacific Journal of Management*, 20(3), pp. 359–74.

Lim, L.L. and Oishi, N. 1996. International labour migration of Asian women: Distinctive characteristics and policy concerns. *Asian and Pacific Migration Journal*, 5(1), pp. 85–116.

Limoncelli, S.A. 2009. The trouble with trafficking: Conceptualising women's sexual labour and economic human rights. *Women's Studies International Forum*, 32, pp. 261–9.

Link, P. and Phelan, J. 2001. Conceptualizing stigma. *Annual Review of Sociology*, 27, pp. 363–85.

Lithur, N.O. 2004. Destigmatising abortion: Expanding community awareness of abortion as a reproductive health issue in Ghana. *African Journal of Reproductive Health*, 8(1), pp. 70–74.

Liu, A.Y.C. 2001. Flying ducks? Girls' schooling in rural Vietnam. *Asian Economic Journal*, 15(4), pp. 385–403.

Loff, B. and Sanghera, J. 2004. Distortions and difficulties in data for trafficking. *Lancet*, 363(9408), p. 566.

Long, L.D. 2004. Anthropological perspectives on the trafficking of women for sexual exploitation. *International Migration*, 42(1), pp. 5–31.

Lucas, A. 1999. Women and prostitution. In: K.D. Askin and D.M. Koenig, *Women and international human rights law*. Ardsley, US: Transnational Press, Vol. 1, pp. 683–726.

Mackenzie, C. 2010. Autonomy: Individualistic or social and relational. In: G. Marston, J. Moss and J. Quiggin, eds. *Risk, welfare and work*. Melbourne, Australia: Melbourne University Press.

Mackenzie, C. and Stoljar, N. eds. 1999. *Relational autonomy: feminist perspectives on autonomy, agency and the social self*. Oxford: Oxford University Press.

Madhok, S., Phillips, A. and Wilson, K., eds. 2012 *Gender, agency and coercion*. London, UK: Palgrave Macmillan.

MacKinnon, C.A. 2004. Pornography as trafficking. *Michigan Journal of International Law*, 26, pp. 993–1012.

MacKinnon, C.A. 1993. Prostitution and civil rights. *Michigan Journal of Gender and Law*, 1, pp. 13–31.

Madhok, S. and Phillips, A. and Wilson, K. 2012. *Gender, agency and coercion*. London: Palgrave MacMillan.

Macklin, A. 2004. At the border of rights: Migration, sex work and trafficking. In: N. Gordon, ed. *From the margins of globalisation: Critical perspectives on human rights*. Lanham, US: Lexington Books, pp. 161–91.

Mahalik, J.R., Good, G.E., and Englar-Carlson, M. 2003. Masculinity scripts, presenting concerns, and help seeking: Implications for practice and training. *Professional Psychology: Research and Practice*, 34, pp. 123–31.

Mahdavi, P. 2011. *Labour, migration and human trafficking in Dubai*. Stanford, US: Stanford University Press.

Mahmoud, T.O. and Trebesch, C. 2010. The economics of human trafficking and labour migration: Micro-evidence from Eastern Europe, *Journal of Comparative Economics*, 38, pp. 173–88.

Marcus, A., Horning, A., Curtis, R., Sanson, J. and Thompson, E. 2014. Conflict and agency among sex workers and pimps: A closer look at domestic minor sex trafficking. *The Annals of the American Academy of Political and Social Science*, 653(1), pp. 225–46.

Marr, D. 1976. The 1920s women's rights debate in Vietnam. *The Journal of Asian Studies*. 35(3), pp. 371–89.

Marshall, P. 2006. From the beginning … Strengthening return, recovery and reintegration procedures for trafficking victims in Viet Nam, Unpublished.

Marshall, P. 2005. Raising our own awareness: Getting to grips with trafficking in persons and related problems in South-East Asia and beyond. *Asia-Pacific Population Journal*, 20(3), pp. 143–63.

Marshall, P. 2001. Globalization, migration and trafficking: Some thoughts from the South-East Asian region, In: *Globalization Workshop*. 8–10 May 2001, Kuala Lumpur, Malaysia.

Massey, D.S. et al. 2010. Causes of migration. In: M. Guibernau and J. Rex, eds. *The Ethnicity Reader: Nationalism, multiculturalism and migration.* Cambridge, UK: Polity Press, pp. 310–42.

Mattar, M.Y. 2006. Incorporating the five basic elements of a model anti-trafficking in persons legislation in domestic laws: From the United Nations protocol to the European Convention, *Tulane Journal of International and Comparative Law*, 14, pp. 357–419.

Mattar, M.Y. 2004. Trafficking in persons: An annotated legal bibliography. *Law Library Journal*, 96(4), pp. 669–726.

Meyers, D.T. 1987. Personal autonomy and the paradox of female socialization. *Journal of Philosophy*, 84(11), pp. 619–28.

Meyers, D.T. ed., 1997. Feminists rethink the self. Boulder, US: Westview Press.

Meyers, D.T. 2000. Feminism and women's autonomy: The challenge of female genital cutting. *Metaphilosphy*, 31(5), pp. 469–91.

McCabe, K.A. 2008. *The Trafficking of persons: National and International Responses.* New York, USA: Peter Lang Publishing.

McCabe, I. et al. 2011. Male street prostitution in Dublin: A psychological analysis. *Journal of Homosexuality*, 58(8), pp. 998–1021.

McSherry, B. and Kneebone, S. 2008. Trafficking in women and forced marriage: Moving victims across the border of crime into the domain of human rights. *International Journal of Human Rights*, 12(1), pp. 67–87.

Miles, A. 2003. Prostitution, trafficking and the global sex industry: A conversation with Janice Raymond. *Canadian Woman Studies*, 22(3/4), pp. 26–37.

Mill, J.E. 2003. Shrouded in secrecy: Breaking the news of HIV infection to Ghanaian women. *Journal of Transcultural Nursing*, 14(1), pp. 6–16.

Mill, J.E. 2001. I'm not a 'Basabasa' woman: An explanatory model of HIV illness in Ghanaian women. *Clinical Nursing Research*, 10(3), pp. 254–74.

Mill, J.S. 1859. On Liberty. In: J.M. Robson, ed. 1977. *Collected works: Essays on politics and society*, Vol.18. Toronto, Canada: University of Toronto Press and London, UK: Routledge.

Mills, M.B. 1999. *Thai women in the global labour force: Consuming desires, contested selves*. New Brunswick, US: Rutgers University Press.

Miller, R. and Baumeister, S. 2013. Managing Migration: Is border control fundamental to anti-trafficking and anti-smuggling interventions? *Anti-Trafficking Review*, 2, pp. 15–32.

Miller, E., Decker, M.R., Silverman, J.G., and Raj, A. 2007. Migration, sexual exploitation, and women's health: A case report from a community health center. *Violence Against Women*, 13, pp. 486–97.

Miller, J. and Schwartz, M. 1995. Rape myths and violence against street prostitutes. *Deviant Behavior*, 16(1), pp. 1–23.

Milivojevic, S. and Segrave, M. 2011. Evaluating responses to human trafficking: An analysis of the applications of contemporary international, regional and national counter-trafficking mechanisms. In J. Winterdyk, B. Perrin and P. Reichel, eds. *Human Trafficking: International issues and perspectives*. Boca Raton, Florida: Taylor and Francis.

Miriam, K. 2005. Stopping the traffic in women: Power, agency and abolition in feminist debates over sex trafficking. *Journal of Social Philosophy*, 36(1), pp. 1–17.

Mohajerin, S.K. 2006. Human trafficking: Modern day slavery in the 21st century, *Canadian Foreign Policy Journal*, 12(3), pp. 125–32

Molland, S. 2012. T*he Perfect Business? Anti-Trafficking and the Sex Trade along the Mekong*. Honolulu, Hawaii: University of Hawaii Press.

Molland, S. 2011. 'I am helping them'": Traffickers, anti-traffickers and economies of bad faith. *The Australian Journal of Anthropology*, 22, pp. 236–54.

Molland, S. 2010. The value of bodies: Deception, helping and profiteering in human trafficking along the Thai-Lao Border. *Asian Studies Review*, 34, pp. 211–29.

Mon, M. 2010. Burmese labour migration into Thailand: Governance of migration and labour rights. *Journal of Asia Pacific Economy*, 15(1), pp. 33–44.

Moşneaga, V. and Echim, T. 2003. Counteraction towards the trafficking of 'human beings': The experience of the Republic of Moldova. *Migracijske I etničketeme* (2/3), pp. 223–38.

Moyer, E.M. et al. 2012. Sexual and reproductive health status and related knowledge among female migrant workers in Guangzhou, China: A cross-sectional survey. *European Journal of Obstetrics and Gynaecology and Reproductive Biology*, 160(1), pp. 60–65.

Munro V.E. and Della Giusta, M. eds. 2008. *Demanding sex: Critical reflections on the regulation of prostitution*. Surrey, UK: Ashgate.

Munro, V.E. 2006. Stopping Traffic? A comparative study of responses to the trafficking of women for prostitution. *British Journal of Criminology*, 46, pp. 318–33.

Munro, V.E. 2005. A tale of two servitudes: Defining and implementing a domestic response to trafficking of women for prostitution in the UK and Australia. *Social and Legal Studies*, 14(1), pp. 91–114.

Murphy, E. and Ringheim, K. 2005. An interview with Jo Doezema, of the Network of Sex Work Projects: Does attention to trafficking adversely affect sex workers' rights? *Reproductive Health Matters*, pp. 13–15.

Musacchio, V. 2004. Migration, prostitution and trafficking of women: An overview. *German Law Journal*, 5(9), pp. 1015–30.

Musto, J.L. 2009. What's in a name? Conflations and contradictions in contemporary US discourses of human trafficking. *Women Studies International Forum*, 32, pp. 281–7.

Muecke, M.A. 1992. Mother sold food, daughter sells her body: The cultural continuity of prostitution. *Social Science Medicine*, 35, pp. 891–901.

Nadaswaran, S. 2012. Analysing sex trafficking in neo-liberal Nigeria through Nigerian women's writing. *International Journal of Social Sciences and Humanity*, 2(1), pp. 59–64.

Nagle, J. ed., 1997. *Whores and Other Feminists*. New York, US: Routledge.

Nair, P.M and Sen, S. 2005. *Trafficking of women and children in India*. New Delhi, India: Orient Longman.

Nami, O. and Keiko, H. 2009. Japanese perceptions of trafficking in persons: An analysis of the 'demand' for sexual services and policies for dealing with trafficking survivors. *Social Science Japan Journal*, 12(1), pp. 45–70.

Niemi, J. 2010. What we talk about when we talk about buying sex. *Violence Against Women*, 16(2), pp. 159–72.

Nieuwenhuys, C. and Pécoud, A. 2007. Human trafficking, information campaigns, and strategies of migration control. *American Behavioral Scientist*, 50(12), pp. 1674–95.

Ngom, P. et al. 2003. Gate-Keeping and women's health seeking behaviour in Navrongo, Northern Ghana. *African Journal of Reproductive Health*, 7(1), pp. 17–26.

Nguyễn, T.A. et al. 2008. A hidden HIV epidemic among women in Vietnam. BMC *Public Health*, 8, pp. 37–48.

Nussbaum, M.C. 1999. 'Whether from reason or prejudice': Taking money for bodily services. In: *Sex and social justice*. New York, US: Oxford University Press, pp. 276–98.

Nussbaum, M.C. 2000. *Women and Human Development*. New York, US: Cambridge University Press.

O'Brien, E. 2011. Fuelling traffic: Abolitionist claims of a causal nexus between legalised prostitution and trafficking. *Criminal Law and Social Change*, 56, pp. 547–65.

O'Connell Davidson, J. 2006 'Will the real sex slave please stand up?' *Feminist Review*, 83, pp. 4–22.

O'Connell Davidson, J. 2003. 'Sleeping with the enemy?' Some problems with feminist abolitionist calls to penalise those who buy commercial sex. *Social Policy and Society*, 2(1), pp. 55–64.

O'Connell Davidson, J. 1998. *Prostitution, power and freedom*. Ann Arbor, US: University of Michigan Press.

O'Connell Davidson, J. 1995. The anatomy of 'free choice' prostitution. *Gender, Work and Organisation*, 2(1), pp. 1–10.

O'Connor, M. and Healy, G. 2006. *The links between prostitution and sex trafficking: A briefing handbook*. <http://blog.lib.umn.edu/globerem/main/Handbook%20excerpt.pdf> [Accessed 15 May 2012].

O'Neil, J. 2004. Dhandha, dharma and disease: Traditional sex work and HIV/AIDS in rural India. *Social Science & Medicine*, 59(4), pp. 851–60.

O'Neil, T. 2001. Selling girls in Kuwait: Domestic labour migration and trafficking discourse in Nepal. *Anthropologia*, 432(2), pp. 152–64.

Obokata, T. 2003. Human trafficking, human rights and the Nationality, Immigration and Asylum Act 2002. *European Human Rights Law Review*, 4, pp. 410–22.

Ogonor, B. and Osunde, A. The Universal Basic Education Programme and female trafficking in South-South Nigeria. *International Journal of Lifelong Education*, 26(6), pp. 607–20.

Olesen, H. 2002. Migration, return, and development: an institutional perspective. *International Migration*, 40(5), pp. 125–50.

Opdenakker, R. 2006. Advantages and disadvantages of four interview techniques in qualitative research. *Qualitative Social Research*, 7(4). <http://nbn-resolving.de/urn:nbn:de:0114-fqs0604118> [Accessed 15 May 2012].

Outshoorn, J. 2005. The political debates on prostitution and trafficking of women. *Social Policy*, 12, pp. 141–55.

Outshoorn, J. ed. 2004. *The Politics of Prostitution: Women's movements, democratic states and the globalisation of sex commerce*. Cambridge, UK: Cambridge University Press.

Overs, C. 2009. How the development industry imagines sex work. *Development*, 52, pp. 13–17.

Pajnik, M. 2010. Media framing of trafficking. *International Feminist Journal of Politics*, 12(1), pp. 45–64.

Parker, R. and Aggleton, P. 2003. HIV and AIDS-related stigma and discrimination: A conceptual framework and implications for action. *Social Science and Medicine*, 57(1), pp. 13–24.

Parreñas, R.S. 2012. *Illicit flirtations: Labour, migration and sex trafficking in Tokyo*. Palo Alto: Stanford University Press.

Pateman, C. 1998. *The sexual contract*. Cambridge, UK: Polity Press.

Pederson, E.L. and Vogel, D.L. Male gender role conflict and willingness to seek counselling: Testing a mediation model on college-aged men. *Journal of Counselling Psychology*, 54(4), pp. 373–84.

Peil, M. 1995. Ghanaians abroad. *African Affairs*, 94(376), pp. 345–67.

Pauw, I and Brener, L. 2003. 'You are just whores – you can't be raped': Barriers to safer sex practices among women street sex workers in Cape Town. *Culture, Health and Sexuality*, 5(5), pp. 465–81.

Peracca, A., Knodel, J., and Saengtienchai, C. 1998. 'Can prostitutes marry?' Thai attitudes toward female sex workers. *Social Science and Medicine*. 47, pp. 255–67.

Peters, A.W. 2013. 'Things that involve sex are just different': US anti-trafficking law and policy on the books, in their minds and in action. *Anthropological Quarterly*, 86(1), pp. 221–55.

Pham, H.T. and Reilly, B. 2009. Ethnic wage inequality in Vietnam. *International Journal of Manpower*, 30(3), pp. 192–219.

Pham, H.T. and Reilly, B. 2007. The gender pay gap in Vietnam, 1993–2002: A quantile regression approach. *Journal of Asian Economics*, 18(5), pp. 775–808.

Phoenix, J. 2009. *Regulating sex for sale: Prostitution, policy reform and UK*. Bristol: The Policy Press.

Phongpaichit, P., Piriyarangsan, S. and Treerat, N. 1998. *Guns, girls, gambling, ganja: Thailand's illegal economy and public policy*. Chiang Mai, Thailand: Silkworm Books and Washington University Press.

Pheterson, G. 1993. The whore stigma: Female dishonour and male unworthiness. *Social Text*, 37, pp. 39–54.

Phillips, A. 2009. Autonomy, coercion and constraints. In: *Multiculturalism without Culture*. Princeton: US Princeton University Press, pp. 100–132.

Piper, N. 2005. A problem by a different name? A review of research on trafficking in South-East Asia and Oceania. *International Migration*, 43(1/2), pp. 203–33.

Piper, N. 2004. Rights of foreign workers and the politics of migration in South-East and East Asia. *International Migration*, 42(5), pp. 71–97.

Piper, N. 2003. Bridging gender, migration and governance: Theoretical possibilities in the Asian context. *Asian and Pacific Migration Journal*, 12(1–2), pp. 21–48.

Piscitelli, A. and Vasconcelos, M. 2008. Dossiê: Gênero no tráfico de pessoas. *Cadernos Pagu*, 31, pp. 9–28.

Piscitelli, A. 2008. Entre as 'máfias' ea 'ajuda': A construção de conhecimento sobre tráfico de pessoas. *Cadernos Pagu*, 31, pp. 29–63.

Poudel, P. and Carryer, J. 2000. Girl-trafficking, HIV/AIDS, and the position of women in Nepal. *Gender and Development*, 8(2), pp. 74–9.

Poulin, R. 2003. Globalisation and the sex trade: Trafficking and the commodification of women and children. *Canadian Women Studies*, 22, pp. 38–43.

Quinn-Judge, S. 1983. Vietnamese Women: Neglected Promises, *Indochina Issues*, 42: pp. 1–7

Radin, M.J. 1996. *Contested Commodities*. Cambridge, US: Harvard University Press.

Rassam, Y. 2004/2005. International law and contemporary forms of slavery: An economic and social rights-based approach, *Penn State International Law Review*, 23(4), pp. 809–56.

Raymond, J.G. 2004. Prostitution on demand: Legalizing the buyers as sexual consumers. *Violence Against Women*, 10, pp. 1156–86.

Raymond, J.G. 2002. The new UN Trafficking Protocol. *Women's Studies International Forum*, 25(5), pp. 491–502.

Rende-Taylor, L. 2005. Dangerous trade-offs: The behavioural ecology of child labour and prostitution in rural Northern Thailand. *Current Anthropology*, 46(3), pp. 411–32.

Richard, S. 2005. State legislation and human trafficking: Helpful or harmful? *University of Michigan Journal of Law Reform*, 38, pp. 447–77.

Richards, K. 2004. The trafficking of migrant workers: What are the links between labour trafficking and corruption? *International Migration*, 42(5), pp. 147–68.

Rijken, C. 2009. A human rights based approach to trafficking in human beings. *Security and Human Rights*, 3, pp. 212–22.

Rogot, E., Sorlie, P.D. and Johnson, N.J. 1992. Life expectancy by employment status, income and education in the national longitudinal mortality study. *Public Health Reports*, 107(4), pp. 457–61.

Rossman, G.B. and Rallis, S.F. 1998. *Learning in the field: An introduction to qualitative research*. Thousand Oaks, US: Sage.

Rubchak, M.J. 1996. Christian virgin or pagan goddess in feminism in post-communist Ukrainian society. In: *Women in Russia and Ukraine*. Cambridge, UK: Cambridge University Press, pp. 315–30.

Rubin, G. 1975. The traffic in women: Notes on the 'political economy' of sex. In: R.R. Reiter, ed. *Toward an Anthropology of Women*. New York, US: Monthly Review Press, pp. 157–210.

Rushing, R. 2006. Migration and sexual exploitation in Vietnam. *Asian and Pacific Migration Journal*, 15(4), pp. 471–94.

Rydstrøm, H. 2003. Encountering 'hot' anger: Domestic violence in contemporary Vietnam. *Violence Against Women*, 9, pp. 676–97.

Saari, S. 2006. Balancing between inclusion and exclusion: The EU's fight against irregular migration and human trafficking from Ukraine, Moldova and Russia. London School of Economics. <http://www2.lse.ac.uk/internationalRelations/ centresandunits/EFPU/EFPUpdfs/EFPUchallengewp3.pdf> [Accessed 20 July 2012].

Sadruddin, H., Walter, N. and Hidalgo, J. 2005. Human trafficking in the United States: Expanding victim protection beyond prosecution witnesses. *Stanford Law and Policy Review*, 16(2), pp. 379–416.

Samarasinghe, V. and Burton, B. 2007. Strategising prevention: A critical review of local initiatives to prevent female sex trafficking. *Development in Practice*, 17(1), pp. 51–64.

Sanders, T. 2006. Sexing up the subject: Methodological nuances in researching the female sex industry. *Sexualities*, 9(4), pp. 449–68.

Sanghera, J. 2005. Unpacking the trafficking discourse. In: K. Kempadoo, J. Sanghera and B. Pattanaik, eds. *Trafficking and prostitution reconsidered: New perspectives on migration, sex work, and human rights.* Boulder, US: Paradigm Publishers, pp. 3–24.

Saunders, P. 2005. Traffic violations: Determining the meaning of violence in sexual trafficking versus sex work. *Journal of Interpersonal Violence*, 20(3), pp. 343–60.

Scambler, G. 2007. Sex work stigma: Opportunist migrants in London. *Sociology*, 41(6), pp. 1079–93.

Schloenhardt, A. 2011. Case Report on *R v Wei Tang*, (2009) 23 VR 332, University of Queensland, TC Beirne School of Law, Brisbane, Australia. Available at <http://www.law.uq.edu.au/documents/humantraffic/case-reports/wei_tang.pdf>. Accessed 20 September 2013.

Schloenhardt, A. 2001. Trafficking in migrants: Illegal migration and organized crime in Australia and the Asia Pacific region. *International Journal of the Sociology of Law*, 29(4), pp. 331–78.

Schloenhardt, A. and Jolly, J. 2010. Honeymoon from hell: Human trafficking and domestic servitude in Australia. *Sydney Law Review*, 32: 671–92.

Schroeder, J. et al. 1993. Symposium: Decriminalizing prostitution: Liberalization or dehumanization? *Cardozo Women's Law Journal*, 1(1), pp. 101–47.

Schuler, S.R. et al. 2006. Constructions of gender in Vietnam: In pursuit of the 'Three Criteria'. *Culture, Health and Sexuality*, 8(5), pp. 383–94.

Schulhofer, S.J. 1998. *Unwanted Sex: The culture of intimidation and the failure of law.* Cambridge, US: Harvard University Press.

Schultz, V. 2006. Sex and work. *Yale Journal of Law and Feminism*, 18, pp. 223–34.

Segrave, M. 2004. Surely something is better than nothing? The Australian response to the trafficking of women into sexual servitude in Australia. *Current Issues in Criminal Justice*, 16, pp. 85–92.

Segrave, M. and Milivojevic, S. 2005. Sex trafficking – A new agenda. *Social Alternatives*, 24(2), pp. 11–16.

Seng, M.J. 1989. Child abuse and adolescent prostitution. *Adolescence*, 24(95), pp. 665–75.

Schaeur, E. and Wheaton, E.M. Sex trafficking into the United States: A literature review. *Criminal Justice Review*, 31(2), pp. 146–69.

Shah, S.P. 2005. Prostitution, sex work and violence: Discursive and political contexts for five texts on paid sex, 1987–2001. In: S. D'Cruze and A. Rao, eds. *Violence, Vulnerability and Embodiment: Gender and History.* Oxford, UK: Blackwell, pp. 301–19.

Sharma, N. 2005. Anti-trafficking rhetoric and the making of a global apartheid. *National Women Studies Association Journal* (now *Feminist Formations*), 17(3), pp. 88–111.

Sharma, N. 2003. Travel agency: A critique of anti-trafficking campaigns, *Refuge*, 21, pp. 53–65.

Shih, M. 2004. Positive stigma: Examining resilience and empowerment in overcoming stigma. *The Annals of the American Academy of Political and Social Science*, 591, pp. 175–85.

Shelley, L. 2010. *Human Trafficking: A global perspective*. New York, US: Cambridge University Press.

Silverman, D. 2006. *Interpreting qualitative data: Methods for analysing talk, text and interaction*. London, UK: Sage.

Silverman, D. 1998. Analyzing talk and text. In: N. Denzin and Y. Lincoln, eds. *Collecting and Interpreting Qualitative Materials*. Thousand Oaks, US: Sage, Ch. 9, pp. 340–62.

Simm, G. 2004. Negotiating the United Nations Trafficking Protocol: Feminist debates. *Australian Yearbook of International Law*, 23, pp. 135–60.

Simon, H.A. Spurious correlation: A causal interpretation. In: Blalock, H.M. ed. *Causal models in the social sciences*. 2nd ed. New York, US: Aldine de Gruyter, pp. 7–22.

Skeldon, R. 2000. Trafficking: A perspective from Asia. *International Migration*, 38(3), pp. 7–30.

Skinner, BE. 2009. The fight to end global slavery. *World Policy Journal*, pp. 33–41.

Skinner, B.E. 2008a. *A crime so monstrous: Face-to-face with modern day slavery*, New York, US: Free Press.

Skinner, B.E. 2008b. A world enslaved. *Foreign Policy*, 165, pp. 62–7.

Small, J. 2012. Trafficking in truth: Media, sexuality and human rights evidence. *Feminist Studies*, 38(2): 415–43.

Spector, J. 2006. *Prostitution and pornography: Philosophical debate about the sex industry*. Stanford, US: Stanford University Press.

Spener, D. 2011. Global Apartheid, Coyotaje, and the discourse of clandestine migration: Distinctions between personal, structural and cultural violence. In: D. Kyle and R. Koslowski, ed. *Global human smuggling: Comparative perspectives*. 2nd ed. Baltimore, US: Johns Hopkins University Press, pp. 157–85.

Spreen, M. 1992. Rare populations, hidden populations and link-tracing designs: What and why? *Bulletin Methodologie Sociologique*, 36, pp. 34–58.

Stolz, B. 2005. Educating the policymakers and setting the criminal justice policymaking agenda: Interest groups and the 'Victims of Trafficking and Violence Act of 2000'. *Criminal Justice: The International Journal of Policy and Practice*, 5(4), pp. 407–30.

Steinfatt, T.M. 2011. Sex trafficking in Cambodia: Fabricated numbers versus empirical evidence. *Criminal Law and Social Change*, 56, pp. 443–62.

Steinfatt, T.M., Baker, S. and Beesey, A. 2002. Measuring the number of trafficked women in Cambodia. In: *The human rights challenge of globalization in Asia-Pacific-US: The trafficking in persons, especially women and children*. 13–15 November, Honolulu, Hawaii.

Sullivan, M.L. and Jeffreys, S. 2002. Legalization: The Australian experience. *Violence against Women*, 8(9), pp. 1140–48.

Sullivan, B. 2010. When (some) prostitution is legal: The impact of law reform on sex work in Australia. *Journal of Law and Society*, 37(1), pp. 85–104.

Sullivan, B. 1997. *The Politics of Sex: Prostitution and pornography in Australia since 1945*. Cambridge, UK: Cambridge University Press.

Sun-Hee Park, L. 2011. *Entitled To Nothing: The Struggle for immigrant health in the age of welfare reform*. New York: New York University Press.

Sunday, J. 2005. International Protocols for human trafficking and smuggling. *Globalisation and autonomy online compendium*. <http://globalautonomy. uwaterloo.ca/global1/servlet/Glossarypdf?id=CO.0055> [Accessed 15 May 2012].

Sunstein, C.R. 1997. *Free Markets and Social Justice*. New York, US: Oxford University Press.

Sunstein, C.R. 1991a. Preferences and Politics. *Philosophy & Public Affairs*, 20(1), pp. 3–34.

Sunstein, C.R. 1991b. Why Markets Don't Stop Discrimination, *Social Philosophy and Policy*, 8(2), pp. 22–37.

Sunstein, C.R. 1989. Disrupting voluntary transactions. In: J.W. Chapman and J.R. Pennock, eds. *Markets and Justice*. New York, US and London, UK: New York University Press, pp. 279–302.

Sunstein, C.R. 1986. Legal interference with private preferences. *University of Chicago Law Review*, 53(4), pp. 1129–74.

Superson, A. 2010. The deferential wife revisited: Agency and moral responsibility. *Hypatia*. 25(2), pp. 253–75.

Surtees, R. 2008b. Trafficked men as unwilling victims. *St Anthony's International Review*, 4(1), pp. 16–36.

Sutherland, K. 2004. Work, sex, and sex-work: Competing feminist discourses on the international sex trade. *Osgoode Hall Law Journal*, 42(1), pp. 139–67.

Takyi, B.K. 2000. AIDS-related knowledge and risks and contraceptive practices in Ghana: The early 1990s. *African Journal of Reproductive Health*, 4(1), pp. 13–27.

Talleyrand, I. 2000. Military prostitution: How the authorities worldwide aid and abet international trafficking in women. *Syracuse Journal of International Law and Commerce*, 27, pp. 151–76.

Taylor, J.S. 2006. Female sex tourism: A contradiction in terms? *Feminist Review*, 83, pp. 42–59.

Thorsen, D. 2010. The place of migration in girls' imagination. *Journal of Comparative Family Studies*, 41(2), pp. 265–80.

Tiefenbrun, S. 2001. Sex sells but drugs don't talk: Trafficking of women sex workers. *Thomas Jefferson Law Review*, 23, pp. 199–226.

Todres, J. 2011. Widening our lens: Incorporating essential perspectives in the fight against human trafficking. *Michigan Journal of International Law*, 22, pp. 53–76.

Tomasi, L.F. 2000. Globalisation and human trafficking. *Migration World Magazine*, 28, pp. 4.

Townsend, P. 1970. *The concept of poverty: Working papers on methods of investigation and life-styles of the poor in different countries.* London, UK: Heinemann Educational.

Trépanier, M. 2003. Trafficking in women for purposes of sexual exploitation: a matter of consent? *Canadian Woman Studies*, 22, pp. 48–54.

Tyldum, G. 2013. Dependence and human trafficking in the context of transnational marriage. *International Migration*, 51(4), pp. 103–15.

Tyldum, G. and Brunovskis, A. 2005. Describing the unobserved: Methodological challenges in empirical studies on human trafficking. *International Migration*, 43(1/2), pp. 17–34.

Tzvetkova, M. 2002. NGO responses to trafficking in women. In: R. Masika, ed. *Gender, Trafficking and Slavery*. Oxford, UK: Oxfam Publishing.

Uehling, G. 2004. Irregular and illegal migration through Ukraine. *International Migration*, 42(3), pp. 77–109.

Uy, R. 2011. Blinded by Red Lights: Why trafficking discourse should shift away from sex and the 'perfect victim' paradigm. *Berkeley Journal of Gender, Law and Justice*, 26, pp. 204–19.

Vance, C.S. 1984. *Pleasure and Danger: Exploring female sexuality*. Boston, US: Routledge.

Van-Landingham, M. and Trujillo, L. 2002. Recent changes in sexual attitudes, norms, and behaviors among unmarried Thai men: A qualitative analysis. *International Family Planning Perspectives*, 28(1), pp. 6–15.

Van Impe, K. 2000. People for sale: The need for a multi-disciplinary approach towards human trafficking. *International Migration*, 38(3), pp. 113–31.

Van de Walle, D. and Gunewardena, D. 2001. Sources of ethnic inequality in Vietnam. *Journal of Development Economics*, 65, pp. 177–207.

Vijeyarasa, R. 2013a. Stigma, stereotypes and Brazilian soap operas: Roadblocks to ending trafficking in Vietnam, Ghana and Ukraine. *Gender, Place and Culture*, 20(8), pp. 1015–32.

Vijeyarasa, R. 2013b. Roadblocks to counter-trafficking: A comparative analysis of Vietnam, Ghana and Ukraine. In: M.Z. Gonçalves de Abreu, ed. *Women past and present: Biographic and interdisciplinary studies*. Cambridge, UK: Cambridge Scholars Press.

Vijeyarasa, R. 2013c. Hidden Data, Hidden Victims: Trafficking in the context of globalisation and labour exploitation – the case of Vietnam. In: M.C. Rawlinson, W. Vandekerckhove, W.M.S. Commers, eds. *Labour and global justice: Essays on ethics of labour practices in the age of globalisation*. Lanham, US: Lexington Books, pp. 141–64.

Vijeyarasa, R. 2012a. The Cinderella syndrome: Economic expectations, false hopes and the exploitation of trafficked Ukrainian women. *Women Studies International Forum*, 35, pp. 53–62.

Vijeyarasa, R. 2011a. Speak no evil, see no evil, hear no evil: The unspoken story of the traffic of Ghanaian women. In: *Women's Worlds 2011: Inclusions,*

Exclusions Seclusions: Living in a globalised world. 3–7 July 2011, Ottawa, Canada.

Vijeyarasa, R. 2011b. Roadblocks to counter-trafficking: A comparative analysis of Vietnam, Ghana and Ukraine. In: *Debating women: Past and present.* 1–4 June 2011, Funchal, Portugal.

Vijeyarasa, R. 2011c. Review of *Trafficking and human rights: European and Asia-Pacific Perspectives* by L. Holmes and *The international law of human trafficking* by A.T. Gallagher. *Australian Journal of Human Rights*, 17(1), pp. 139–43.

Vijeyarasa, R. 2010a. Exploitation or expectations? Moving beyond consent in prostitution, trafficking and migration discourse. *Women's Policy Journal of Harvard*, 7, pp. 11–22.

Vijeyarasa, R. 2010b. The state, family and language of 'social evils': Re-stigmatising victims of trafficking. *Culture, Health and Sexuality*, 12 (1), pp. 89–102.

Vijeyarasa, R. 2010c. Scrutinizing Vietnam's progress towards gender equality. *Development*, 53(1), pp. 91–7.

Vijeyarasa, R. 2010d.Vietnam's MDG report card: An assessment of progress on reproductive health. In: *Asian Conference on Social Sciences: East Meets West in Pursuit of a Sustainable World.* 18–21 June 2010, Osaka: Japan.

Vijeyarasa, R. 2010e. The impossible victim: Judicial treatment of the trafficked migrant and their unmet expectations. *Alternative Law Journal*, 35(4), pp. 217–22.

Vijeyarasa, R. 2009. Combating stigma: Empowering trafficked returnees to (re) integrate into communities in Vietnam. In: *7th IASSCS Conference: Contested Innocence – Sexual Agency in Public and Private Space.* 15–18 April 2009. Hanoi, Vietnam.

Vijeyarasa, R. and Bello y Villarino, J. 2012. Modern-day slavery? A judicial catchall for trafficking, slavery and labour exploitation: A critique of *Tang* and *Rantsev*. *Journal of International Law and International Relations*, 8(1), pp. 36–61.

Vijeyarasa, R. and Stein, R. 2010. HIV and Human trafficking-related stigma: Health interventions for trafficked populations. *Journal of the American Medical Association*, 304(3), pp. 344–5.

Vines, A. 1991. Mozambique: Slaves and the snake of fire. *Anti-Slavery Reporter*, 13(7), pp. 41–5.

Vocks, J. and Nijboer, J. 2000. The promised land: A study of trafficking in women from Central and Eastern Europe to the Netherlands. *European Journal of Criminal Policy and Research*, 8, pp. 379–88.

Vosko, L.F. 2010. *Managing the margins: Gender, citizenship, and the international regulation of precarious employment*, NY, United States: Oxford University Press.

Vu Ngoc, B. 2006. Trafficking of women and children in Vietnam: Current issues and problems. In: K. Beeks and D. Amir, eds. *Trafficking and the global sex industry*, ed. Lanham, US: Lexington Books, pp. 33–46.

Webber, A. and Shirk, D. 2005. Hidden victims: Evaluating protections for undocumented victims of human trafficking. *Immigration Policy in Focus*, 4(8), pp. 1–10.

Wahab, S. 2002. For their own good? Sex work, social control and social workers: A historical perspective. *Journal of Sociology and Social Welfare*, 29(4), pp. 39–57.

Wahab, S. and Sloan, L. 2004. Ethical dilemmas in sex work research. *Research for Sex Work*, 7, pp. 3–5.

Ward, H. and Day, S. 2006. What happens to women who sell sex? Report of a unique occupational cohort. *Sexually Transmitted Infections*, 82, pp. 413–17.

Weitzer, R. 2014. New directions in research on human trafficking. *The Annals of the American Academy of Political and Social Science*, 653(1), pp. 6–24.

Weitzer, R. 2012. Sex trafficking and the sex industry: The need for evidenced-based theory and legislation. *Journal of Criminal Law & Criminology*, 101(4), pp. 1337–70.

Weitzer, R. 2010. The movement to criminalize sex work in the United States. *Journal of Law and Society*, 37(1), pp. 61–84.

Weitzer, R. 2010. The mythology of prostitution: Advocacy research and public policy. *Sexuality Research and Social Policy*, 7, pp. 15–29.

Weitzer, R. 2007. The social construction of sex trafficking: Ideology and institutionalization of a moral crusade. *Politics and Society*, 35(3), pp. 447–75.

Weitzer, R. and Ditmore, M. 2010. Sex trafficking: Facts and fiction. 2nd ed. In: R, Weitzer, ed. *Sex for sale: Prostitution, pornography and sex industry*, New York, US: Routledge, pp. 325–51.

Wheaton, E.M., Schauer, E.J. and Galli, T.V. 2010. Economics of human trafficking. *International Migration*, 48(4), pp. 114–41.

Wheaton, E.M. and Schauer, E.J. 2016. Sex trafficking into the US: A literature review. *Criminal Justice Review*, 31(2), pp. 146–69.

White, R. 2013. *Invisible Women: Examining the political, economic, cultural and social factors that lead to human trafficking and sex slavery of young girls and women*. PhD thesis, University of New Orleans, New Orleans, US.

Yegidis, B.L. et al. 2005. Ukrainian women in the new economy. *International social work*, 48(2), pp. 213–22.

Zatz, N.D. 1997. Sex work/sex act: Law, labor, and desire in constructions of prostitution. *Signs*, 22(2), pp. 277–308.

Zhang, S.X. 2009. Beyond the 'Natasha' story: A review and critique of current research on sex trafficking. *Global Crime*, 10(3), pp. 178–95.

Zheng, T. 2010. *Sex trafficking, human rights, and social justice*. New York, US: Routledge.

Zherebkina, I. 2001. 'Who is Afraid of Feminism in Ukraine?' How Feminism is Possible as a Post-Soviet Political Project. In: G. Jahnert et al. eds. Gender in *Transition in Eastern and Central Europe Proceedings*. Berlin, Germany: TrafoVerlag, pp. 142–7.

Zhurzhenko, T. 2001. Free market ideology and new women's identities in post-socialist Ukraine. *European Journal of Women's Studies*, 8, pp. 29–49.

Zimmerman, C. 2007. Documenting the effects of trafficking in women. In: C. Beyrer and H. Pizer, eds. *Public health and human rights*, Baltimore, US: Johns Hopkins University Press, 2007, pp. 143–76.

Zimmerman, C. 2004. Risks and responsibilities: Guidelines for interviewing trafficked women. *The Lancet*, 363, p. 565.

Zimmerman, C., Hossain, M., and Watts, C. 2011. Human trafficking and health: A conceptual model to inform policy, intervention and research. *Social Science and Medicine*, 72(2), pp. 327–35.

Zimmerman, C. et al. 2008. The health of trafficked women: A survey of women entering post-trafficking services in Europe. *American Journal of Immigrant Health*, 98(1), pp. 55–9.

News Articles and Opinion Pieces

BBC News. 2010. 'Spain breaks up male-sex trafficking ring', 31 August 2010. <http://www.bbc.co.uk/news/world-europe-11142264>.

Birchall, J. 2009. 'Sex trafficking: Inside the Business of Modern Slavery', *The Financial Times*, 24 January 2009. <http://www.ft.com/cms/s/0/339b0ee8-e8db-11dd-a4d0-0000779fd2ac.html.

CNN Freedom Project. 2011. 'Breaking the chains: Freedom's successes', 19 December 2011. <http://thecnnfreedomproject.blogs.cnn.com/2011/12/19/breaking-the-chains-freedoms-successes/>.

Degen, G. 2007. 'UNICEF Ukraine helps re-unite abandoned siblings and encourages family-based care', 9 November 2007. < http://www.unicef.org/ceecis/media_7871.html>

Evans, M. 2012. 'First case of people trafficking for organs uncovered in UK', *The Telegraph*, 25 April 2012. <http://www.telegraph.co.uk/news/uknews/crime/9227137/First-case-of-people-trafficking-for-organs-uncovered-in-UK.html>.

Fuller, T. 2014. Cambodian activist's fall exposes broad deception. *The New York Times*, 14 June 2014.<http://www.nytimes.com/2014/06/15/world/asia/cambodian-activists-fall-exposes-broad-deception.html?_r=0>

The Ghanaian Times, 13 charged with child trafficking, 18 August 2010.

Marks, S. 2014. Somaly Mam: The holy saint (and sinner) of human trafficking, *Newsweek*, 30 May 2014. <http://www.newsweek.com/2014/05/30/somaly-mam-holy-saint-and-sinner-sex-trafficking-251642.html>

Scheerer, M. 2012. Human trafficking: New EU strategy to combat modern slavery. *Commission en direct*, 638, p. 3.

Skinner, B.E. 2010. The new slave trade. Time, 175(2): 54–7.

Viet Nam News. 2009. 'Rural women fall prey to city evils', 7 January 2009. <http://vietnamnews.vn/social-issues/population--development/184084/rural-women-fall-prey-to-city-evils.html>.

Index

Gender in a Global/Local World

Also published in this series

Turkey's Engagement with Global Women's Human Rights
Nüket Kardam
ISBN 978-0-7546-4168-1

(Un)thinking Citizenship
Feminist Debates in Contemporary South Africa
Edited by Amanda Gouws
ISBN 978-0-7546-3878-0

Vulnerable Bodies
Gender, the UN and the Global Refugee Crisis
Erin K. Baines
ISBN 978-0-7546-3734-9

Setting the Agenda for Global Peace
Conflict and Consensus Building
Anna C. Snyder
ISBN 978-0-7546-1933-8